CH00690755

The Major Phases of Philip Roth

Also Available from Continuum:

Philip Roth: American Pastoral, The Human Stain, The Plot Against America
Edited by Debra Shostak

The Major Phases of Philip Roth

David Gooblar

continuum

Continuum International Publishing Group

The Tower Building	80 Maiden Lane
11 York Road	Suite 704
London SE1 7NX	New York NY 10038

www.continuumbooks.com

© David Gooblar 2011

David Gooblar has asserted his right under the Copyright, Designs and Patents Act, 1988, to be identified as Author of this work.

All rights reserved. No part of this publication may be reproduced or transmitted in any form or by any means, electronic or mechanical, including photocopying, recording, or any information storage or retrieval system, without prior permission in writing from the publishers.

British Library Cataloguing-in-Publication Data
A catalogue record for this book is available from the British Library.

ISBN: 978-1-4411-7540-3 (hardback)
      978-1-4411-6970-9 (paperback)

Library of Congress Cataloging-in-Publication Data
A catalog record of this book is available from the Library of Congress.

Typeset by Newgen Imaging Systems Pvt Ltd, Chennai, India
Printed and bound in India

To my parents

Contents

Acknowledgments

The first words of this book were written in 2003, and, while rereading the manuscript for the 500th time recently, I was struck by how many of the ideas came from suggestions made by Kasia Boddy. I am hugely grateful for her guidance and wisdom, without which this book would simply not exist. Thanks, also, must go to Pam Thurschwell and Sarah Wintle for their help along the way, as well as to the English Department at University College London for providing such a stimulating and friendly environment for learning the trade. I would like to acknowledge my gratitude to the UCL Graduate School, which funded my research at the Library of Congress, as well as to Alice Lotvin Birney and the other manuscript historians and archivists at the Library of Congress for making my trawl through Roth's archives a fruitful and enjoyable experience. I would like to thank Colleen Coalter and everyone else at Continuum for making the publishing process such a pleasure. Many of my peers deserve thanks for helping me come to grips with Roth and find my way to finishing this project, in particular Jim Clements, Kelso Cratsley, Oliver Herford, Yohei Igarashi, Julia Jordan, David McAllister, Ruth Maxey, and John Morton. I thank Miodrag and Natalija Perović for all of their support and love, and my parents, Howard and Linda Gooblar, for much more than I can express here. Most of all, I thank Katarina Perović, for, well, everything.

I also gratefully acknowledge permission to reproduce in slightly different form portions of the following previously published articles:

Portions of "'Oh Freud do I know!' Philip Roth, Freud, and Narrative Therapy" appear in revised form in Chapter 4. Reprinted from *Philip Roth Studies* 1.1: 67–85, by permission of Purdue University Press.
"The Truth Hurts: The Ethics of Philip Roth's 'Autobiographical' Books," *Journal of Modern Literature* 32.1: 33–53, appears in revised form in Chapter 5. © Indiana University Press, 2008. Reprinted by permission of Indiana University Press.

List of Abbreviations

AP	*American Pastoral*
AL	*The Anatomy Lesson*
C	*The Counterlife*
D	*Deception*
E	*Everyman*
F	*The Facts*
GW	*The Ghost Writer*
GC	*Goodbye, Columbus*
HS	*The Human Stain*
IMAC	*I Married a Communist*
"Kafka"	"'I Always Wanted You to Admire My Fasting'; or, 'Looking at Kafka'"
MLM	*My Life as a Man*
OS	*Operation Shylock*
P	*Patrimony*
PC	*Portnoy's Complaint*
PD	*The Professor of Desire*
"Writing"	"Writing American Fiction"

Timeline

Date	Personal	Publications	Cultural
March 19, 1933	Philip Milton Roth born, Newark, NJ, to Herman Roth (born in 1901) and Bess Finkel Roth (born in 1904). His older brother Sandy was born in 1927.		
1934			Philip Rahv and William Phillips launch *Partisan Review*.
1941			The United States enters World War II.
1945			World War II comes to an end. American Jewish Committee launches *Commentary*.
1949			Philip Rahv publishes *Image and Idea*.
1950	Graduates from Weequahic High School; enters Newark Colleges of Rutgers University as a pre-law student.		Lionel Trilling publishes *The Liberal Imagination*.
Sept. 1951	Transfers to Bucknell University (Lewisburg, PA).		
1952	Switches to English major; helps found Bucknell literary journal *Et Cetera*.		*The Diary of a Young Girl*, by Anne Frank, published in the United States.
1953			Saul Bellow publishes *The Adventures of Augie March*.

Date	Personal	Publications	Cultural
1954	Graduates from Bucknell; begins graduate school at the University of Chicago; publishes "The Day it Snowed" in the *Chicago Review* (first story published outside of *Et Cetera*).		
1955	Receives MA from University of Chicago; enlists in army; suffers back injury during basic training at Fort Dix.		*The Diary of Anne Frank* opens at the Cort Theatre on Broadway. R. W. B. Lewish publishes *The American Adam.* Lionel Trilling publishes *The Opposing Self.*
1956	Spends two months in hospital for complications from spinal injury; granted honorable discharge from army; returns to University of Chicago to teach and begin PhD, dropping out of program after one term.		
1958	Resigns from teaching at University of Chicago; moves to New York.		The Jewish population of Newark declines from approximately 58,000 (in 1948) to around 41,000.
1959	Marries Margaret Martinson Williams.	*Goodbye, Columbus and Five Short Stories*	Philip Rieff publishes *Freud: The Mind of the Moralist.*
1960	Receives National Book Award for *Goodbye, Columbus*; joins teaching faculty at the Writers' Workshop at the University of Iowa (1960–62).		Leslie Fiedler publishes *Love and Death in the American Novel.*
1961	Publishes "Writing American Fiction" in *Commentary.*		
1962	Becomes writer-in-residence at Princeton University (1962–64).	*Letting Go*	

Date	Personal	Publications	Cultural
1963	Legally separates from wife; begins five years of psychoanalysis; publishes "Writing About Jews" in *Commentary*.		
1965	Begins to teach comparative literature at the University of Pennsylvania one semester a year (1965–77).		
1967	"A Jewish Patient Begins His Analysis," first excerpt from *Portnoy's Complaint*, published in *Esquire*.	*When She Was Good*	Riots rip through Newark, the culmination of decades of demographic change.
1968	Margaret Martinson Roth dies in car accident.		Soviet tanks invade Czechoslovakia, ending the "Prague Spring," and beginning an occupation that would last until 1990.
1969	Rents house in Woodstock, NY, where he lives mainly until 1972.	*Portnoy's Complaint*	
1970	Elected to National Institute of Arts and Letters.		
1971		*Our Gang*	
1972	Buys eighteenth-century farmhouse in northwest Connecticut; travels to Prague for the first time (returns annually until denied entry visa in 1977).	*The Breast*	Irving Howe publishes "Philip Roth Reconsidered" in *Commentary*.
1973	Publishes "'I Always Wanted You to Admire My Fasting'; or, Looking at Kafka" in *New American Review*.	*The Great American Novel*	
1974	Proposes and becomes general editor of Penguin's "Writers from the Other Europe" series.	*My Life as a Man*	John N. McDaniel publishes *The Fiction of Philip Roth*, the first academic monograph wholly devoted to Roth's work.

Date	Personal	Publications	Cultural
1975		*Reading Myself and Others*	
1976	Moves to London with Claire Bloom (the couple alternate between London and Connecticut for the next 12 years); begins to travel regularly to Israel.		
1977		*The Professor of Desire*	
1979		*The Ghost Writer*	
1981	Bess Roth dies.	*Zuckerman Unbound*	
1983		*The Anatomy Lesson*	
1985		*Zuckerman Bound: A Trilogy and Epilogue* (includes *The Prague Orgy*)	
1986		*The Counterlife*	
1987	Receives National Book Critics Circle Award for *The Counterlife*.		
1988	Begins teaching at Hunter College (1988–92).	*The Facts: A Novelist's Autobiography*	The Israeli Supreme Court finds John Demjanjuk guilty of war crimes and sentences him to death. The sentence would be overturned in 1993.
1989	Undergoes quintuple bypass surgery; Herman Roth dies.		
1990	Marries Claire Bloom.	*Deception: A Novel*	Michael White and David Epston publish *Narrative Means to Therapeutic Ends*, outlining Narrative Therapy.
1991	Receives National Book Critics Circle Award for biography for *Patrimony*.	*Patrimony: A True Story*	

Date	Personal	Publications	Cultural
1993	Receives PEN/Faulkner Award for *Operation Shylock*; separates from Claire Bloom.	*Operation Shylock: A Confession*	
1995	Receives National Book Award for *Sabbath's Theater*.	*Sabbath's Theater*	
1996			Claire Bloom publishes *Leaving a Doll's House*.
1997	Receives Pulitzer Prize for *American Pastoral*.	*American Pastoral*	
1998		*I Married a Communist*	The House of Representatives impeaches President Clinton.
2000	Receives PEN/Faulkner Award for *The Human Stain*.	*The Human Stain*	
2001	Receives the Gold Medal in fiction from the American Academy of Arts and Letters.	*The Dying Animal; Shop Talk: A Writer and His Colleagues and Their Work*	
2002	Receives National Book Foundation's Medal for Distinguished Contribution to American Letters.		
2004		*The Plot Against America*	
2005	Becomes the third living American author (after Eudora Welty and Saul Bellow) to have his works collected and published by the Library of America.		
2006	Becomes the fourth recipient of the PEN/Nabokov award.	*Everyman*	
2007	Receives inaugural PEN/Bellow Award; receives PEN/Faulkner Award for *Everyman*.	*Exit Ghost*	
2008		*Indignation*	
2009		*The Humbling*	
2010		*Nemesis*	

Introduction

Inward/Outward

Updike and Bellow hold their flashlights out into the world, reveal the real world as it is now. I dig a hole and shine my flashlight into the hole.

Philip Roth

What I keep forgetting about you, and shouldn't, is that when you talk about yourself digging a hole and shining a flashlight into it you're talking just to try it on for five minutes to see what it looks like.

David Plante

In 1973, at the age of 40, having published seven books, Philip Roth took a moment to sit back, reflect, and interview himself on the subject of the shape of his career to date. For a writer who has claimed that "the art of impersonation" is "the fundamental novelistic gift," impersonating his own interviewer came naturally enough ("Art of Fiction" 221). Asking himself a question about his alternation between the "serious" and the "reckless," Roth allowed himself a long response that, after taking in his early battles with Jewish critics over his debut publication, *Goodbye, Columbus* (1959), eventually cites Philip Rahv's 1939 essay "Paleface and Redskin," which posited two polarized types of American writer. Paleface writers, like T. S. Eliot and Henry James, were refined, educated, East Coast figures, exhibiting an old world interest in moral concerns. Redskins, like Walt Whitman and Mark Twain, were the writers of the frontier and the big city: emotional, vernacular, energetic writers who reflected the new world's vitality and the explorer's spirit of curiosity. After introducing Rahv's dichotomy, Roth claims membership in a new, hybrid category of American writer—the "redface," who remains "fundamentally ill at ease in, and at odds with, both worlds." It is telling that Roth does not go on to claim that he writes like some combination of paleface and redskin—there is no assertion of the ways in which he has been influenced by, say, both James and Twain—but rather it is the alternation between opposing modes, the awkward uncertainty as to which path to choose, that is emphasized:

To my mind, being a redface accounts as much as anything for the self-conscious and deliberate zig-zag that my own career has taken, each book veering sharply away from the one before, as though the author was mortified at having written it as he did and preferred to put as much light as possible between that kind of book and himself. ("Reading Myself" 410–11)

This "self-conscious and deliberate zig-zag" has continued to define Roth's career to the present day, creating a body of work as varied and fertile as that of any writer in recent memory. Is there another writer of fiction who has been so many things to so many readers? At one time or another, Roth has been seen as the sharp-eyed chronicler of the affluent Jewish-American suburbs; the best-selling celebrity author of sexual transgression; the keeper of the flame of Jewish humor; the self-hating Jewish writer, eager to drag his people in the mud to sell a few more copies of his books; the politically incisive satirist in the tradition of Swift and Orwell; the self-obsessed teller of psychoanalytic tales of the self; the champion of the work and traditions of Eastern European writers behind the Iron Curtain; the playful postmodernist, blurring the lines between fiction and fact; the nostalgic bard of Newark, New Jersey; and the unabashed Great American Novelist, writing works that condense and comment upon whole decades of American experience. How are we to make sense of such a career?

In another interview 11 years later, in 1984 (this time with Hermione Lee as the interviewer), Roth spoke of Nathan Zuckerman's actions in *The Anatomy Lesson* (1984)—in which he both decides to become a doctor and spontaneously impersonates a pornographer who publishes a magazine called, appropriately enough, *Lickety Split*—in terms that seem to recall his earlier vision of himself as a redface:

> There had to be willed extremism at either end of the moral spectrum, each of his escape-dreams of self-transformation subverting the meaning and mocking the intention of the other [. . .] The thing about Zuckerman that interests me is that everybody's split, but few so openly as this.

Later in the same interview, Lee asked Roth about his alternation between first- and third-person narration in the *Zuckerman Bound* novels; Roth's explanation again describes a balancing act, a movement between two poles:

> *The Ghost Writer* is narrated in the first person, probably because what's being described is largely a world Zuckerman's discovered outside of himself, the book of a young explorer. The older and more scarred he gets, the more *inward*-looking he gets, the further out *I* have to get. The crisis of solipsism he suffers in *The Anatomy Lesson* is better seen from a bit of a distance. ("Art of Fiction" 221, 241)

Alternating between inward and outward perspectives, between the willed extreme of a noble profession and the willed extreme of a sordid one, between paleface and redskin, Roth has made a career out of such shifts, and this study argues that this has been a defining characteristic of Roth's writing from its beginnings to the start of the present century.

* * *

In the introduction to his 2006 monograph on Roth's work, Ross Posnock sounds the bell for an understanding of Roth as much more than a Jewish-American writer with a handful of, by now, familiar settings and concerns. Posnock claims that Roth is "a writer usually regarded as a wholly known quantity, confined to a particular region (New Jersey), a particular aesthetic tradition (American literary realism and naturalism), and, above all, a particular ethnicity (third-generation American Jew)." Posnock argues that seeing Roth only in these terms is unfair to a writer who "long ago slipped the bonds of particularism not least by exemplifying that the local cannot be thought apart from the worldly." In contrast to "the pigeonholing critics who would anchor him to his historical coordinates," Posnock aims to place Roth's writing in the much wider, looser contexts of world literature:

> I hope readers expecting (yet one more) discussion about Roth and being Jewish in America will come to be persuaded that this topic has for too long been isolated from a more capacious inquiry into larger dimensions of his art and broader questions of what it means to be human. (xii)

Asserting that Roth is not "merely" a Jewish-American writer has long been a favorite pursuit of academic critics of Roth's work.[1] But this "pigeonholing" approach still retains its familiarity and power, especially in the popular press, even though the famous firm of Bellow, Malamud, and Roth is now down to one member. Posnock's sentiment seems to be shared by other authors of recent book-length studies of Roth's work. Along with Posnock, Mark Shechner, Debra Shostak, Elaine B. Safer, and David Brauner have all recently written books on Roth that reckon with a career that has now lasted more than 50 years. Beyond the mere fact that Roth has written more than 25 books, making it particularly difficult to quickly sum up the sort of writer he is, his most recent books have been almost universally hailed as more ambitious, wider in scope, and more concerned with "the human" than with "the Jewish." None of these new studies, in fact, takes Roth's Jewishness or his treatment of Jewish themes as the main subject of their inquiry. Rather, each takes a different, broad, somewhat vague, unifying concept to be the backbone of his or her study. Posnock ties together Roth's works through an exploration of his interest in immaturity and provocation. Shostak sees an intense concern with the various aspects of subjectivity as the common element of Roth's long career. Both Safer and Brauner restrict their focus to Roth's books since *The Ghost Writer* (1979), with Safer arguing that Roth's comedy, as used to comment on culture and society, is the unifying feature of his career. Brauner uses paradox, "both as a rhetorical device of which Roth is particularly fond, and also as an organising intellectual and ideological principle that inflects all of his work," as a thread that runs through his study (*Philip Roth* 8). Shechner, even broader in his thesis, allows himself only this by way of an explanation of Roth's methods: "Roth does what he does because he does what he does" (*Up Society's Ass* 4).[2]

This is not to say that these recent studies are vague or unfocused in their engagement with Roth's works; on the contrary, these five works, as well as a number of new essay collections on Roth and a journal devoted to him, have contributed substantially to a newfound depth and breadth of serious criticism on Roth. Rather, the general concepts around which these studies are organized—immaturity, subjectivity, comedy, paradox, willfulness—suggest that it is no longer the case that Roth is spoken of as a "wholly known quantity." These are terms with which to discuss a writer concerned with subjects that concern us all. But beyond an acknowledgment of Roth's universality, this is also, I suspect, a token of the extraordinary variety to be found within Roth's work, and the extraordinary difficulty (or perhaps even inappropriateness) of an attempt to unify it all. When attempting to unify the fiction under one of these general headings, one often concludes that such unity is impossible to declare.

I would suggest that even some of the best critical work on Roth has tended to overlook the ways in which Roth's career frustrates most attempts at imposing unity. Consider, for example, the recent monographs by Shostak and Posnock. Both take on the entirety of Roth's career with a willingness to rethink common assumptions about familiar works and a capacity for spotting both the overlooked details as well as the larger threads that run through the fiction. But although, as noted above, both works take broad concepts as central to their efforts to do justice to Roth's multiplicity of concerns, their approaches tend to focus on two different, perhaps opposing, sides of Roth.

Shostak's central argument is that Roth has a handful of characteristic concerns, all revolving around the enigma of subjectivity. This Roth, by turning inward to focus on "masculinity, embodiment, Jewish American identity, storytelling as an act of both fictive imagination and quasi-autobiographical disclosure, and the position of the subject within American history," can provide "an index into the shifting ideologies of the time, both social and literary" (viii). But despite his repeated explorations of such topics, Roth has never "solved" any of his self-imposed problems. Rather, Shostak argues, taking a page from *The Counterlife* (1986), Roth's books are a series of "countertexts," each testing out a number of speculative situations to explore the many implications of selfhood. Shostak's focus, in widening the scope of Roth studies from traditional takes that would see him as "merely" a Jewish writer or "merely" a comic writer, is to examine the ways that Roth has made human subjectivity, the way that we inhabit ourselves, his most significant enduring concern. "Roth has chosen to explore the process of how one comes to rest at a position, how one thinks about what one really thinks, by tracing the journeys of imagined selves through a series of subject-positions" (7). This is the Roth who has said that "Updike and Bellow hold their flashlights out into the world, reveal the world as it is now. I dig a hole and shine my flashlight into the hole" (Plante 3).

Posnock, by contrast, presents a Roth who has been shining his flashlight out into the world, or at least into the library, since his earliest writings. In a study distinguished by its wide range of reference points, Posnock makes the case that Roth, rather than Jewish Newark's native son, actually resides in the "republic of culture," a space defined by his reading, instead of his geographical, or even biographical, origins (xiii). Borrowing Ellison's concept of "the appropriation game" (a concept which, Posnock points out, originates in Goethe and Emerson), Posnock sees this, rather than assimilation, as the key to Roth's movement from the particular circumstances of his origins to the universal ground of world literature:

> To rewrite assimilation as appropriation banishes the whole melodrama of assimilation whereby the outsider is required to cast off old (ethnic) ways for new and submit to a culture assumed to possess a stable, homogenous identity; this sacrificial process affirms a hierarchy of insider/outsider, native/ alien grounded in blood and origin.
>
> By contrast, all that appropriation requires is a good library. (5)

The library from which Roth has appropriated, Posnock insists, is much larger and idiosyncratic than is often claimed. Along with such familiar names as Henry James and Milan Kundera, Posnock ties Roth into a distinctive tradition that includes Montaigne, Emerson, Witold Gombrowicz, Robert Musil, William James, Dostoevsky, and Ellison. Uniting all of these writers with Roth is an attraction to aspects of the broadly defined concept of immaturity: resistance to bourgeois notions of civilized adulthood, rejection of belief in a transparently static and comprehensible reality, willingness to transform and be transformed, and a generally anarchic spirit of provocation. Included within this definition of immaturity is the very concept of appropriation itself, which rejects the assumed boundaries of biographical circumstance in favor of an approach that promiscuously takes from wherever the individual chooses. Roth "negotiates his identity as an American citizen and writer" through "a freewheeling approach to culture that rewrites heritage not as a passive inheritance but as an assemblage produced by the act of seizing or appropriating from the past and present" (90, 91–2). Posnock elucidates this approach through a series of wide-ranging case studies. For example, instead of merely focusing on the much-noted influence of Henry James on Roth's early career, Posnock argues that, in the final chapter of *American Pastoral*, Roth appropriates and revises a crucial moment of *The Golden Bowl* for his own purposes, illuminating Swede Levov through an implied comparison with Maggie Verver (114–16). This is a Roth pointed outwards, perched, like one of his first protagonists, Neil Klugman, on a high chair in a grand library, roaming through a "republic of culture," entrance to which is granted to anyone curious enough to spend most of his time reading.[3]

Whereas Shostak tends to focus on the ways in which Roth turns inward in his interest in the creation of subjectivity, and Posnock tends to focus on Roth's outward trajectory toward the appropriation of literary models and discourses, I hope to show that my approach requires a modulation between the two directions. Roth's intense and durable self-consciousness has ensured a focus on the formation of identity, both in the ways in which the self is constructed and understood and in the ways in which the self is affected by the world "out there," by culture, but also by history, by other people. This inward/outward, or inside/outside, distinction, is a useful one in discussing Roth's career, especially because he has tended toward a refusal to choose one over the other. The critical firestorm that greeted his debut centered on just this distinction: Roth was accused of betraying his people by writing about them in a way that, while perhaps acceptable when speaking within the community, was tantamount to "informing" when spread to the world at large, outside the community.[4] Roth's fiction in the 1970s and early 1980s shows him, on the one hand, apparently turning inward, focusing on the trials and comic effects of a psychoanalytically defined self, while, on the other hand, turning outward to describe and make use of a culture decidedly not his own, that of Eastern Europe. Roth's work of the late 1980s and early 1990s seemed again to reflect an inward turn, with four books of varyingly autobiographical concerns. Soon after, however, Roth was seen to apparently change tack, shifting his focus directly outward to the effects of American history in his late 1990s trilogy. Roth's comment above, about shining his flashlight into a hole, seems to indicate that he sees his vocation as mainly an inward-looking one. However, we should keep in mind the response of the American writer David Plante, to whom Roth directed those remarks, when considering the shape of Roth's career as a whole: "What I keep forgetting about you, and shouldn't, is that when you talk about yourself digging a hole and shining a flashlight into it you're talking just to try it on for five minutes to see what it looks like" (3). If there is one constant to Roth's career, now nearing five decades long, it's that he has never stopped "trying on" such positions for himself, pointing both inward and outward.

There are a few baseline assumptions that will guide my approach to Roth's career. First, the long procession of Roth's fiction unsurprisingly shows a variety of preoccupations: obviously Roth's interests and approaches have changed over the years, the product of an intensely curious and often impetuous writer who has taken great pleasure in changing tack from book to book, often it sometimes seems trying to frustrate those readers who would pin him down as a certain type of writer.[5] Therefore I have found it necessary to break Roth's career down into clusters of books, positing "phases" of Rothian preoccupation, while trying not to lose sight of the cumulative whole. Sometimes these phases overlap, reflecting the messy interplay of a writer's primary concerns as they are tailored to the needs of the individual books. For example, *Portnoy's Complaint* (1969) serves both as the culmination of Roth's early attempts to define himself through both high and low culture, as well as the beginning of a period of intense fascination with the processes and literary uses of psychoanalysis, a preoccupation which would last for nearly two decades.

Secondly, Roth's self-consciousness, compounded by (perhaps birthed by) the defining scrutiny he suffered over his early work, makes a chronological approach preferable. Roth has spoken about the "exuberance of being a literary orphan," the freedom that he felt upon writing his first book: "Not as yet informed that he is a realistic writer, or a Jewish writer, or an academic writer, or a controversial writer, he is not tempted either to satisfy the expectation or to subvert it" ("From the First" 1). Implied here is that, since writing *Goodbye, Columbus*, Roth has *always* felt the temptation to satisfy or subvert the expectations that have circled his career. Roth has always been acutely aware of how his books have been received, of the shape of his career to date, and, as the initial Zuckerman trilogy shows, he is attuned to the way a writer's life and career make a compelling narrative. Such a narrative is also implied by the definite development of his preoccupations, tied to the chronological points of his career. In the early books, he is most concerned with the initial definition of the self, especially through early experiences of culture. In the middle period, the preoccupations become more self-consciously intellectual, as he pursues topics that interest him as an established author, as a teacher, and as an adult. The later period seems most concerned with looking back on his career as a writer to date and evaluating the culture that has shaped him as a writer and as an American.

Thirdly, Roth's fiction shows a writer particularly open to the culture around him. The interplay between the writer of fiction and his contemporary culture is a central topic in Roth's early forays into literary criticism as a young author. His oft-quoted remark that "the American writer in the middle of the 20th century has his hands full in trying to understand, and then describe, and then make *credible* much of American reality," although its meanings have been contested, certainly implies that Roth thinks part of an American writer's job is to address the reality around him ("Writing" 224). *Portnoy's Complaint* alone, to pick an obvious example, contains literary allusion, both high and low, reference to popular song, Hollywood movies, the golden age of radio, baseball and its myths, presidential politics, advertisements, tabloid headlines, and the television quiz show scandal, to name just some of the cultural artifacts which find their way into Portnoy's monologue. To follow on from Posnock's conception of Roth as a promiscuous, cosmopolitan appropriator, I think it is necessary when writing about Roth to remain open to unexpected cultural connections. As I work chronologically through Roth's career, I bring to the discussion certain discourses that I feel can show Roth's writing in a new light. These include the progression of liberal thought from socialist left to anti-Stalinist right, the costs of the New York Intellectuals' embrace of seriousness, the

Broadway production of *The Diary of Anne Frank*, the psychotherapeutic practice of narrative therapy, and many others.

* * *

Each of my chapters will follow an inward or outward turn from Roth, always remembering that, of course, as he turns inward, he very often also turns outward, and vice versa. The first two chapters examine Roth's early career, showing that, as Roth established himself, he, often through the crucible of controversy, worked at defining himself as an American writer, often revising the definition as he went along. Roth's initial attempts at definition show a writer made keenly aware of his readership and their expectations for his fiction. In Chapter 1, I look at how, in *Goodbye, Columbus*, while apparently performing the role of the outsider (he who would violate the code of the ethnic group through allegiance to the wider conscripts of literature), Roth actually enacts and seems to anticipate the internal debate of the American Jewish community that would come to the surface upon the book's publication. With a similar Janus-faced approach, in Chapter 2, I examine how *Portnoy's Complaint*, which apparently breaks with Roth's earlier ardent pursuit of literary seriousness in exchange for the wild "new sensibility" of the 1960s, tends to concern itself precisely with the "assimilation-by-culture trail"—Jonathan Freedman's phrase for the highbrow road many Jewish intellectuals attempted to follow into America—as a path toward identity formation (Freedman 8). Both chapters refer frequently to the work of the New York Intellectuals, both as a cultural barometer of the times and as a sort of baseline indication of the way that American Jews made their way into the mainstream of American letters.

Chapters 3 and 4 are concerned with the period that followed the cataclysmic popular success of *Portnoy's Complaint*, signaling Roth's entrance into mainstream American culture and also granting him the cultural capital to shift from his initial definitions of himself to the more self-consciously intellectual interests of an established author. Chapter 3 sees Roth turn outward to address models outside of his immediate experience, in the form of Franz Kafka and Anne Frank. Characteristically, these appropriative moves allow Roth to further define himself and his personae. In Chapter 4, I follow what might be called Roth's psychoanalytic period, as a fascination with Freudian ways of conceiving of, dealing with, and talking about the self reveals itself to be central to the work of the 15-year period that begins with *Portnoy's Complaint*. As the period progresses, I detail how a growing frustration with the limits of a psychoanalytic mindset leads Roth to introduce a radically different vision of the self in *The Counterlife*, the book that David Brauner has called "the beginning of Roth's second coming" (*Philip Roth* 3).

The final two chapters follow Roth's work from his memoir *The Facts* (1988) through his American trilogy, which culminates in *The Human Stain* (2000). Increasingly established as one of the most significant authors of the second half of the twentieth century, Roth begins to look backward, sizing up, taking stock, and revising his own, and his culture's, history. This involves both inward and outward moves. Chapter 5 examines Roth's four "autobiographical" works that begin with *The Facts*. Although in many senses this is an inward turn, a late-career reappraisal of the self seemingly provoked by a series of near-fatal medical scares, I work to show how writing about his self so explicitly leads Roth into a consideration of how writing affects others—an ethical consideration with roots going back to the very beginning of his career. Chapter 6 is concerned with the three books most cited as responsible for Roth's "career resurgence" in the late nineties, *American Pastoral* (1997), *I Married a Communist* (1998), and *The Human Stain* (2000). As Roth seems to turn recognizably outward again, the chapter makes the case that the trilogy shares many concerns with Roth's earliest work, demonstrating that this new Roth is much like the old one. Ultimately, I hope to show that Roth's "self-conscious and deliberate zig-zag" has resulted in a body of work that is both remarkably diverse and unmistakably his.

Chapter 1

The American Jewish Experience and the New York Intellectuals: *Goodbye, Columbus*

As long as the Jews were isolated in their own communities, there was no problem of group personality. However, with emancipation and settlement in an open society, the problem of identity became crucial.

Milton Plesur, Jewish Life in Twentieth-Century America

Is it me? Is it me ME ME ME ME! It has to be me—but is it!

Ozzie Freedman, *"The Conversion of the Jews"*

On January 8th, 1914, Franz Kafka wrote in his diary: "What have I in common with Jews? I have hardly anything in common with myself and should stand very quietly in a corner, content that I can breathe" (252). This statement should remind us of the dangers inherent in assigning group loyalties to essentially individualistic artists.[1] How would Kafka, that most uncomfortable and lonely of writers, have reacted if told that one day he would be hailed as "the most quint-essentially Jewish of writers"? (Brauner, *Post-War* 8). How would Kafka have responded to calls from the Jewish community for him to represent the virtues of that community to the wider world? Of course, Kafka only published a hand-ful of stories during his lifetime, and wrote before there was much of a literary industry eager to categorize writers into ethnic and religious "schools." But one can assume that if he had been born 50 years later and had emigrated to America, he would be lumped in with Saul Bellow and Bernard Malamud in the "Jewish-American school," with all the assumptions and expectations that such a title implies.

Philip Roth was born in 1933, 50 years after Kafka, and, as such, would go on to become the third name in that magical triumvirate, Bellow-Malamud-Roth, upon the publication of his debut, *Goodbye, Columbus*, in 1959. He also found himself in the middle of a storm of controversy among ordinary Jewish readers and Jewish community leaders as a result of the portrayal of Jews in his stories. Due to many factors (at the very least, the economic gains of the Jewish-American community, the explosion of popular Jewish-American fiction, and the prominent Jewish presence at such highbrow journals as *Commentary* and *Partisan Review*), questions of Jewish literary identity were of great interest to many in 1959. Writing when he did, and writing about Jews, Roth could not merely be a writer who happened to be Jewish. Rather, the pressures exerted by the Jewish-American community, and the specific nature of that community at the time, in many ways dictated the formation of Roth's literary sensibility, and his sense of himself as a writer for years to come.

Goodbye, Columbus consists of the title novella as well as five short stories, all of which were initially published in magazines over the previous year and a half. Each of the stories centers on contemporary Jewish life in American suburbia, save "Defender of the Faith," which transposes its Jews onto a US army base in Missouri near the end of World War II. Much of the appeal of the collection lies in the sharp eye it directs toward the Jewish suburbs. The Jewish-American population went through a remarkable demographic shift in the 15 years following the war. As second- and third-generation American Jews moved into the middle and upper-middle class, there was a tremendous migration out of the cities and into the suburbs. The New Jersey city of Newark, where Philip Roth grew up, had 58,000 Jewish residents in 1948. By 1958, that number had fallen to 41,000. By contrast, the Jewish population of West Orange, just one of the many suburbs within 20 miles of Newark, rose from 1,600 to 7,000 within the same ten-year period (Shapiro 145). The nature of Jewish life, for so long poor and urban, had become, seemingly overnight, wealthy and suburban.[2] As Saul Bellow noted in his review of *Goodbye, Columbus*, "nothing in history has so quickly and radically transformed any group of Jews" ("Swamp" 79). It is this transformation that informs the stories of Roth's debut.

This significant demographic shift must be taken into account when looking at the Jewish response to *Goodbye, Columbus*. The response was remarkably polarized, reflecting the great changes affecting the Jewish-American community, and problematizing the notion of the Jewish-American writer. As I will argue, the simmering issues reflected in the book's reception are ones that the book itself takes up.

Any analysis of the Jewish response to a book published in the 1940s or 1950s must begin with the so-called New York Intellectuals. First coming together in the 1930s, the New York Intellectuals were a (largely Jewish) group of critics, writers, and thinkers who made their mark in the pages of such journals as *Partisan Review*, *Commentary*, and *Dissent*. Perhaps the most useful way of understanding this disparate group comes from Norman Podhoretz's conception of the New York Intellectuals as a Jewish family, made up of three generations. The founding generation included Philip Rahv, Lionel Trilling, Clement Greenberg, and Sidney Hook, all active in New York in the 1930s. Rahv, along with William Phillips, launched *Partisan Review* in 1934, perhaps the most influential American intellectual journal of the mid-twentieth century. The second generation, arriving in the 1940s, included Irving Howe, Leslie Fiedler, Alfred Kazin, Irving Kristol, and Saul Bellow (Podhoretz, *Making It* 111, 120).[3] The third generation brought Podhoretz, Susan Sontag, and Midge Decter into the fold (Bloom 277). Although Roth is considered by some to be a part of this third generation, the link seems tenuous. He did initially publish two of the stories from *Goodbye, Columbus* ("Eli, the Fanatic" and "You Can't Tell a Man by the Song He Sings") in *Commentary*, as well as the essays "Writing About Jews" and "Writing American Fiction," but he tended to run in different circles, and is rarely mentioned in the various histories of the group. Like a family, all of these figures "found themselves stuck with one another against the rest of the world whether they liked it or not" (Podhoretz, *Making It* 110).

The various reviews of *Goodbye, Columbus* by the New York Intellectuals are remarkable in their similarity. Almost unanimously positive, each reviewer noted Roth's sharp portrayal of suburban Jewish communities in similar terms. Irving Howe praised Roth for his "ruthless" depiction of the Jewish suburbs, calling it "ferociously exact" ("Suburbs" 37). Alfred Kazin approvingly noted Roth's "refusal of a merely sentimental Jewish solidarity [. . .] He cast[s] a cold eye on Jews as a group" (145). Harvey Swados, something of a distant Jewish cousin to the New York core group, admired Roth's "fiendishly accurate eye for the minutiae of middle-class Jewish life" (459). Perhaps Saul Bellow's assessment, in a review in *Commentary*, best sums up the response of the New York Intellectuals:

> Here and there one meets people who feel that the business of a Jewish writer in America is to write public relations releases, to publicize everything that is nice in the Jewish community and to suppress the rest, loyally. This is not at all the business of Jewish writers or of writers of any kind. [. . .] The loss to our sense of reality is not worth the gain (if there is one) in public relations. ("Swamp" 79)[4]

Reviews such as these strive to paint a picture of what a Jewish-American writer should be. He should be "ruthless" and "ferocious"; the eye he casts toward his community should be "cold" and "fiendishly accurate"; and he must be "exact," responsible for portraying "our sense of reality." This is the modernist idea of the artist as alienated from, and independent of, his community. But the aspects of *Goodbye, Columbus* that these Jewish critics praised—Roth's "refusal of a merely sentimental Jewish solidarity"—seemed precisely the aspects that sparked a strikingly different response from Roth's more middlebrow Jewish readers.

"What is being done to silence this man?"

The controversy began with the publication of "Defender of the Faith" in the *New Yorker* in March of 1959 and continued when the story was reprinted as part of *Goodbye, Columbus*, in June of that year. "Defender of the Faith," narrated by US army sergeant Nathan Marx, takes place on a base in Missouri during World War II. One of the base's new recruits, Sheldon Grossbart, proceeds to extract a series of favors and privileges from Marx, based upon their shared Jewish heritage. Although Marx is deeply uncomfortable and confused about giving Grossbart special treatment, Grossbart takes advantage of Marx's basically compassionate nature for his own ends. The story is essentially about Marx's troubled conscience, as he must eventually decide between his allegiance to a fellow Jew and his allegiance to his own sense of justice.

This moral dilemma was not what had enraged the readers who denounced the story and its author. Rather it was the character of Sheldon Grossbart. The portrayal of a Jew who is manipulative, conniving, and greedy, they argued, would only provide fuel to the fire of anti-Semites, who are eager to characterize all Jews as such. Almost immediately after the story was initially published, letters poured in, both to the *New Yorker*'s editorial office and to Roth himself. One reader wrote, in a personal letter to Roth, "With your one story, 'Defender of the Faith,' you have done as much harm as all the organized anti-Semitic organizations have done to make people believe that all Jews are cheats, liars, connivers" (Farberow). Another letter, to the *New Yorker*, imparted the message that "we cannot escape the conclusion that [this story] will do irreparable damage to the Jewish people. [. . .] Cliches like 'this being art' will not be acceptable" (Levy).

The controversy soon spread to American synagogues, where Roth and his work became the subject of intense debate. Rabbis made Roth the topic of their sermons, pointing out the dangers that lurked within *Goodbye, Columbus.* One rabbi wrote, in his synagogue newsletter, that "the only logical conclusion any intelligent reader could draw from [Roth's] stories or books, is that this country—nay that the world—would be a much better and happier place without the 'Jews'" (*Temple Topics*). Another rabbi wrote to the Anti-Defamation League, asking, "What is being done to silence this man? Medieval Jews would have known what to do with him" (Roth, "Writing About Jews" 450). At the age of 26, with but one slim book to his name, Roth suddenly had more notoriety within the Jewish community than anyone could have predicted.

What should emerge from this account of the controversy surrounding *Goodbye, Columbus* is a sense of the late 1950s Jewish-American community as very sensitive to the ways in which Jews were portrayed to the wider world, and a sense that the community was willing and able to exert tremendous pressure upon those who would attempt to make those portrayals. I would argue that there were two main historical reasons for this sensitivity.

The first aspect to consider is the effect of the Holocaust. The extermination of six million European Jews had an immense impact on their American counterparts. As American Jews became more prosperous and left the traditional Jewish neighborhoods of the cities for anonymous American suburbs, the nature of Jewish life in America was in rapid flux. And yet, as Irving Howe points out, "Memories of the Holocaust pressed deep into the consciousness of Jews, all, or almost all, making them feel that whatever being a Jew meant, it required of them that they try to remain Jews." No matter how secure and

Americanized Jews became, the Holocaust remained fixed in the collective Jewish psyche as a permanent reminder of the tenuous survival of the Jewish people. This manifested itself most noticeably in a heightened suspicion of the existence of anti-Semitism. Howe goes on to state that,

> [h]aunted by the demons of modern history, most of the immigrants and many of their children kept a fear, somewhere in their minds, that anti-Semitism might again become a serious problem in America. By mid-century, it was often less an actual fear than a persuasion that they *should* keep this fear, all past experience warranting alertness even if there was no immediate reason for anxiety. (*World* 627, 630)

When Philip Roth's story "Defender of the Faith" portrayed a Jew such as Sheldon Grossbart as selfish, greedy, and manipulative, many Jewish readers seemed to fear what an American anti-Semite would make of it.

The second aspect of the Jewish-American community that needs to be considered has to do with its socioeconomic position at the time. As already noted, the overall trend for American Jews after the war was toward the upper-middle class and toward the suburbs. After centuries as a wandering people without a nation, never secure for very long, Jews had seemingly found, in America, a place where they could be successful members of the broader community. Albert Gordon, in his 1959 sociological study *Jews in Suburbia*, noted, "The uniqueness of present-day Jewish suburbanites, then, is associated with the fact that they, unlike their fathers' generation, feel 'at home' and secure in their Americanism" (16). Having finally attained comfort and security, there was a tremendous collective desire to protect and maintain it. Jews had finally established safe and prosperous communities, and, understandably, they wanted to keep them that way. Jewish historian Milton Plesur claims that, in the new suburban communities, or "Golden Ghettoes," "one's affiliation with the Jewish community is compulsive; he is subject to its claims and demands in the way the metropolitan Jew has never been" (166). Philip Roth certainly felt these claims and demands after the publication of *Goodbye, Columbus*.

The Jewish response to *Goodbye, Columbus* had two distinct strains. The New York Intellectuals praised Roth's cutting portrayal of the prosperous Jewish suburbs, affirming a modernist view of the artist who must maintain a critical eye toward his or her community. The outraged readers, by contrast, were precisely concerned with protecting that community, especially in regard to the way it was seen by outsiders. The contrast raises the question of the artist's, or in fact any individual's, responsibility to his community. Can, or should, an artist be a representative of his ethnic or religious community? How much are any individual's actions constricted by the collective desires of his community? What is most interesting about the questions that the Jewish response to *Goodbye, Columbus* raised is that they seemed to echo the questions raised in the stories themselves. In the best stories in the collection, Roth focuses upon the complicated relationship between an individual protagonist and the Jewish community of which he is a part.

"Eli, the Fanatic"

The question of an artist's responsibility to represent his community is most explicitly on display in the book's final story, "Eli, the Fanatic," as the eponymous hero must literally represent his community. As a lawyer, Eli has been hired by the Jews of his town to evict, by appeal to zoning laws, the members of the newly arrived Yeshiva—a Talmudic boarding school that houses two adults and eighteen Hasidic children. The town of Woodenton, Eli informs the Hasidic headmaster (in especially apt terms), is a community in which both Jews and non-Jews "are anxious that their families live in comfort and beauty and serenity" (*GC* 242). It seems that Woodenton's comfort, beauty, and serenity have all been disturbed by the Yeshiva, whose ancient practices and strange dress will threaten the delicate balance of assimilation.

Much of the story centers on the pressures that Eli's townsmen exert upon him, underlining the importance of his mission. Eli's every spare moment is spoiled by a ringing phone, bringing with it another townsman's plea that he rid the town of the Yeshiva. The individual characterization of Woodenton's concerned citizenry is minimal—the community as a whole becomes a character, shouting its demands into Eli's ear. Through these pressures, Roth portrays a modern suburban Jewish community in which the protection of comfort and prosperity trumps all other considerations.

It quickly becomes clear that what prompts the Jewish community of Woodenton to want to evict the Yeshiva is a desire to maintain their assimilated suburban community, with its homogenized culture that has no room for such "extreme" practices. The conception of the suburbs as an escape from traditional American Jewish urban communities is made clear enough by one of Eli's neighbors, who, speaking of the yeshiva, exclaims, "when I left the city, Eli, I didn't plan the city should come to me" (*GC* 237). This is in line with one accepted view of twentieth-century Jewish suburbia, in which "[w]hatever spoke too emphatically of traditional ways in religious practice, or too stridently of traditional ideologies in Yiddish secular life, was left behind" (Howe, *World* 614). But Roth goes further than this claim, depicting the rejection of even fundamental Jewish religious values and practices in such communities.

One townsman expresses his worry that soon the town will be filled with Hasidic children, wearing yarmulkes and chanting their prayers through the center of town. Even the religious education he's not so crazy about: "This Abraham in the Bible was going to kill his own *kid* for a sacrifice. [. . .] Today a guy like that they'd lock him up" (*GC* 256). The distaste shown for the Yeshiva's traditional religious practices highlights the extent to which a desire for normalcy has gripped the modern Jewish community, eclipsing even the most fundamental aspects of religion, the ostensible source of Jewish identity. The same townsman even goes on to imply that it was the European Jews' inability to "blend in" that led to the atrocities of the Holocaust: "There's going to be no pogroms in Woodenton. Right? 'Cause there's no fanatics, no crazy people [. . .] just people who respect each other, and leave each other be" (*GC* 257).

The mention of the Nazi pogroms is not merely incidental to the story, as the 20 residents of the Yeshiva are all D.P.s—"displaced persons"—Jewish survivors of the Holocaust, left without any family, community, or home. The Yeshiva in suburban Woodenton is their refuge; America, with its traditions of religious tolerance, will offer them a place to live as Jews. The irony Roth introduces here is clear. The rise of American Jews from poor immigrants at the end of the nineteenth century to prosperous suburbanites by the 1950s was perhaps the most remarkable demographic shift in twentieth-century American history. Jews, for whom the world had seemingly no home for centuries, could finally feel comfortable and secure. But, in this story at least, this comfort and security comes at a steep price. Holocaust survivors, the modern age's most striking symbol of the homeless Jewish people, chased from their homes by the Nazi atrocities, do not fit in to the Woodenton Jews' plan for their community. Here, it is the Jews themselves who initiate a pogrom.[5]

Eli stands out as the only member of the Woodenton Jewish community who seeks to understand the elements of the conflict. Keeping in mind Roth's experience with the outraged Jewish readers of *Goodbye, Columbus*, Eli might be seen as something like an artist figure for Roth, pushed and pulled by the claims of his society, struggling to maintain his individual perspective. Throughout, he is filled with self-doubt and self-questioning. This self-doubt stands in stark contrast to the assured, unified voice of the community, which only states that it wants the Yeshiva gone. But Eli's investigative approach leads him toward an understanding of the motives of both sides of the conflict, and, eventually, to a sort of resolution. He understands the town's desires, and, for most of the story, tries to be conciliatory in carrying out their demands. Driving through the prosperous suburb, he thinks of his ancestors, who struggled for generations in Eastern Europe to establish a stable, safe community, like the one the Jews of Woodenton seemingly have: "After all these centuries, maybe there just had to be this communal toughness—or numbness—to protect such a blessing" (*GC* 259). At the same time, Eli spends time speaking with the Hasidic headmaster, listening to the survivors' story. He feels compassion for their situation and attempts to strike a compromise that would allow the Yeshiva to stay. The compromise, in which the Yeshiva's two adults agree to wear modern dress (actually suits that Eli gives them) when in the town, shows an understanding that most of the town's grievances concern the outward appearance of normalcy. Eli's final act, however, transgresses Woodenton's conventions of normalcy, emphasizing his rebellious character. In a sort of epiphany of empathy and understanding for the Hasids, he dresses in the traditional Hasidic suit and hat, and parades down the main street of town. It is only a token act of defiance, perhaps, but it is sufficiently subversive to convince his fellow towns-men that he is having a nervous breakdown.

The sensitivity of the suburban Jewish community in "Eli, the Fanatic" is a product of that community's fervent desire to be normal, American, and incon-spicuous to the broader, secular world. This fictional community uncannily foreshadowed the outspoken opponents of *Goodbye, Columbus*, who saw Roth as playing Eli's role, parading down the street and exposing to America what should be hidden.

"The Conversion of the Jews"

In another, more lighthearted story in the collection, "The Conversion of the Jews," Roth depicts the sensitivity of another suburban Jewish community, and depicts its suspicious attitude toward individual dissent and self-questioning. Ozzie Freedman, the story's 13-year-old protagonist, is in trouble with Rabbi Binder, the teacher of his Hebrew school class. For the third time in recent memory, Ozzie's mother will have to come in to discuss Ozzie's transgressions with the rabbi. Each of these meetings is prompted by Ozzie's persistent curios-ity and questioning of accepted Jewish practices. This time, Ozzie's offense results from a theological discussion in class. Rabbi Binder explains to the class that although, like Christians, Jews believe that Jesus Christ existed, they do not believe that he was the son of God. He appeals to the students' common sense to convince them that Jesus Christ could not have been conceived without sex-ual congress. His explanation, however, does not fly with Ozzie. If God could create the whole world in six days, he wonders aloud, isn't it possible that he could let a woman have a baby without having intercourse? Rabbi Binder takes Ozzie's remarks as pure impudence and tells him that his mother will have to come in. In the meantime, the rabbi tells Ozzie that he should think over what he has said. Ozzie later admits to his friend Itzie: "Itz, I thought it over for a solid hour, and now I'm convinced God could do it" (*GC* 130).

This phrasing of Ozzie's ostensible blasphemy is important to the main thrust of the story, as Ozzie's transgression comes in the form of a statement of belief. Whereas in "Eli, the Fanatic," Roth depicts a nonreligious Jewish community that pursues a homogenized state of assimilation at the expense of conspicu-ously strange religious Jews, here Roth operates within a specifically religious Jewish setting. In "The Conversion of the Jews," instead of suburbia, it is an institutionalized and intellectually stagnant Judaism that resists individual dif-ference. Ozzie is punished because his honest, ingenuous belief differs from accepted dogma.

Rabbi Binder, as the leader of Ozzie's synagogue and Hebrew school class, is depicted as an authoritarian figure, or at the very least someone who aspires to such a position. As the figurative voice of the Jewish community, it is striking that it is his voice that receives the most descriptive detail from Roth. It is first described as "the monumental voice of Rabbi Binder" (*GC* 127). Later, Ozzie compares the rabbi's voice, when in full scolding mode, to "a statue, real slow and deep" (*GC* 130). Finally, the narrator reports that the rabbi's voice, "could it have been seen, would have looked like the writing on scroll" (*GC* 135).[6] The pressures of the Jewish community are brought to bear on the individual through a voice that strives toward an unquestionable authority. Of course, Rabbi Binder's role in the story is clearly signaled by his very name. His attempts to bind his students, to restrict their responses to the ideas they are being taught, are frustrated by Ozzie Freedman, whose own name suggests that he cannot be bound.

The rabbi uses his authoritarian voice in the service of an institutionalized, lifeless Judaism. For example, he scolds Ozzie in class for reading too slowly from the Hebrew prayer book. But if Ozzie were to read faster, we are told, "he was sure not to understand what he was reading." When Ozzie continues to read at his snail's pace, the rabbi administers a "soul-battering" to the boy (*GC* 132). Ozzie's meticulous reading is clearly contrasted with the perpetual mumbling of Yakov Blotnik, the 71-year-old custodian who seems as integral to the synagogue's structure as its roof or walls. "To Ozzie the mumbling had always seemed a monotonous, curious prayer [. . .] Ozzie suspected he had memorized the prayers and forgotten all about God" (*GC* 131–2).

In their 1961 sociological study of three generations of Jewish-American immigrants, Judith R. Kramer and Seymour Leventman argued that, for third generation American Jews in the suburbs, religious practice had more to do with a desire for group survival than authentic belief. For these Jews, they argued, "religious observance has been reduced to an occasional acknowledgment of synagogue and ritual. Sentiment exceeds commitment in the third generation, sufficing to assuage the conscience without isolating the Jew from the general community." In this way, the suburban community in "The Conversion of the Jews" differs little from the community in "Eli, the Fanatic." Whereas the Jews in the latter are suspicious of any visibly religious practices, the community of the former seems to maintain these practices merely for their own sake, suspicious of any religious practices that differ from the norm. It is a memorized, anaesthetized Judaism that Ozzie runs up against. Kramer and Leventman continue:

> The third generation's religious observance, such as it is, continues to be rationalized by a desire to perpetuate Jewish identity. Only a few young intellectuals, puzzled voices in a Philistine wilderness, wonder whether the religion justifies the people or the people the religion. (17)

Rabbi Binder's voice can be monumental, like a statue, or like the writing on a scroll, but it is never puzzled. It is Ozzie who fits the role of the wondering young intellectual.

The second half of "The Conversion of the Jews" contains the story's most memorable scene, with Ozzie standing on the roof of the synagogue and a large crowd of people down below watching him. Ozzie has escaped to the roof following a confrontation with Rabbi Binder. The boy shouted at the rabbi and the rabbi (accidentally) hit Ozzie, causing the latter to flee to the roof. The scene that follows borders on the ridiculous, ending as it does with the whole crowd following Ozzie's orders to go down on their knees. But it works because it clearly juxtaposes the individual (Ozzie) and his community (the crowd below, made up of many people, including Rabbi Binder, Yakov Blotnik, and Ozzie's mother). This allows Roth to develop his theme in a clear progression, as self-questioning and iconoclasm leads to a questioning of the broader community and collective action.

When Ozzie first finds himself up on the roof, a question runs through his mind: "Is it me? Is it me ME ME ME ME! It has to be me—but is it!" (*GC* 135). He might be asking himself if it was he who called his religious leader a bastard after the rabbi hit him. Or he might be wondering if it is really him on top of his synagogue roof. Either way, this streak of self-questioning runs through him, just as it runs through Eli. It is the bizarre scene that ensues, with the rabbi and Ozzie's mother pleading that the boy not jump to his death, and Ozzie's gleefully anarchic classmates shouting that he *should* jump, that prompts Ozzie to think: "If there was a question to be asked now it was not 'Is it me?' but rather 'Is it us?'" (*GC* 142). He might as well be asking, "Who are we?" Eventually, realizing his power over the crowd of people below him, Ozzie makes everyone get down on their knees—otherwise he'll jump. He then proceeds to make everyone say that God can let a woman have a child without having intercourse. Finally, he asks that his mother promise that she will "never hit anyone about God." "He had asked only his mother, but for some reason everyone kneeling in the street promised he would never hit anybody about God" (*GC* 145). What had begun with a child's honest, brazen question meeting rebuke from an impatient rabbi has led to a small community's pledge to change its ways. Like "Eli, the Fanatic," "The Conversion of the Jews" suggests the ways that an individual's actions can change his community, if that individual is sufficiently inquisitive and independent. Once again, we can see the figure of the artist manifest in the story's protagonist. This scene, with Ozzie on the roof, and his community down below, listening to him, giving credence to his ideas, even following his orders, is something of an artist's fantasy. Roth, who would insist to his community that Jews in America need to be more inquisitive and self-questioning, could only dream of such an audience in 1959.

"Defender of the Faith"

Unlike "Eli, the Fanatic" and "The Conversion of the Jews," "Defender of the Faith" does not take place within a Jewish community. But, in the distinctly non-Jewish environment of a US army base, Sheldon Grossbart effectively imports the coercive power of the Jewish community to manipulate Sergeant Nathan Marx. Grossbart is keenly aware of the power of the conviction that

Jews need conformity for survival and harnesses that power to his own selfish ends.

Initially, his efforts are relatively benign. Guessing (correctly) that Sergeant Marx, his superior, is Jewish, Grossbart asks Marx to make clear to the other soldiers that, when the Jewish soldiers leave their duties to attend religious services, they're not just "goofing off." Sergeant Thurston, Marx's predecessor, would never make such a statement, Grossbart says, "but we thought that with you here things might be a little different" (*GC* 151). Insinuation colors many of Grossbart's statements to Marx. Asking Marx for a weekend pass, Grossbart lies and says that he wants to go to his aunt's house for a Seder, the ceremonial meal that marks the beginning of the Jewish holiday Passover. Some things are important for Jews, Grossbart hints, and Jews must rely on each other to maintain them in a Gentile world. Grossbart's persuasive powers should not be underestimated, and Marx eventually writes him the pass, only to learn, later, that Grossbart's "Seder" was actually a meal at a Chinese restaurant.

As the events of the Holocaust played a large role in the creation of this particular group mentality in American Jews, it is not surprising that Grossbart evokes the decimated European Jewish population in his efforts. Early in the story, Marx sees Grossbart and his two Jewish tagalongs, Mickey Halpern and Larry Fishbein, talking and laughing through the prayers at the aforementioned religious services. He asks them if services are important to them, and Fishbein responds that they're more important away from home, away from their Jewish communities. "That's what happened in Germany," Grossbart chimes in, eager to keep up his pressure on Marx, "they didn't stick together. They let themselves get pushed around" (*GC* 160). As in "Eli, the Fanatic," the reference to the Holocaust increases the power of the community's coercive argument. Whereas in "Eli" the purported lesson of the Holocaust was that the Jews did not "blend in" enough, here it is that they were not unified. Later, when Marx initially denies Grossbart his request for the weekend pass, Grossbart wildly lashes out, in terms that would be repeated by Roth's detractors: "Ashamed, that's what you are [. . .] So you take it out on the rest of us. They say Hitler himself was half a Jew. Hearing you, I wouldn't doubt it" (*GC* 172–3). For Grossbart, the Jewish fear of a repetition of the Holocaust's atrocities becomes another tool for his own aims, and the story becomes, in Michael Rothberg's words, "a warning to avoid turning [the Holocaust] into ethnic property and cultural capital" (57).

Marx is not a hard-hearted man. He does feel for his fellow soldiers and, from time to time, is touched by Grossbart's appeals for Jewish compassion. At one point, he chides himself for his coldness to Grossbart's seemingly honest desire to go visit his aunt, remembering his own grandmother's gentle way with her misbehaving grandson. He asks himself, "Who was Nathan Marx to be such a penny pincher with kindness?" (*GC* 177). He tells Fishbein, "you understand I'm not trying to deny you anything, don't you? If it was my army, I'd serve gefilte fish in the mess hall, I'd sell *kugel* in the PX, honest to God" (*GC* 176).

The story's richness derives from the fact that Roth is alive to the complexities of the situation. This is accomplished through the character of Nathan Marx, who, like Eli and Ozzie, seems to represent the figure of the artist for Roth, always questioning both himself and the situation, agonizingly pursuing the right decision. No matter how distasteful Grossbart is, Marx cannot ignore the young soldier's humanity, or his own compassionate feelings for his Jewish community.

Nonetheless, when Grossbart's manipulations defy Marx's sense of morality, the latter acts. Marx informs Grossbart that all of the trainees will soon be shipped off to the Pacific war. After Grossbart fails in his attempt to get Marx to somehow change his orders, Marx learns that Grossbart has found another Jewish string to pull. By befriending a Corporal Shulman, Grossbart has managed to become the only trainee to be sent to duty in peaceful Monmouth, New Jersey. This Marx cannot abide. He makes a phone call and makes sure Grossbart is on the list to go to the Pacific, along with all the other trainees. He is not proud of his vindictiveness, but the act is something that Marx feels he must do to answer to his own conscience.

"Doesn't Mr. Uris?"

Amid all the controversy that his first book roused, Roth quickly became schooled in defending himself and his work, insisting on his freedom to write literature, not pro-Jewish propaganda. Many of the angry correspondents may have been surprised to find Roth's even-tempered, thorough refutations of their letters waiting in their mailboxes. He went to many synagogues and Jewish community centers to speak and take questions from the often angry audience members (Roth, "Interview" 115–16). And in 1963, Roth published "Writing About Jews" in *Commentary*, an essay that went into great detail in the description and analysis of the attacks upon him and his work. The entire experience was certainly a demanding one; looking back on it in 1975, Roth states that "I seem to have felt called upon both to assert a literary position and to defend my moral flank the instant after I had taken my first steps" (*Reading Myself and Others* xiii). One particular exchange with a correspondent illuminates this literary and moral position.

One of the letters Roth received in this period asked him what grudge he held against his heritage, and, to reinforce the point, included a clipping of an interview given by Leon Uris in the *New York Post*. Uris was a Jewish cultural star at the time, following the 1958 publication of *Exodus*, his unabashedly pro-Israel work of historical fiction. The correspondent marked off a section of the piece, in which Uris states, "There is a whole school of Jewish American writers who spend their time damning their fathers, hating their mothers, wringing their hands and wondering why they were born. [. . .] Their work is obnoxious and makes me sick to my stomach" (Wershiba 34). Roth's response to the implication of this passage is telling, and sheds light upon his attitude toward the Jewish-American community that he investigates in *Goodbye, Columbus*:

> I take it that the inked section of Uris' speech is meant somehow to refer to me. Am I right? If it does, I am deeply sorry you find in my work that I damn my father and that I hate my mother. As for wringing my hands and wondering why I was born, I will admit to it. I do wonder about that. Doesn't Mr. Uris? (Roth, Letter to Mrs. Strausberg)

Roth's insistence here on self-questioning speaks to the brand of artistic individualism he has adopted, a stance that is evident in the three stories discussed here, and throughout his entire body of work. Each of these stories features a Jewish community striving toward a conformity and forced unity that places immense pressure on any individual as intellectually curious as Roth insists that he remain. *Goodbye, Columbus*, unlike many of Roth's later books, does not feature protagonists who are writers. Nonetheless, seen in relation to Roth's public response to the Jewish community's reception of the book, these protagonists are perhaps the predecessors of Peter Tarnopol and Nathan Zuckerman, Roth's future alter egos. Self-questioning, ambivalent, and struggling to remain independent, Eli, Ozzie, and Nathan are proto-Rothian writers by other names.[7] And, like Roth, they must fight against a community that would dictate their actions. In "Eli, the Fanatic," the community pursues an American ideal of normalcy and assimilation at the expense of any other vision of Jewishness. In "The Conversion of the Jews," the community desires an institutionalized, stable Judaism at the expense of individual questioning and curiosity. And in "Defender of the Faith," Grossbart takes advantage of a broad Jewish desire for unity and solidarity at the expense of individual justice. These communities all, in some way, prompt the individual protagonists to question these pressures, to swim against the tide.

The New York Intellectuals and the New Liberalism

Writing in the late 1950s, Roth was by no means alone in his portrayal of the individual resisting the collective desires of community or mass society. *Goodbye, Columbus* must be seen within the changing discourse of liberal thought in postwar America, a narrative particularly well told in Thomas Hill Schaub's *American Fiction in the Cold War*. Schaub's study argues that, from the late 1930s onward, "the nature and obligations of writing were altered in response to the decline of the left, to the fact of Hiroshima, Nagasaki and the Holocaust, and to the anticommunism which dominated politics and culture for some years afterward" (vii). He charts a narrative that runs through the work of a great number of liberal intellectuals and writers; simply, the rejection of staunch socialism following the disillusionment with Russian Communism under Stalin, leading to a move rightward, toward a chastened, more realistic, de-idealized liberalism. This "new liberalism," as it was often called, embodied a host of powerful cultural norms that were expressed throughout the literature and critical writing of the time, and could not have helped but to influence Roth.

This fundamental change in liberal thought is perhaps most thoroughly exemplified by the evolution of the New York Intellectuals. The group's beginnings are usually traced to the birth of *Partisan Review*, in 1934. The journal was launched by Philip Rahv and William Philips under the sponsorship of the New York John Reed Club, a Communist organization that aimed to advance the cause of American proletarian literature. Leaving *New Masses* to focus strictly on politics, *Partisan Review* would take up literary and cultural matters from a socialist perspective (Jumonville 49). Nearly the whole of the first generation of the New York Intellectuals were socialists of some sort in the 1930s, and they brought this orientation to bear on their literary and cultural criticism.

In the years that followed, however, nearly all of these individuals moved steadily to the right. Although the individual paths were idiosyncratic, a pattern of political affiliation can be discerned. After the revelations of the Moscow trials (begun in 1936) and Stalin's nonaggression pact with the Nazis, revolutionary socialism, in full-fledged support of the Soviet Union, became anti-Stalinist Marxism. This, in turn, became pro-American liberalism after the war, often falling in line with Cold War anticommunism. As Alan Wald points out, "[w]hat remained most consistent in their ideological outlook in the postwar era was their virulent hostility to Stalinism, which increasingly became redefined to mean Leninism, and ultimately any form of revolutionary Marxism" (268).[8] This is a simplified version of the twists and turns that led each individual from one affiliation to another, but it is useful in providing an archetype of postwar liberal thought, often haunted by memories of failed or compromised socialist ideals.

Within this political and cultural narrative, one of the most crucial changes was the repositioning of the liberal attitude toward collective action and the power of the masses. What had been a socialist belief in mass uprising toward revolutionary ends became the postwar fear of totalitarianism, the crass products of mass culture, and the specter of widespread cultural conformity.

> [T]he "masses"—once the hope of revolutionary change—became transformed into the disappointing and potentially threatening "mass society." "Alienation," once defined as the separation of the worker from the fruits of his labor, now became a badge of radicalism and autonomy—a sign that one was not a member of "mass society." (Schaub 150)

The liberal's faith in the benevolence of social institutions, in the positive power of mass action, in the socialist society of the Soviet Union, was broken by the revelations of the Soviets' crimes against their own people, the Holocaust, and the detonation of two atomic bombs. The postwar American boom, bringing with it a seemingly all-pervasive, dumbed-down, mass-produced culture indus-try, only strengthened the suspicion that the masses were not a force for good. Instead, what becomes apparent in much of the liberal thinking in the postwar era is a widespread championing of nonconformity, dissent, and individual rebellion against what was seen as a dangerous cultural consensus.

In 1955, R. W. B. Lewis published *The American Adam*, a study of nineteenth-century American literature that traces a narrative of "the authentic American as a figure of heroic innocence and vast potentialities, poised at the start of a new history" (1). He finds this "Adamic tradition" running through the work of Whitman, Hawthorne, and Melville, among others, but the way he sees this tradition adapted in the best literature of the 1950s is telling. Lewis praises Ralph Ellison's *Invisible Man* (1952), J. D. Salinger's *The Catcher in the Rye* (1951), and Saul Bellow's *The Adventures of Augie March* (1953) because, in each, "the hero is willing, with marvelously inadequate equipment, to take on as much of the world as is available to him, without ever fully submitting to any of the world's determining categories" (199). This idea of the individual who must resist and fight against submission to society's "determining categories" is cen-tral to Schaub's portrait of American liberal thought in the Cold War era, and, of course, central to the three stories discussed above. Everywhere—in fiction, in critical texts, even in popular cinema—the dissenting, defiant individual was championed for resisting the bland, homogenizing effects of cultural confor-mity. Even a seemingly radical text such as Norman Mailer's "The White Negro" (1957), which posited a revolutionary power in the defiantly nonconformist "hipster," affirmed this widespread mentality. "[Mailer] was merely indulging a commonplace of the cold war consensus, familiar to mass, mid, and high culture alike. Everyone feared the effects of conformity. Everyone lionized the 'individual'" (Schaub 142).

Along with this widespread emphasis on individual freedom and resistance to "determining categories," the new liberalism was institutionally conscious of the failures of past liberal thought, the seeming naiveté of the belief in the perfectibility of social institutions, the liberal utopia. "The list of charges that liberals brought against themselves [included]: the old liberalism was unimagi-native, it subscribed to 'facile' ideas of progress and 'history,' it wavered in its rejection of totalitarian politics" (Schaub 7). Having vehemently believed in socialist ideals that, under Stalin, were perverted into totalitarianism, many liberals, including the bulk of the New York Intellectuals, were determined to learn from their mistakes. These mistakes were very often attributed to youthful innocence and naiveté, an unwillingness to acknowledge and deal with life's complexity and man's imperfections. In 1955, Lionel Trilling wrote:

> We tried as hard as we could to believe that politics might be an idyll, only to
> discover that what we took to be a political pastoral was really a grim military
> campaign or a murderous betrayal of political allies. [. . .] The evidence
> of this is to be found in a whole literary genre with which we have become

familiar in the last decade, the personal confession of involvement and then disillusionment with Communism. ("George Orwell" 152)

This political narrative, a movement from innocence to a chastened, world-weary maturity, would have a great effect on the nature of the literary and cultural criticism that was produced by these new liberals, especially by the New York Intellectuals.

Just as an apparently naïve socialism was eschewed in favor of a more complex, measured, ambiguous view of the political landscape, so many liberal critics began to reject literary works of naturalism, the traditional vehicle for proletarian literature, for a more modernist aesthetic. Naturalism, with its often simplified assumptions of the individual determined by societal forces, clashed with the new liberalism, both in the former's disavowal of significant individual freedom, and in its supposed positivist portrayal of a black and white world. As Schaub points out, the New York Intellectuals in particular were drawn to a modernist aesthetic for ideological reasons, as modernism's watchwords of ambiguity, contradiction, tension, and complexity appealed to a group that attributed the failure of their erstwhile political affiliations to a simplified, naïve view of the world (25–49). By championing modernism, these critics could continue to insist upon literature's relevance to the social and political world, without falling back upon the simplified ideas of the revolutionary proletarian novel. "On the one hand it grounds the literary idea in the emotions produced by history; on the other it establishes the aesthetic, or formal, standard of contradiction and paradox as the central quality of great art" (Schaub 34). The new liberalism's twin preoccupations with individual freedom and a complex, measured view of the world found a compatible aesthetic in modernism.

The three stories discussed above all seem to have been born of this new liberalism. Emphasizing the dangers of collective societies, here in the form of Jewish communities, each story seems to be most concerned with the fate of the individual within these communities. Roth's individuals are each marked off from the collective by their ambivalence, self-questioning, and, often, self-contradiction—qualities that, in line with the new liberalism, are presented as in vital opposition to the idea of collective will. Even more than the other stories, the title novella of the collection embodies the spirit of the new liberalism, as it follows an ambivalent protagonist whose very ambivalence sets him apart from the culture surrounding him.

"Goodbye, Columbus"

Twenty-three-year-old Neil Klugman lives in Newark with his Aunt Gladys. "Goodbye, Columbus" is the story of the romance that blossoms (and then dies) between Neil and Brenda Patimkin, but it is shadowed by the larger story of the Jewish-American community, in flux between its urban past and its rapidly suburban present. The Patimkins are a nouveau riche Jewish family living in Short Hills, a prosperous New Jersey suburb less than ten miles away from Newark on the map, but much further in terms of lifestyle. Early in the story, Neil asks his aunt where she keeps the suburban phone book, so he can call Brenda. Aunt Gladys is typically exasperated: "That skinny book? What, I gotta clutter my house with that, I never use it?" (*GC* 4). Later, Aunt Gladys, ever the voice of urban Jewishness, asks, "Since when do Jewish people live in Short Hills? They couldn't be real Jews believe me" (*GC* 53). Real Jews or not, suburban families like the Patimkins were now a fact of Jewish life in America, and "Goodbye, Columbus" was Roth's attempt to come to grips with the new Jewish-American reality, through the eyes of his ambivalent narrator. Sanford Pinsker notes that "for all its initial difficulties, the battle for assimilation was a relatively short skirmish. The harder task of assessing the 'victory' fell to contemporary American-Jewish writers like Philip Roth" (22).

From the beginning of the novella, the reader is made aware of the differences between Newark and Short Hills, and of the different Jewish lifestyle each represents. Aunt Gladys's greatest worry in life is that the food she buys might go uneaten by her family. As Neil eats, she sits across the table, rapt with attention, monitoring what he eats. A stereotypical Jewish matriarch, Aunt Gladys seems to spend most of her time warning, in Yiddish-inflected English, about the dangers of wasting food. If this reads as a typically Jewish concern, it is reflective of the accepted socioeconomic status of urban Jewish immigrants. When money is scarce, food must not be wasted.

For the Patimkins, by contrast, food and other material goods are so abundant that, to Neil at least, they do not need to be bought at all; they seem to sprout from the soil. Looking out through the window of the suburban house, Neil sees, under two oak trees, "like fruit dropped from their limbs," an abundance of sporting goods—the accessories of the Patimkins' preferred recreations (*GC* 20). Later, Neil discovers an old refrigerator in the Patimkin basement, overflowing with fruit of every kind. He is astonished: "Oh Patimkin! Fruit grew in their refrigerator and sporting goods dropped from their trees!" (*GC* 40). And when Brenda wonders if the cherry and watermelon pits that the young couple spit onto the grass will take root and bear fruit, Neil responds, "If they took root in this yard, sweetie, they'd grow refrigerators and Westinghouse Preferred" (*GC* 50). This repeated motif of material possessions growing in suburban Short Hills, without even the unseemliness of purchase, emphasizes Neil's vision of Brenda and her family in both socioeconomic and literary terms. In this way, Neil's sometimes ardent, often conflicted love affair with Brenda is also a love affair with Short Hills, with the increasingly prosperous lifestyle of American Jews. Near the end of the novella, when Neil is apprehensive about his future with Brenda, he wanders into a cathedral and informally addresses God. What is he after? What is he pursuing? Which prize will be his reward? "Which prize do you think, *schmuck?* Gold dinnerware, sporting-goods trees, nectarines, garbage disposals, bumpless noses, Patimkin Sink, Bonwit Teller—" (*GC* 92).

In both "Eli, the Fanatic" and "The Conversion of the Jews," Roth provides vivid Jewish communities whose collective desires clash with those of the protagonists, who are, by their nature, conflicted and uncertain. In "Defender of the Faith" there is no such community, but the idea of a collective will is sufficiently expressed through Grossbart's intimations of Jewish solidarity. Similarly, there is no explicit community in "Goodbye, Columbus" that is in conflict with Neil. But something like a collective will is present. It is the seemingly foregone conclusion of Jewish-American upward mobility—the certainty that Aunt Gladys and Newark belong to the past and that Brenda Patimkin and Short Hills belong to the future. Neil's sensitivity to this force is often expressed somewhat bitterly, in small signs of resentment that occasionally appear amid the seeming idyll of budding romance. When Brenda vaguely indicates that she goes to college in Boston, Neil tells the reader, testily, that he's not embarrassed to tell people he attended Newark Colleges of Rutgers (*GC* 10). When Brenda casually mentions that she "lived in Newark when [she] was a baby," Neil is suddenly, unaccountably, angry (*GC* 12). And when Brenda unwittingly derides Newark in chastising her mother for not properly adapting to the family's affluence, Neil cannot "shake from [his] elephant's brain that she-still-thinks-we-live-in-Newark remark" (*GC* 24). Throughout their time together, Neil is unable to forget the difference in status between Brenda and himself. The implicit rejection of urban Jewish life that seems inherent in the Jewish suburbs and the ease with which Brenda takes for granted her affluence are a constant nagging presence in Neil's perception of their relationship.

The certainty and momentum of this change in Jewish lifestyles is rendered in a meditation Neil makes while driving through Newark's Third Ward: "The neighborhood had changed: the old Jews like my grandparents had struggled and died, and their offspring had struggled and prospered, and moved further and further west, towards the edge of Newark, then out of it [. . .]" This is the master story of the Americanization of immigrants, grounded in the specific story of the end of Newark Jewry. It is a story that is told again and again throughout Roth's work, whether by Zuckerman, in *Zuckerman Unbound* and *American Pastoral*, David Kepesh's father, in *The Professor of Desire*, or Roth's own father, in *Patrimony*. But whereas in those works the tone is generally mournful or nostalgic for Newark's Jewish past, here, because Neil is caught up between the life of Aunt Gladys and that of the Patimkins, the tone is more bitter. Continuing his thoughts, Neil predicts that "someday these streets [. . .] would be empty and we would all of us have moved to the crest of the Orange Mountains, and wouldn't the dead stop kicking at the slats in their coffins then?" (*GC* 82–3). This invocation of "the dead" is the closest Neil gets to explicitly condemning the suburbs. For the majority of the story his attitude to Short Hills, like his attitude to Brenda, is typically conflicted; he is simultaneously tempted and repulsed.

In his review of *Goodbye, Columbus* in *The Nation*, George P. Elliott praises the stories, but faults the novella for its romantic plot. The problem is that Neil "is represented as being so detached and ironic an observer that whether he marries [Brenda] or not doesn't matter very much to the reader" (346). Elliott's assessment of Neil's character is astute, but his emphasis on the romance as the main thrust of the story seems off the mark. Neil is most definitely a detached and ironic observer, and this does detract somewhat from the dramatic tension in the portrayal of his relationship with the satirically depicted Brenda. But if that relationship is seen as tied up with another relationship—that between Neil and the broader Jewish-American community, so rapidly enacting changes to the very nature of Jewish life in America—then irony and detachment do not seem so inappropriate a response. Neil's character is essential to Roth's greater purpose: an exploration of how one is to live as a Jew in mid-twentieth-century America.

Neil's burgeoning love for Brenda often takes the form of putting her upon a pedestal, elevating her above the majority of her peers, of whom Neil is generally disdainful. Among the women of the country club, whose gaudy dress betray an abundance of wealth and a corresponding lack of taste, Brenda is "elegantly simple, like a sailor's dream of a Polynesian maiden" (*GC* 13–14). But Neil can never quite convince himself of his belief in Brenda and tends to undercut this sentiment as well. He sees Brenda's mother as one who has been "tamed and made the servant to the king's daughter—who was Brenda" (*GC* 20). This still demonstrates some of Neil's esteem for Brenda, envisioning her as the king's daughter, but also intimates something of his disdain for her spoiled and pampered existence.

One day, when Brenda goes shopping in New York, Neil drives down to a park in the Orange Mountains, an echo of the forgotten wilderness amid the many suburbs that so recently exploded around it. Instead of merely finding deer there, he has occasion to observe the young suburban mothers who chatter all day, comparing their "suntans, supermarkets and vacations." "They looked immortal sitting there. Their hair would always stay the color they desired, their clothes the right texture and shade." It is a vision of conformity and mindless, tasteless materialism. Neil justifies his newfound presence in this crass community by believing that Brenda is somehow better than these "immortals," somehow uncorrupted by her affluence. But his enduring ambivalence, both toward Brenda and toward himself, does not allow him to fully believe: "Only Brenda shone. Money and comfort would not erase her singleness—they hadn't yet, or had they? What was I loving, I wondered" (*GC* 87–8). Neil wonders what he is loving throughout his time with Brenda, never forgetting that she is a part of the materialistic suburbs that have earned his contempt. He strives to keep in check "that hideous emotion I always felt for her, and is the underside of love" (*GC* 25).

Roth's use of ambivalent protagonists can be seen from two different, though complementary, perspectives. As it was for many liberal thinkers in the mid-twentieth century, focusing on the conflicted individual was an artistic and ideological stance, a statement of belief in the concepts of difficulty, contradiction, and paradox in the face of social institutions that seemed to be conspicuously lacking these traits. Stories told through the voice of an ambivalent narrator were perhaps the most noticeable product of the new liberalism within the literature of the time. But an ambivalent narrator or protagonist also serves another purpose for Roth. By keeping Neil aloof and non-committal, Roth is better able to capture his complex subject. As heavily contested a topic as the idea of American Jewishness was (and still is), "Goodbye, Columbus" manages to investigate an often confusing crossroads in Jewish-American life without seeming to advocate one direction or another. Saul Bellow's review of *Goodbye, Columbus* insists that the Jewish writer's responsibility is to "our sense of reality," rather than "public relations." A narrator like Neil allows Roth to better portray this sense of reality, to see clearly. For Neil, as well as Roth, individual autonomy seems connected to accuracy of vision.

Seeing, being able to observe his surroundings, knowing exactly where he is, is paramount for Neil. Brenda, by contrast, has no such need. In the Jewish-American community, the novella implies, there are those who see, who choose to open their eyes to reality, and there are those who choose to remain blind. It is perhaps no surprise that Neil, hailing from lower-middle-class Jewish Newark sees, whereas Brenda, wealthy and suburban, does not. The difference is introduced in the novella's first lines: "The first time I saw Brenda she asked me to hold her glasses. Then she stepped out to the edge of the diving board and looked foggily into the pool; it could have been drained, myopic Brenda would never have known it" (*GC* 4). Neil reports this first encounter in visual terms—it was the first time he saw Brenda, not the first time he met her. And his first impression of Brenda is that she cannot see. On two other occasions Neil holds Brenda's glasses, emphasizing his need to see, and her corresponding lack thereof. At one point he has to remind her that he is holding them. Brenda responds, "Oh break the goddam things. I hate them" (*GC* 14).

Neil's need to see is often evoked through his discomfort in the darkness, where he cannot trust his vision. Playing basketball with Brenda's younger sister in the dying light of the evening, he has a frightful premonition. "I had one of those instantaneous waking dreams that plague me from time to time, and send, my friends tell me, deadly cataracts over my eyes" (*GC* 25). He suddenly envisions himself locked in an interminable game with the sister, forever in darkness. When Neil and Brenda sneak into Brenda's country club after hours, Neil begins to panic only when the lights go out ("*we should go,* I thought"; *GC* 45). Nonetheless, they stay and play a game in which one person goes into the water, while the other waits at the side of the pool, eyes closed, waiting to be surprised by a wet embrace. As Neil dives into the water, he becomes momentarily desperate and frightened in the darkness, worried that Brenda has disappeared. Again he fears that he will have to be out in the blind darkness until morning and prays for the sun to rise "if only for the comfort of its light" (*GC* 49).

Vision is Neil's security, and he needs it to feel comfortable with Brenda. She has her big house, Radcliffe education, and cashmere sweaters, and he has his sight. Brenda, accordingly, is exceedingly comfortable without her glasses, and in the darkness. Watching her play tennis as the sun goes down, Neil notices that "[t]he darker it got the more savagely did Brenda rush the net" (*GC* 9). When it's light out, Brenda stays back, worried about the effects a tennis ball might have on her expensively "fixed" nose. But in the dark, she goes for broke.

This emphasis on vision seems particularly relevant to the overall thrust of the novella, a focus alluded to by its title. The phrase, "Goodbye, Columbus," comes from a record that Brenda's brother Ron plays for Neil. The record is an audio highlight reel of Ron's final year at Ohio State University in Columbus, Ohio, and concludes with a nostalgia-laden, wistful farewell to the ivy-covered campus of the university: "some day we shall return. Till then, goodbye, Ohio State, [. . .] goodbye, Columbus . . . goodbye, Columbus . . . goodbye . . ." (*GC* 96). The words are a signal to the graduates that their picturesque days at the university are over and that they now must enter the "real world," with all of the complications and uncertainty that that clichéd catchall implies. But it can also be seen as a more general farewell to idyllic illusions, signaling a chastened, clear-eyed view of reality. Neil's relationship with Brenda must eventually end; although their breakup is nominally triggered by Brenda's mother's discovery of her daughter's diaphragm, there is a sense that Neil is not able to whole-heartedly commit to a life as an affluent suburban husband. For Neil, seeing clearly means saying goodbye to the dream of unproblematic love. The title's historical suggestion, bringing to mind the storied discoverer of the new world, implies also a farewell to an unproblematic American dream. As in "Eli, the Fanatic," "The Conversion of the Jews" and "Defender of the Faith," Roth portrays the difficulty in reconciling an identity as a Jew and as an American. The mostly suburban America that is portrayed in *Goodbye, Columbus* is neither a utopia for the Jews, offering them a perfect blend of assimilation and accep-tance, nor the end of Jewish identity altogether.

"A broken wall of books, imperfectly shelved"

It is clear that, as a young writer, Philip Roth had already internalized many of the precepts of the new liberalism. In its implicit preference for the auto-nomous individual over the conformist masses, complexity over simplicity, and ambiguity over certainty, *Goodbye, Columbus* takes its place within the discourse of dissent, difficulty, and contradiction so in fashion among liberal intellectuals of the 1950s. The sensitivity of the Jewish-American community at the time, in part produced by their rapidly changing socioeconomic status, provided Roth with a deeply known subculture within which he could express his autonomy. The similarity of the communities evoked in these stories to the community that responded so vehemently to *Goodbye, Columbus* suggests not only that Roth had an astute understanding of the Jewish-American community when he wrote it, but also that the particular nature of the community at the time, with its all-encompassing drive toward normalcy and comfort, may have played a large role in the formation of his defiantly individualistic artistic stance. The forces that combined to create the response to Roth's debut were the very same ones that played a part in its creation. There seems to have been a synchronicity of influences on Roth, from the intellectuals of the time who extolled the conflicted, ambivalent, autonomous individual, and from the sensitive and coercive community imposed by his identity as an American Jew.

At one point in "Goodbye, Columbus," Neil's awareness of his own detachment from the life around him emerges in a section concerning his employment at the library. He fears that one day he will be like his fellow employees, lifeless, uninteresting, and uninterested, each of whom seem to have "a thin cushion of air separating the blood from the flesh." Looking at himself in the bathroom mirror, Neil has a vision of the future in which his life "would not be a throwing off, as it was for Aunt Gladys, and not a gathering in, as it was for Brenda, but a bouncing off, a numbness" (*GC* 30). It is a telling moment for Neil, defining him, as it does, against both Aunt Gladys and Brenda, the representatives of the two ways of life seemingly available to him. Having distanced himself from both worlds, preferring to remain a non-committal observer, would "numbness" be the necessary result? In such times, what role can an observer play? What is left for the man who will not "submit to any of the world's determining categories?"

Perhaps Roth's answer is to be found in another moment when Neil looks at his reflection, at the end of the novella. Having ended his relationship with Brenda in Boston, where she is at university, Neil wanders over to the Harvard library, and catches sight of himself in the darkened windows. Staring at himself, he tries to make sense of his situation. "I looked hard at the image of me, at that darkening of the glass, and then my gaze pushed through it, over the cool floor, to a broken wall of books, imperfectly shelved" (*GC* 124). This image, of Neil's reflection merging with a wall of books, shows Roth's protagonist simultaneously looking both inward and outward. For Alan W. France, this is an image of resignation, a signal that "[f]or Neil there is no alternative to the hollowness of 1950s commodity culture; he must go back to the Newark Public Library" (89). But the Newark Public Library *is* an alternative to a life among the Patimkins or with Aunt Gladys; the library offers up a different sort of community than the ones presented in *Goodbye, Columbus*—the community of literature.[9] The novella's final image, in contrast to Neil's ostensible position between the poles of Jewish life represented by Aunt Gladys and Brenda Patimkin, posits Neil as a characteristically Rothian figure, poised between an inward focus on the experience of the self (Shostak's situated subject) and an outward focus on the boundless world of literature (Posnock's republic of culture). The image's ingenuity, the window acting as both mirror and lens, obviates the need for Neil to choose between the two. For Roth, himself a questioning, iconoclastic individual, who, at the start of his career, felt the full brunt of the Jewish-American community's coercive force, the only determining category ever fully submitted to has been that of the writer.

Chapter 2

The Idea of Seriousness: *Portnoy's Complaint*

This phenomenon is known to students of literary survey courses as the writer changing his style.

Philip Roth

Serious in the Sixties: "Writing American Fiction" and "Writing About Jews"

In 1971, reflecting on the experience of writing *Goodbye, Columbus*, Roth remembered "the exuberance of being a literary orphan." "Not as yet informed that he is a realistic writer, or a Jewish writer, or an academic writer, or a controversial writer, he is not tempted either to satisfy the expectation or to subvert it" ("From the First" 1). As the 1960s dawned, those days were over for Roth, and having been informed that he was both a Jewish writer and a controversial writer, he immediately set out to subvert those expectations. For most of the sixties, Roth chose a path that served to reject both the narrowness of subject matter implied by the "Jewish-American writer" label and the irresponsibility that he was accused of demonstrating in his first book. Explaining that because he felt that it was "my seriousness, my sense of proportion and consequence that was under attack" by the angry Jewish readers of *Goodbye, Columbus*, "I did not have the nerve to appear frivolous in any way" ("Reading Myself" 408). Roth is describing here his very earnest response to these critics in the essay "Writing About Jews," but he might just as well be characterizing his writing throughout much of the sixties, a period in which, in a number of essays and two novels, the maintenance of seriousness and the banishing of frivolity seem just as central as the works' ostensible content. Although not entirely a "literary orphan" anymore, Roth's writings in the early sixties seemed concerned with establishing a place for himself in the cultural landscape, quickly casting him in the role of the serious intellectual.

This word, "serious," is worth unpacking. For I feel it is the best term to characterize Roth's overall output until 1967, the year in which the first installment of that deeply unserious book, *Portnoy's Complaint*, was published in *Esquire*. There is the everyday, dictionary definition, which is pretty close to Roth's usage above, his "sense of proportion and consequence." For to be serious is to consider the issues carefully, thoughtfully, instead of frivolously. Distinguished from the comic by its earnestness, seriousness implies the ability to recognize the significance of significant things, and to address them as such. But seriousness can also refer to significance itself, that which is *taken seriously*. Looked at this way, the nature of seriousness changes with context; one era's serious or significant writers or works often differ from another's. Attaining *literary* seriousness often involves aligning yourself with certain writers or literary works to demonstrate your credibility, to show that, like these serious writers and works, you need to be taken seriously. In addition, setting yourself up as an arbiter of seriousness, telling others what is serious and what is not, is a surefire way of demonstrating your own seriousness. In one of his first published pieces of writing after *Goodbye, Columbus*, Roth put himself forward as someone who should be taken seriously as a writer and an intellectual. Thoughtful, earnest, and serious in the right ways for the time and milieu, "Writing American Fiction" established the sort of seriousness that would characterize Roth's writing for much of the sixties.

First given as a speech at a symposium on "Writing in America Today," held at Stanford University in November 1960, "Writing American Fiction" was published in *Commentary* magazine in March 1961. The essay, in attempting to tackle head-on the problems of writing fiction in contemporary America, was a rite of passage for Roth, a declaration of intent, a bold statement from a young writer who dared to criticize, albeit with intellectual decorum, his better-established and well-respected fellow writers. Roth begins the essay by recounting the story of the Grimes sisters, two teenage girls who were killed a few years earlier in Chicago, when Roth was living there. In what Roth sees as particularly American fashion, the crime soon turns into a media circus; as the papers fly off the newsstands, the mother of the girls, the alleged murderer, and *his* mother all become local celebrities, and Mrs. Grimes ends up with a brand new kitchen, the gift of a concerned philanthropist. In the most-quoted passage of the essay, Roth gives us the moral of the story:

> [T]he American writer in the middle of the 20th century has his hands full in trying to understand, and then describe, and then make *credible* much of American reality. It stupefies, it sickens, it infuriates, and finally it is even a kind of embarrassment to one's own meager imagination. The actuality is continually outdoing our talents, and the culture tosses up figures almost daily that are the envy of any novelist. ("Writing" 224)

That American reality is increasingly unreal is a particularly vexing problem for the American writer, for, in Roth's consideration, a writer's world must be understandable to him, must feel like it is *his* world, for him to write. "For a writer of fiction to feel that he does not really live in the country in which he lives [. . .] must certainly seem a serious occupational impediment. For what will be his subject? His landscape?" ("Writing" 225). There are two points to untangle here. The first is that the outlandishness of contemporary America makes it very difficult for the writer of fiction to keep up, to write believable fiction in an unbelievable time. The second is that the task of writing is doubly difficult if the writer feels estranged from his culture, for his culture inevitably furnishes both his subject and his landscape. The rest of the piece sizes up the writing of a number of Roth's contemporaries and finds evidence to support "the notion that the world we have been given, the society and the community, has ceased to be as suitable or as manageable a subject for the novelist as it once may have been" ("Writing" 227).

It is a confident, wide-ranging essay, and it has since become much-discussed in studies of Roth, and in broader studies of postwar American fiction as well. Critics have interpreted the essay in many different ways in applying it to their own view of Roth's fiction. Some, seemingly taking Roth at his word, paint him as a social realist, committed to an accurate portrayal of American reality (McDaniel 3–8, Rodgers Jr., 9–18). Others have detected the essay's polemical intent in Roth's novels and claim that Roth is always trying to make a point through his fiction, rather than letting his stories come to life.[1] I would focus instead on the cultural move that Roth made here with his first significant piece of published criticism. The essay declared Roth a serious intellectual, taking on the biggest writers of the era, making judgments about the culture as a whole, deciding which writers seriously engage with the times, and which do not. Following *Goodbye, Columbus*, with its probing view of American Jewish life, Roth was often discussed as part of a wave of Jewish-American writers who had come to prominence in the fifties. But this essay is titled "Writing American Fiction," not "Writing Jewish-American Fiction." Roth here takes a larger scope than might be expected of him, laying claim to the whole of American fiction, instead of just his small allotted cultural space. Also indicative of his sensibility is the marked distaste shown for popular culture and its products. The reader gets the definite feeling that most of what "sickens" and "stupefies" Roth about the Grimes case is the popular media's role in creating an event. The tabloid coverage, a song about the case on the radio, a newspaper's fundraiser to help redecorate Mrs. Grimes's house, all of these seem to add to Roth's dismay. As evidence of the increasing feeling of a descent into the absurd, he offers an example: "my wife turned on the radio and heard the announcer offering a series of cash prizes for the three best television plays of five minutes' duration written by children. At such moments it is difficult to find one's way around the kitchen" ("Writing" 225). At points, the writer sounds more like Edmund Wilson (to whom Roth alludes in the next paragraph) than the man who would write the raucous, pop culture–steeped *Portnoy's Complaint*. It is no surprise then, that he finds the novels that sit atop the best-seller list insufficiently "serious" to provide "the investigation of our times and the impact of those times upon human personality" ("Writing" 226).

What emerges from Roth's look at "Writing American Fiction" is a hierarchy of cultural seriousness. American reality, as it is filtered through mass culture, is, by Roth's definition, deeply unserious. The problem in trying to "make *credible* much of American reality" is that American reality is something that Roth cannot take seriously. It is outlandish, vulgar, and often unbelievable, terms that, if used in a book review, would condemn a piece of serious literature. Herman Wouk, Sloan Wilson, and best-selling novelists in general fare no better; Roth spends little time on them, and ties them in with television and the "*amor-vincit-omnia* boys" of sentimental Broadway musicals ("Writing" 226). Saul Bellow, Bernard Malamud, and J. D. Salinger are certainly much more serious, even if they seem to have withdrawn from engaging with contemporary American reality; Roth can forgive this, because "what is particularly tough about the times is writing about them, as a serious novelist or storyteller" ("Writing" 227). Ralph Ellison, brought up in the essay's final paragraph, has pride of place as the most serious of all, seemingly because *Invisible Man*'s pessimistic final image of a man bitterly retreating from America fits in well with Roth's picture of American reality. A similar hierarchy emerges in a 1961 piece, "Some New Jewish Stereotypes," in which Roth looks at recent cultural representations of the Jew.[2] Here it is Leon Uris, whose *Exodus* had recently been turned into a Hollywood movie (complete with a theme song sung by Pat Boone), and Harry Golden, whose nostalgic novels of the Jewish Lower East Side had met with great commercial success, who come in for Roth's derision. To provide a counterbalancing example of a serious Jewish novelist, Roth invokes Elie Wiesel, in whose *Dawn* Roth finds ambiguity, complexity, and legitimate tragedy (*Reading Myself and Others* 184–6, 191–2). Again, that which is popular, accessible, and embraced by American pop culture is eschewed in favor of the highbrow, difficult, and complex.

Perhaps it is not surprising that Roth set himself up as an arbiter of seriousness in "Writing American Fiction" and "Some New Jewish Stereotypes." The two are works of literary criticism, and a literary critic is supposed to make judgments. But it is clear that the nature of these judgments, the grounds for approval or disapproval, stems from a sensibility much more attuned to high culture than to mass culture. This particular aspect of Roth's sensibility is further revealed in a quite different piece, "Writing About Jews," Roth's response to the Jewish critics of *Goodbye, Columbus*, published in *Commentary* in December 1963. In laying out, and then picking apart, the case brought against him by rabbis, community leaders, and ordinary Jewish readers, Roth uses examples from the "World Literature Pantheon" to justify whatever offense *Goodbye, Columbus* had caused ("Reading Myself" 408). One outraged reader wrote a letter to Roth concerning "Epstein," a story in which the eponymous, middle-aged Jew cheats on his wife, with unfortunate results. The reader asked Roth why he thought adultery was a Jewish trait. Roth's answer, in the essay, is by way of Tolstoy: "Anna Karenina commits adultery with Vronsky, with consequences more disastrous than those Epstein brings about. Who thinks to ask, 'Is it a Russian trait?'" To the rabbis who would want Jewish writers' novels to represent, as in sociological works, the full range of Jewish life, Roth invokes Flaubert:

"*Madame Bovary* is hardly recognizable as a sociological study either, having at its center only a single, dreamy, provincial Frenchwoman." Continuing on to respond to those readers who did not find in *Goodbye, Columbus* a "balanced portrayal" of Jews, Roth brings in some more distinguished authors: "Dear Fyodor Dostoevsky—[. . .] do you call Raskolnikov a balanced portrayal of students as we know them? [. . .] Dear Mark Twain—[. . .] Dear Vladimir Nabokov—.' ("Writing About Jews" 442, 448). Although the essay is a brilliant defense of his work, it *is* defensive, and in his defensiveness Roth reaches for his high art credentials—Tolstoy, Flaubert, and Dostoevsky. One wonders how the reader who wrote to the *New Yorker* insisting that "cliches like 'this being art' will not be acceptable" would respond to Roth's justification for his writing (Levy).

In 1973, looking back on the controversy and his response, Roth regretted this defensiveness and admitted that he was totally unprepared for such accusations:

> I might turn out to be a bad artist, or no artist at all, but having declared myself *for* art—the art of Tolstoy, James, Flaubert, and Mann, whose appeal was as much in their heroic literary integrity as in their work—I imagined I had sealed myself off from being a morally unacceptable person, in others' eyes as well as my own.
>
> The last thing I expected, having chosen this vocation—*the* vocation— was to be charged with heartlessness, vengeance, malice, and treachery. ("Reading Myself" 406)

This formulation intimates the level of investment which Roth put into the idea of literary seriousness in his youth. He was "instinctively fanatical about seriousness," and cast his lot with the causes of literary integrity, artistic ambition, and intellectual scrutiny ("Just a Lively Boy" 127). And yet he found himself completely out of touch with this very vocal segment of his reading public. This could not have been too much of a surprise, for at least some part of this drive to be serious was prompted by a rejection of all that seemed to be unserious in America and the fear that the philistines would soon be taking over.

> Alienated in America, a stranger to its pleasures and preoccupations—that was how many young people like me saw their situation in the fifties. It was a perfectly honorable stance, I think, shaped by our literary aspirations and modernist enthusiasms, the high-minded of the second post-immigrant generation coming into conflict with the first great eruption of postwar media garbage. ("Art of Fiction" 235)

What Roth leaves unsaid here is an explanation of why the second post-immigrant generation was so high-minded. For this idea of seriousness cannot be taken as a culturally neutral term, especially when discussing an American Jew.

Jewish Matthew Arnolds

The critic and editor Theodore Solotaroff met Philip Roth in the fall of 1957 when they were both graduate students at the University of Chicago. In a seminar on Henry James, Solotaroff and the "handsome, well-groomed young man" who spoke in a "very precise and concrete way," teamed up to argue against another student, who was expounding "one of those symbolic religious interpretations" of *Daisy Miller* (Solotaroff 64). The two met properly after the class and discovered that they had in common a Jewish upbringing in New Jersey, as well as similar ambitions of literary seriousness. They were both in the midst of a "journey from the halfway house of semi-acculturation [. . .] into the realm of literature and culture." Solotaroff explains: "In our revolt against the exotic but intransigent materialism of our first-generation bourgeois parents, we were not in school to learn how to earn a living but to become civilized. Hence our shared interest in James" (65). The pull of Henry James, seen as a representative of serious, moral scrutiny of the highest (and lowest) of life's concerns, was but one aspect of the atmosphere of high-mindedness and difficulty that characterized graduate life in the late fifties for Solotaroff and Roth. Looking back on those times from the vantage point of 1969, Solotaroff claims:

> It was a time when the deferred gratifications of graduate school and the climb to tenure and the problems of premature adjustment seemed the warranty of "seriousness" and "responsibility": those solemn passwords of a generation that practiced a Freudian/Jamesian concern about motives, pondered E. M. Forster's "only connect," and subscribed to Lionel Trilling's "moral realism" and "tragic sense of life." In contrast to today, everyone came on as though he were thirty. (67)

The mention of Trilling, in addition to James, does not seem accidental, for, if James became a central talisman of seriousness and artistic integrity to second-generation American Jews like Solotaroff and Roth, he played an even larger role in the intellectual lives of older Jewish intellectuals such as Trilling. In fact, without the work of Trilling, and other Jewish intellectuals in the forties and fifties, it is very likely that Roth and Solotaroff would not have had the option of taking a course on Henry James at all.

As detailed in Chapter 1, the New York Intellectuals' move from staunch socialists to "new liberals," as well as their analogous move from championing proletarian, naturalistic fiction to the exaltation of works of high modernism, was part of a broader liberal narrative among American intellectuals in the decades surrounding World War II. But it must be remembered that most of these men (and, for the most part, they were men) were also Jews. And, as Jonathan Freedman demonstrates in *The Temple of Culture*, the alignment with difficult, serious, highbrow culture, and James in particular, performed powerful cultural work for these first- and second-generation American Jews in their

quest to escape the provincial world of their immigrant upbringing and establish themselves as successful American intellectuals. The New York Intellectuals
were merely the most visible representatives of a trend that manifested itself
in a wide number of assimilating American Jews who felt "a persistent sense of
inadequacy in the face of the cultures of the West and [made] an earnest
attempt to slough off immigrant garb and beliefs in order to pass as 'real' Americans" (Freedman 164). The irony, of course, was that mainstream America was
scarcely less suspicious of highbrow culture as it was of Jewish immigrants.
Nonetheless, a life devoted to "the best that has been thought and said" became
a "middle ground between a hostile and seemingly anti-Semitic American society and the suffocating family and neighborhood—a place where they could
stake their own fates, make their own futures, outside the constraints both
within and without the Jewish community." For many of these Jewish intellectuals on the "assimilation-by-culture trail," it was Henry James, whose books often
exhibited a less than wholly positive view of Jews, who was to become the epit-
ome of the literary seriousness that was to be exalted (Freedman 166–7, 8).

   In 1943, Philip Rahv, the Russian-born Jewish critic and one of the founders
of *Partisan Review,* wrote an essay, "Attitudes Toward Henry James," that detailed
the almost wholly negative contemporary reception of James. Rahv quoted
from a wide variety of sources, including *The College Book of American Literature,*
which stated, "It is not certain that Henry James really belongs to American
literature, for he was critical of America and admired Europe." Rahv argued
forcefully for a renewed appreciation of "the depth and quality of [James's]
contradictions" (77, 83). Note again the tendency of the New York Intellectuals
to seek out and uphold "contradictions," paradox, and difficulty as key features
of a modernist aesthetic. The essay was later published as part of Rahv's collection, *Image and Idea,* in 1949. Eight years later, in the preface to that book's
second edition, Rahv felt compelled to note that the essay was written before
the "James revival": "I was quite as surprised as anyone else by the unexpected
dimensions of the interest in him and by the collapse of the resistance to his
appeal in some of the literary and academic circles characterized in ['Attitudes
Toward Henry James']" (ix). This note, while communicating just how swiftly
and broadly the "James revival" took hold, leaves unsaid the integral part Rahv,
and other Jewish intellectuals, played in resurrecting James to his exalted place
in the canon and to his stable place in college curricula. As Freedman points
out, "the so-called James revival of the 1940s and 1950s was the first effort in
American canon formation in which Jews participated on an equal footing with
gentiles" (12). Rahv wrote a number of essays on James in *Partisan Review* in the
late thirties and early forties, casting James as "a model who might stand both
within and without a culture from which Rahv [felt] profoundly alienated"
(Freedman 191). Trilling wrote often, and influentially, on James; among the
13 essays of Trilling's landmark collection, *The Liberal Imagination,* James figures
in nine of them. And Trilling's only published novel, *The Middle of the Journey,* is
a distinctly Jamesian work, in both spirit and tone. Leon Edel, a Russian-born

Jewish immigrant, became, in the 1940s, perhaps the leading James scholar, publishing a number of anthologies of James's neglected works, writing a five-volume biography and casting himself as the owner and protector of James's legacy (Freedman 199–200). Without the work of these men, it is unlikely that James would hold such appeal for younger Jews such as Roth and Solotaroff. James became an important touchstone for many Jewish intellectuals in the thirties and forties, and if their work on him helped to elevate him to the canonical status he continues to hold, it also validated their own still-tenuous positions in the American literary world.

   What is missing from this very brief summation of the role Jewish intellectuals played in the revival of Henry James, that representative of genteel, highbrow seriousness, is what Freedman calls the "unstable amalgam of affect" that was the necessary product of such a role (192). Irving Howe has noted that the New York Intellectuals were nothing if not ambitious as critics, working under the implicit assumption that a critic should comment on as wide a range of culture as possible; this assumption seems to underlie Roth's own wide-angle lens, so boldly exhibited in "Writing American Fiction." Howe explained this ambition by saying that "behind this is a very profoundly Jewish impulse: namely, you've got to beat the goyim at their own game. So you have to dazzle them a little" (Rosenberg and Goldstein 284). The idea put across here is that to succeed in the very gentile world of literary criticism, Jews had to work harder and attempt more, but also, I think, there is the implication that these Jews felt they had to be more goyish than the goyim, so to speak. This negotiation is a complicated one, defined by ambition and insecurity, attraction and repulsion. It brings to the surface a seemingly contradictory set of relationships. The Jewish intellectual aligns himself with highbrow culture, at least partly as a way to demonstrate his full capabilities, to pull himself out of the role of the alien, as only Jewish. But this culture that is sought out, championed, and used as a foothold to some sort of assimilation, has itself played a large role in the construction of the Jew as alien. Alfred Kazin, in reminiscing about his beginnings as a Jewish critic in New York in the late thirties, simultaneously notes the anti-Semitism he felt in the literary milieu and his "[falling] in love with American literature and the native Protestant tradition." In a remarkable passage, he (perhaps unwittingly) yokes together his feelings of otherness with his attachment to Henry James:

   As a young reviewer and writer, a freelancer in New York, I was invited everywhere. I had experiences which made me realize that I was regarded as a Jew. It had to do with a phenomenon Henry James touched upon in *The American Scene*. Coming back to New York, James noted the obvious "lowness" of the people. It's something you can observe everywhere in the city. I was being watched, and judged. It struck me as being a question of *manners*. (Rosenberg and Goldstein 197)

This intimates something of the psychic toll that must have been the product of the alignment with serious, highbrow culture for many Jewish intellectuals. Kazin's appreciation and analysis of the serious writers of high culture was his ticket into the literary world. But it also served as a lens through which he was cast as an alien too "low" for that world. The emphasis on "manners" here is telling, for it indicates the importance of expression and decorum in the quest to be taken seriously. Early in his career at Columbia, Lionel Trilling faced a number of instances of anti-Semitism, at one point nearly losing his job because he was "a Jew, a Marxist, and a Freudian." As Freedman details, Trilling's response to such affronts was always a suppression of his anger, "a stiff upper lip, a gentlemanly reserve, an elegant silence." "The best revenge for Trilling, it would seem, was to perform the equanimity that Jews, stereotyped as being passionate and overemotional, were accused of lacking" (Freedman 195). This display of manners seemed to play a large role in Trilling's demonstration of his own seriousness; indeed among all of the Jewish intellectuals who made their name through an attachment to highbrow culture, Trilling showed the least signs of there being any contradiction in this move. But that does not mean that it was without its negative effects.

Trilling was perhaps the most successful of the Jewish intellectuals who came to prominence in the 1930s and 1940s, and provided the most visible model for those younger Jews, like Roth and Solotaroff, who had ambitions of seriousness. Solotaroff has written that Trilling

> functioned as a guide, for young Jews like myself, to the Anglo-American literary tradition and to the higher style of criticism. [. . .] Trilling could show you the way to Henry James; he came to seem like the best model for the academic I was becoming: a Jewish Matthew Arnold, full of graceful energy and high public concerns. (Rosenberg and Goldstein 409)

For Trilling did put himself across as a twentieth-century Matthew Arnold, but without the ethnic adjective that Solotaroff applies. In 40 years of critical writing, Trilling was perhaps the most prominent and committed exponent of the Arnoldian vision of the value of high culture of any figure, Jewish or not, and seemed determined never to admit that his Jewishness played any role, for good or for bad, in his professional endeavors.[3] Although he never denied his Jewishness,[4] he stated directly:

> I cannot discover anything in my professional intellectual life which I can significantly trace back to my Jewish birth and rearing. I do not think of myself as a "Jewish writer." I do not have it in mind to serve by my writing any Jewish purpose. ("Under Forty" 12)

This statement is borne out by Trilling's writings, which never displayed a "Jewish perspective," never showed any apparent effects of the anti-Semitism he faced in entering the literary world, and rarely allowed any cracks in his serious façade to show at all.

In a 2002 essay, Adam Phillips concurs with Freedman's view of Trilling's performed seriousness, suggesting that it was prompted by his desire to avoid being a victim:

> Being a Jew for Trilling meant not submitting to the myths of being a Jew, which meant not only not fighting the myths, which would be to acknowledge that one was already victimized by them, but also not accepting them to his own advantage, which would be to consent to them. ("Lionel Trilling's" 168)

But Phillips notes that, in private, Trilling expressed regret over his inability to surrender his seriousness and tied his lifelong commitment to literary seriousness to his perceived failure as a novelist. Phillips calls attention to two journal entries, in which Trilling praises Hemingway for his "foolish postures" and his "self-revealing, arrogant" expression. Trilling felt:

> How [Hemingway's] life which he could expose without dignity and which is anarchic and "childish" is a better life than anyone I know could live, and right for his job. And how far-far-far I am going from being a writer—and how less and less I have the material and the mind and the will. ("Lionel Trilling's" 164)

It seems that Trilling, whose career-long performance of seriousness in print may or may not have been prompted by a desire to not be seen as a Jewish other, and who admitted, late in life, that "I am always surprised when I hear myself referred to as a critic," conceived of this attachment to seriousness as something like a neurosis which prevented him from fulfilling his abiding ambition to be a significant novelist (Trilling "Some Notes" 227). "[Trilling] stages it in terms of an opposition: himself and the 'good minds' of his university life versus himself as a potential novelist and Hemingway, who could expose his life without dignity" (Phillips, "Lionel Trilling's" 167).[5]

A more explicit version of this narrative was voiced by Saul Bellow in a 1965 interview. Speaking of his years in university, Bellow noted that "[i]t was made clear to me [. . .] that as a Jew and the son of Russian Jews I would probably never have the right *feeling* for Anglo-Saxon traditions, for English words." This experience, Bellow implied, contributed to the shortcomings of his first two, "well made," novels, *Dangling Man* and *The Victim*: "I still felt the incredible effrontery of announcing myself to the world (in part I mean the WASP world) as a writer and an artist. [. . .] I was afraid to let myself go." It was only with the writing of *The Adventures of Augie March*, a breakthrough for Bellow in much the same way that *Portnoy's Complaint* would be for Roth, that the former was able to escape the constraints of received notions of seriousness:

Why should [a writer] hobble himself with formalities? With a borrowed sensibility? With the desire to be "correct"? Why should I force myself to write like an Englishman or a contributor to *The New Yorker*? I soon saw that it was simply not in me to be a mandarin. (Bellow, Interview 182–3)

Likewise, Roth has spoken of a confidence he discovered in the writing of *Portnoy's Complaint*, something that carried over into his next three books, all something other than serious: "This confidence expressed itself partly in a greater willingness to be deliberately, programmatically perverse—subversive not merely of the 'serious' values of official literary culture [. . .] but subversive of my own considerable investment [. . .] in seriousness" ("Reading Myself" 413). In these cases, overcoming the need to be serious, the need to be "correct," is seen as the key to reaching full potential as a writer of fiction. Phillips claims that Trilling felt he could not "expose his life without dignity," because a critic, "by definition, as it were, cannot be disreputable in his self-presentation." But Phillips concludes his essay by noting that "the option he and others did have, however, was psychoanalysis, in which one is invited, as a therapeutic measure, [. . .] to abrogate one's 'conscious effort for dignity' in the service of something putatively better" ("Lionel Trilling's" 165, 174). It is surely telling that it was only when Roth utilized the freedom of a psychoanalytic monologue, in *Portnoy's Complaint*, that he was able to "[free] himself of the voice that dominated *Letting Go* and *When She Was Good*, the measured voice of his 'master,' Henry James" (Shostak 83).

In an interview on the subject of his time in Chicago, the period Solotaroff remembers as a time of shared ambitions of seriousness, Roth notes his awareness of the dangers of the "assimilation-by-culture trail." "One had to be careful about the temptation to become a gentleman. So many bright Jewish boys of my generation—and background—gravitated to literature because it was a prestigious form of assimilation that didn't *look* like assimilation" ("Just a Lively Boy" 128). Significantly, the way to avoid "becom[ing] a gentleman" was to affirm the elements that made the graduate school milieu so attractive to both Roth and Solotaroff, the clash of seemingly unalike upbringings and interests, the collision of provincial backgrounds and the wider world, the pleasures of "being the insider/outsider." "We took a lot of pleasure in having humble origins and high-minded pursuits. Either without the other was boring and looked to us like an affectation" ("Just a Lively Boy" 124, 128). Crucially, it was Roth's ability to unite seemingly incongruent elements—the "assimilation-by-culture trail" and wild, irreverent, sixties-style comedy—that would lead to the success of *Portnoy's Complaint.*

Letting Go and *When She Was Good*, the two novels Roth published in between *Goodbye, Columbus* and *Portnoy's Complaint*, are works that noticeably play out under the shadow of James. *Letting Go* (1962), a very long, somber, pain-filled novel, begins with a mention of *The Portrait of a Lady*, and Roth's novel seems to be patterned after James's fiction, which Gabe Wallach, the protagonist of *Letting Go*, succinctly summarizes as concerned with "heroes and heroines tempting one another into a complex and often tragic fate" (3). The novel is set in the academic world, and that world comes across as dreary and difficult as Solotaroff claims it was for Roth and himself at the University of Chicago. It exhibits a very Jamesian concern with moral decisions and how those decisions affect others; Wallach's central dilemma is how much or how little he should involve himself in the lives of those around him, and it is unclear, at the novel's end, whether he has figured this out or not. *When She Was Good* (1967) begins with this line, describing Willard Carroll and echoing Solotaroff's explanation of the attraction of Henry James: "Not to be rich, not to be famous, not to be mighty, not even to be happy, but to be civilized—that was the dream of his life" (9). The novel's protagonist, Lucy Nelson, Willard's granddaughter, has ambitions that go further than her grandfather's: she pursues, with tragic consequences, something like moral perfection in a world that constantly thwarts her dreams. Set in Wisconsin, without any Jews, and without any of the vibrant, comic, Jewish speech Roth made his name with in *Goodbye, Columbus*, it is as dreary and earnest as *Letting Go*. The characters' desperate pursuit of civilization and justice, and their Midwestern milieu, dictates a prose style that has no place for levity or colorful language. Both *Letting Go* and *When She Was Good* have moments of real power, but they are by no means easy books to like, with their unremitting tone of gloom. The two books are often seen as footnotes in Roth's long career. From the present vantage point, they seem idiosyncratic among Roth's other works—two somber, dreary, melodramatic novels set mostly in the Midwest. Although I do not want to spend much time on these books, it is important to emphasize that they are, if nothing else, serious books, in the sense that they demonstrate Roth's continued allegiance to a difficult, complex, morally earnest art, and in the sense that they are distinctly non-comic.[6] In 1967, perhaps not everyone liked Philip Roth's books, but there was no question that he was a serious writer, with deeply intellectual concerns, who brought the highest scrutiny to the investigation of those concerns.

Portnoy's Complaint Arrives

In the summer of 1967, just one month after the publication of *When She Was Good*, Philip Roth, serious author, winner of the National Book Award, and distinguished contributor to such journals as *Commentary*, published a story in *Partisan Review*, the storied mainstay of the New York Intellectuals. Entitled "Whacking Off," it begins, in medias res, with the following sentence:

> Then came the years when half my waking life was spent locked behind the bathroom door, firing my wad down the toilet, or into the soiled clothes of the laundry hamper, or with a thick splat, up against the medicine chest

mirror, before which I stood in my dropped drawers to see how it looked coming out. (385)

Now *this* was certainly different. One of four excerpts from *Portnoy's Complaint* published in various magazines over the next year and a half, "Whacking Off" is a segment of the psychoanalytic monologue of Alexander Portnoy, Jewish son of Newark, New Jersey, sex-obsessed chronic masturbator, guilt-filled bearer of his parents' love and expectations, and the Assistant Commissioner of Human Opportunity for the City of New York. With each excerpt that was published, it became clearer and clearer that *Portnoy's Complaint* would be a marked departure from Roth's earlier work. Filled with Portnoy's graphic descriptions of his sexual exploits (both with women and on his own), written in the first person, in prose equally informed by pop culture and Freud, and very, very funny, Roth's fourth book was his big break—both in literary terms, as a break with the seriousness that had characterized his earlier writings, and in cultural terms, as the book that would make Roth a celebrity.

For, as each excerpt came out, the hype over *Portnoy* grew and grew. When the book was published in February 1969, it was already clear that it would not merely be a work of literature, it would be a cultural commodity, a pop artifact. Profiles of Roth appeared in major magazines and newspapers, each trumpeting the book's outrageous subject matter and sure commercial success. Most of these revealed that Roth had already made a million dollars from the book, and gushed about the royalty advances, paperback rights, movie rights, and book-club rights that now swirled around the author. In an interview six weeks before *Portnoy*'s publication, Roth seemed resigned to the book's fate. "'The moment the book arrives on the scene it will be an event,' he said, with a trace of resignation in his voice. 'In a year or two it'll be a book again.'" Random House, not minding that *Portnoy* was not yet a book, duly raised its price, from $5.95 to $6.95 (Raymont 20).[7] The expectations were confirmed upon the book's publication; it quickly climbed to the top of the *New York Times* best-seller list, and stayed there for 14 consecutive weeks, until it was pushed to number two (where it stayed for some time), by Jacqueline Susann's *The Love Machine*.[8] By Roth's own count, *Portnoy* sold 420,000 hardcover copies, more than seven times as many as his first three books' combined hardcover sales (Roth, *Reading Myself and Others* 256). From January through May of 1969, there were no less than 11 pieces on Roth and *Portnoy* in the *New York Times* alone, including two reviews of the book, two parodies of reviews of the book, two interviews with Roth, and a piece in which prominent Jewish mothers "wonder what Portnoy had to complain about" (Klemesrud 42). All of this suggests that, aside from its break from the seriousness of prose style and subject matter that had characterized Roth's earlier work, *Portnoy* was unserious in the role it played in the culture: a sensational, obscene best seller, quite in tune with the "new sensibility" that was apparently taking over America's culture in the late sixties. Unsurprisingly, many reviewers saw *Portnoy* as part of the era's apparent cultural conflicts: the "new sensibility" versus tradition; blatant vulgarity versus decorum; and popular culture, with its commercial imperatives, versus serious literature.

J. Mitchell Morse, writing in the *Hudson Review*, derided *Portnoy* for its reliance on stereotypes—but also, one senses, for its commercial success. Portnoy is "the hottest brand name in the market. By now everybody knows about him, and I don't find him worth discussing at length." Roth is nothing but the "'pimp of his particularity,' a professional Jew-boy [who] gets his kicks from catering to condescension" (320). An editorial in the *New York Times*, alluding to *Portnoy*, reminded its readers that

> the fact that the legally enforceable standards of public decency have been interpreted away by the courts almost to the point of no return does not absolve artists, producers or publishers from all responsibility or restraint in pandering to the lowest possible public taste in quest of the largest possible monetary reward. ("Beyond" 46)[9]

The same polarities were invoked by *Portnoy*'s defenders, like Raymond A. Sokolov, who wrote in *Newsweek* that "Philip Roth at 35 is a serious writer of the first rank and no sales-hungry smut peddler" (56). Rather, bringing up Roth's prior, serious, books, Sokolov claimed that with *Portnoy* Roth had finally "let go" and found his voice.

Similarly, many commentators saw Roth and Portnoy as bearers of the new, as representative of the "new sensibility," as a product of the sixties' apparent cultural shifts. Marya Mannes wrote that Portnoy's sexual exploits were "one more noxious instance of the writer-intellectual being 'with it.' [. . .] All this comes under the heading of the New Truth, the New Freedom, the end of hypocrisy, the nitty gritty, or whatever you want to call it" (39). Isa Kapp, in the *New Leader*, also saw *Portnoy* as a product of the age, and Roth as a leader of the new class. Roth's novel "is here to tell us that the sexual revolution has triumphed, and to proclaim him leader of the Junta. [. . .] He reaps what our culture has sowed, and emerges in the limelight as the heir of his age" (21). And Sokolov called *Portnoy* "the most explosive example yet of the new permissiveness in language." This "new permissiveness" is utilized in order "to probe at all of our half-stifled conflicts over an emerging 'freer' new morality" (55, 56).

Many of these critics, in casting *Portnoy* as a banner for the new sensibility, saw this "newness" as against old ideas of literary seriousness. Anatole Broyard claimed that *Portnoy* was part of a rebellion against "the old highbrow or 'orthodox' Jewish novel of ideas," like Bellow's *Herzog*. This is a natural progression, though. "Like a statue in a public park, the Jew in literature is a prey to the climate. The climate now is sexy: Portnoy, then, is a sexual prodigy, a real (matzoh) ballsy guy" (21). Jay L. Halio saw the book as nothing more than "a *tour de force*, an inevitable and logical culmination of the fantasy life that *Playboy* magazine has so studiously fostered among us." He contrasted this new, pop-informed fiction with the kind of writing that Iris Murdoch called for in a 1961 essay, with "a renewed sense of the difficulty and complexity of the moral life and the opacity of persons" (Halio 635–6, 639).[10] In becoming a pied piper for the new, Roth, claimed Kapp, mentions the unmentionable "to liberate us not only from our sexual but also from our literary conventions." He does away with literature's "obligation to see life whole," and wants us to throw away the "pieties" of "manliness, discretion, and ethics" (21, 22).

The Comedy of Seriousness

In one interview upon the publication of *Portnoy's Complaint*, George Plimpton asked Roth if the book was at all inspired by the stand-up comedy of Lenny Bruce. Roth, still, apparently, taking the high road, denied that Bruce was an influence, and instead declared that he was influenced by "a sit-down comic named Franz Kafka" ("Philip Roth's Exact Intent" 2). A few years previous, in the course of teaching Kafka, among other serious, gloomy masterpieces of European literature, he had begun to see the absurdity inherent in such books' perpetual focus on guilt and persecution. He remembered hearing somewhere that Kafka used to giggle to himself while writing, and suddenly understood why:

> Of course! It was all so *funny*, this morbid preoccupation with punishment and guilt. Hideous, but funny. Hadn't I recently sat smirking through a performance of "Othello"? And not just because it was badly done either, but because something in that bad performance revealed how *dumb* Othello is. Isn't there something ludicrous about Anna Karenina throwing herself under that train? For what? What after all had she done? ("Philip Roth's Exact Intent" 2)[11]

Sixteen years later, in a 1985 interview with Asher Z. Milbauer and Donald G. Watson, Roth explained the nature of the comedy of *Zuckerman Bound*:

> What's laughable in *Zuckerman Bound* is [Zuckerman's] insatiable desire to be a serious man taken seriously by all the serious men like his father and his brother and Milton Appel. A stage direction that appears in *The Prague Orgy* could have been the trilogy's title: *Enter Zuckerman, a serious person.* [. . .] His superseriousness is what the comedy's *about*. (9)

Without making an equivalence between Anna Karenina and Zuckerman, I think Roth's later, more explicit statement about his comic technique sheds light on his earlier remarks. For what is it about Othello, Anna Karenina, and Kafka's heroes that Roth finds so funny, if not their seriousness? What is "ludicrous" about Tolstoy's heroine is that she takes her predicament so very seriously. The comedy that lurks within man's pretensions of seriousness, the absurdity of an unremitting focus on life's difficulties and tragedies, the comedy that springs from a character's explicit desire *not* to be comedic—this becomes an important aspect of Roth's work, beginning with *Portnoy's Complaint*. For although the book is a comedic performance from the first page to the last, Portnoy wishes it wasn't so funny: "I am the son in the Jewish joke—*only it ain't no joke!*" (*PC* 36–7).

What the similarity in Roth's two explanations above suggests, and what is often overlooked, is that much of the comedy in *Portnoy's Complaint*, like that of *Zuckerman Bound*, springs from the protagonist's desperate desire to be taken seriously. David Brauner has pointed this out, connecting it with Roth's stated intention to move away from his earlier over-seriousness:

> Whereas Roth was taking himself too seriously, Portnoy's complaint is that no one (least of all himself) will take him seriously at all. Like Roth, Alex seeks relief, but in his case it is relief *from* comedy, from the absurd indignities of his life, and from the "Jewish joke" in which he feels he is trapped.

Brauner is most concerned with the interaction between what he sees as the novel's two impulses, "to treat psychoanalysis comically, and to treat comedy psychoanalytically" ("Masturbation" 76). But it is worth looking more closely at the ways in which Roth has Portnoy seek "relief from comedy." Portnoy's pursuit of seriousness is consistently mediated through various encounters with a wide array of cultural reference points, both serious and "not so serious," suggesting that Portnoy's dilemma is informed by Roth's own experiences in the role of the serious intellectual and writer. In addition, Portnoy's desire to be taken seriously exhibits something of the "unstable amalgam of affect" that often characterized the New York Intellectuals' pursuit of seriousness, but rarely showed itself in Roth's own performed seriousness through much of the 1960s. There is no evidence that Roth felt, like Kazin, any alienation in aligning himself with a culture which often cast the Jew as the other, or, like Trilling, a desire to defy the image of the Jew as victim by embracing seriousness. But in Portnoy's anguished and hilarious self-analysis, the emotional causes, and costs, of the pursuit of seriousness often become fodder for Roth's comedy. It is perhaps not as immediately apparent, but Portnoy, like Zuckerman, enacts the comedy that is always the paradoxical product of the desire to be taken seriously in Roth's late 1960s America.

Serious Portnoy

In an essay detailing the genesis of the ideas that became *Portnoy's Complaint*, Roth explains that some of the many inspirations for the Portnoy family were his memories of the Jewish families who lived in his neighborhood during his childhood, "whose squabbles over French-fried potatoes, synagogue attendance, and shiksas were, admittedly, of an Olympian magnitude and splendor"

(*Reading Myself and Others* 35). The rhetorical technique used here, comparing the quotidian arguments of a family in Newark to the battles between Greek gods, is one that Portnoy utilizes within Roth's novel. Peppered throughout Portnoy's childhood reminiscences are literary references that serve to indicate something of his ambitions of seriousness, while demonstrating, by means of the comical distance between his family and their literary analogues, the mix of shame and pride he feels for his uncultured origins. Although growing up in the Portnoy household was not a bookish experience (their library, apart from schoolbooks, consisted of three distinctly nonliterary works), Portnoy, in a nostalgic mood, casts his parents as poets, with the remembrance of his mother's "a real fall sky" and his father's "good winter piney air" making him remark that "I couldn't be more thrilled if I were Wordsworth's kid!" (*PC* 28–9). Most of the time, this yoking of literary references to his memories of his family's day-to-day life is used to humorous effect, emphasizing the outsized emotions and general lack of decorum in the Portnoy household. At the age of five, having misbehaved in some way, little Alex hid under the bed to escape punishment. Recounting this story, Portnoy suddenly remembers that his mother began swinging a broom under the bed to force the little boy out, causing the patient to exclaim, "Why, shades of Gregor Samsa! Hello Alex, goodbye Franz!" (*PC* 121). The ensuing shouted reproaches from his parents change the scene into "some farce version of *King Lear*, with me in the role of Cordelia!" (*PC* 123). And remembering the many nicknames he earned during his childhood for his unruly temper, Portnoy makes a Flaubertian confession: "'Mr. Conniption-Fit'—*c'est moi!*" (*PC* 229).

Portnoy sprinkles these literary references throughout his monologue, often demonstrating how woefully his parents fail to measure up to the grandeur and dignity of high culture, but also, more simply, demonstrating Portnoy's learning and aspirations to seriousness (as well as his eagerness to show off his learning). Portnoy's mother may take his misbehavior overly seriously, but Portnoy knows that Gregor Samsa and Cordelia had it a little harder. For a book that seemed to instantly take its place in contemporary popular culture, *Portnoy's Complaint* contains more literary references and allusions than most, perhaps indicating Roth's inability to completely abandon his own literary seriousness. In addition to Kafka, Shakespeare, and Flaubert, Portnoy, in the course of what is meant to be an uninhibited and unadorned outpouring to his analyst, alludes to Dickens, Tolstoy, Dostoevsky, Homer, Beckett, Keats, Dos Passos, and Yeats, not to mention Marx and Freud. His aspirations to high culture reveal themselves through his allusive speech.

The seriousness that Portnoy hopes to attain is, at least in part, a literary one and clearly tied to his relationship with his father. His father's lack of learning offends Portnoy's sensibilities just as much as his lack of manners, and the two are tied together in Portnoy's mind. He is stirred to anger whenever his father "ate from the serving bowl with his own fork," but also when he tries "to express an opinion on any subject whatsoever" (*PC* 41). This tying together of manners and decorum with intellectual prowess seems part of the New York Intellectuals' version of Jamesian seriousness, a concept that springs from an idea of culture as a civilizing force. Portnoy, as much as Neil Klugman, pursues a version of this seriousness, prompted in part by his shame over his father's lack of both culture and manners. In a doubling back typical of Portnoy's confusion, he laments that he should have learned something from his father's vulgarity, "instead of that too becoming a source of shame" (*PC* 50).

His father's vulgarity does become a source of shame, but also a source of sadness and sympathy. Just as his comparisons of his family to immortal literary characters simultaneously satirize their smallness and elevate them to something like grandeur, so Portnoy derides his father's lack of learning and manners while expressing a deep-seated desire to pull him up to the heights of civilized culture. He remarks that, even at age 33, there are still times when he reads something in a book that makes him think, "If only he could read *this*. Yes! Read, and understand—!" (*PC* 9). Intriguingly, and perhaps indicative of the sort of seriousness Portnoy aspires to, in college he orders an anonymous gift subscription of *Partisan Review* for his father. *Partisan Review*, the flagship journal of the New York Intellectuals, and the badge of honor for young American Jews with ambitions of literary seriousness in the forties and fifties, would grant Jake Portnoy access to the wondrous world of high culture. But when Alex returns home for the holidays, the issues of *Partisan Review* are nowhere to be found: "Thrown out unopened—I thought in my arrogance and heartbreak—discarded unread, considered *junk*-mail by this schmuck, this moron, this Philistine father of mine!" (*PC* 9). The mix of "arrogance and heartbreak" is typical of Portnoy's attitude toward his father, feeling superior to him, then wishing it weren't so. He calls his father a philistine, but he also makes an effort to turn him on to the wonderful intellectual journal that he's fallen in love with. Jake Portnoy never becomes a reader of *Partisan Review*, Alex jokingly claims that the only subject that truly interests his father is the New Jersey Turnpike (*PC* 35). How different this father is from the ideal husband and father that Portnoy projects himself to become: "a man guaranteed to give them kiddies to rear and Kafka to read" (*PC* 153).

Shikses

Of course, one of the primary motivations behind Portnoy's initial bids for seriousness is his pursuit of *shikses*, the Christian girls of Irvington, the town just outside of Newark filled with goyish girls "so gorgeous, so healthy, *so blond*" (*PC* 145). He is obsessed by ways through which he can get these girls to take him seriously, as he is sure "they'll laugh and laugh, howl and hoot" (*PC* 150). They'll be laughing because Portnoy is a Jew with an inescapable "Jewish nose" forever marking him off (in his mind, at least) as an undesirable alien. He is forever imagining the reproaches of his pursuit: "That ain't a nose, it's a hose! Screw

off, Jewboy!" (*PC* 150). Within the ten-page section that introduces his obsession, Portnoy's desperate desire to be taken seriously by *shikses* is mediated
through images and strategies taken from pop culture and high culture alike.
He is heartened by the thought that the goyish actress Debbie Reynolds married the Jewish pop singer and movie actor Eddie Fisher, but also that Marilyn
Monroe fell in love with serious playwright Arthur Miller (*PC* 152). Because
both Eddie Fisher and Arthur Miller "got the girl," they can both serve as models for Portnoy in his quest.

To be sure, Portnoy's primary cultural reference point for *shikses* is the pop
culture of the forties and fifties. Whereas for his parents and grandparents, the
beckoning myth of America was embodied in "a chicken in every pot" or "gold
in the streets," for Portnoy, the attraction is the *shikse,* first encountered at the
movies, in the form of actresses Ann Rutherford and Alice Faye (*PC* 146). The
shikses and their gentile families are "the kids who are always asking for 'the
jalopy' and getting into 'jams' and then out of them again in time for the final
commercial" (*PC* 145–6). He imagines their fathers straight out of the movies'
stock images of respectable paternal masculinity, "with white hair and deep
voices who never use double negatives" (*PC* 145). And any of their mothers
could be a "Gold Star Mom" introduced on "Truth or Consequences," whose
reward is "a bottle of seltzer squirted at her snatch, followed by a brand-new
refrigerator for her kitchen" (*PC* 143). This image, strikingly similar to that of
the mother of the Grimes sisters presented in "Writing American Fiction," is as
familiar and intoxicating to Portnoy as it was sickening and stupefying to Roth.
Portnoy, unlike the serious intellectual that Roth embodied through most of
the sixties, is drawn to the world portrayed in American pop culture and aspires
to be a part of it, if only so that the *shikses* will take him seriously.[12] But if it is
through pop culture that Portnoy comes to know gentiles, it is also how he
comes to know his difference from them. It is because "we ate our meals with
that radio blaring away right through to the dessert" that Portnoy knows that he
and his family are not "Americans just like they are" (*PC* 146). And so he dreams
of somehow becoming Oogie Pringle in the MGM musical *A Date with Judy,* or
Jack Armstrong, hero of the radio show "Jack Armstrong, the All-American
Boy" (*PC* 145–6).

But Portnoy also has another simultaneous strategy (no less doomed to fail)
to attain this particular seriousness, much more in line with the sort of literary
seriousness Roth seemed to be pursuing before he wrote *Portnoy.* This is a strategy of elevation, with an emphasis on language that belies the fact that unlike
Zuckerman, Kepesh, and Tarnopol, Portnoy is not a literary man. He invents an
etymology for his name that will perhaps serve to hide his Jewishness. "Portnoy,
yes, it's an old French name, a corruption of *porte noir,* meaning black door or
gate. Apparently in the Middle Ages in France the door to our family manor
was painted . . . " (*PC* 149). The pursuit of gentile girls inspires Portnoy to something like poetic invention, as he wonders whether, at the skating rink, there
is "a nosegay of *shikses,*" or, alliteratively, "a garland of gentile girls" (*PC* 144).

The days spent gazing at these forbidden love objects teach 13-year-old Alex the meaning of the words "longing" and "pang" (*PC* 147). And it is very often the language that Portnoy imagines is spoken in the *shikses'* houses that points up the difference between his social station and theirs. As the daughter of a father "who never use[s] double negatives," Portnoy imagines a *shikse* turning to him and saying, "And thank you ever so much for a wonderful wonderful evening" (*PC* 151). The pleasantness and modulation of this imagined gentile speech is contrasted with the wild and inventive (if less pleasant) language used in the Portnoy household, where "conversation [is] crossfire where you shoot and get shot at," where people say, "*Shah!*" and "I only hope your children will do the same to you someday!" (*PC* 221, 151). If only Portnoy could escape his undignified origins and be as respectable and eloquent as he imagines "Mr. Porte-Noir" to be, the *shikses* would take him seriously.

When Portnoy reaches maturity, he realizes his adolescent dream of dating *shikses*; indeed, it seems he only dates non-Jewish girls. Within his monologue, he details his relationships with three of these girls: "The Pumpkin," Kay Campbell, whom he dates in college; "The Pilgrim," Sarah Abbott Maulsby, a girlfriend during his early twenties; and "The Monkey," Mary Jane Reed, whom he has just broken up with prior to his entering therapy. Looking at these relationships chronologically, it seems that Portnoy's sense of inferiority in the face of these *shikses'* seriousness (primarily exhibited through their language) rapidly develops into a sense of superiority, indicating both his eagerness to see himself as serious and his defensiveness over his "uncultured" origins. As a 14-year-old, he agonizes over his approach to the ideal *shikse* he sees skating at Irvington Park, making sure to speak "absolutely perfect English. Not a word of Jew in it" (*PC* 164). Nineteen years later, in therapy, reminiscing about his various relationships with *shikses*, he admits, "I'm always telling these girls how to talk right, me with my five-hundred-word New Jersey vocabulary" (*PC* 233).

Talking about Kay Campbell, whom Portnoy names "the Pumpkin," he describes his visit to her home in Iowa for Thanksgiving at the age of 17. Portnoy is utterly fascinated by the Campbells, their gentile blandness, their perfectly dignified manners, the fact that they live on a street named "Elm." It is the way they speak that Portnoy seizes on most, their eternal politeness and equanimity. The Campbells are the embodiment of perfect gentile decorum—at least as Portnoy imagined it growing up watching movies and listening to the radio. Entering into a gentile home for the first time at age 17, confronted by his fantasy of Christian America, Portnoy is both attracted and made insecure by the Campbells. Their radio-ready speech brings to the surface Portnoy's insecurity over his lack of culture, his status as a religious minority, his class. Kay introduces Portnoy to her parents as a "weekend guest," her "friend from school." Portnoy is taken aback: "I am something called 'a weekend guest'? I am something called 'a friend from school'? What tongue is she speaking? I am 'the *bonditt*,' 'the *vantz*,' I am the insurance man's son" (*PC* 220). The polite language reinforces Portnoy's sense of difference, and he identifies himself through

Yiddish, or through his lower-middle-class origins, as someone who is not worthy of such dignified descriptions. Even as he is a confident, headstrong 17-year-old with his parents, deriding them for their philistinism and rejecting their Judaism, in the face of this gentile speech, the Campbell's effortless dignity of expression, he is reduced to a caricature of the uncultured, uncivilized alien. Whereas Alvy Singer, in Woody Allen's *Annie Hall,* imagines himself as a Hasidic rabbi when confronted with the gentile decorum of the Halls' dinner table, Portnoy casts himself as a different Jewish stereotype, that of the passionate, overemotional, unmannered Jewish immigrant just off the boat. In describing the impression that Kay's modulation of speech and ability to keep her calm made on him, Portnoy incidentally provides a contrasting portrait of himself. She is "unencumbered by the garbled syntax of the apocalypse or the ill-mannered vocabulary of desperation, without the perspiring upper lip, the constricted and air-hungry throat, the flush of loathing on the forehead" (*PC* 219).

Similarly, in describing the abundance of polite greetings dispensed within the Campbell household, Portnoy portrays the communication in his own home as being almost devoid of all linguistic content. He expresses amazement at the realization that "the English language is *a form of communication!* [. . .] Words aren't only bombs and bullets—no, they're little gifts, containing *meanings!*" (*PC* 221–2). Although, as Brauner points out, the effect of Portnoy's description of the Campbells' radio-ready speech is "to highlight—comically— the conventionality, the *banality* of their language," this effect is the product of Portnoy's retrospective presentation of the scenes in the Campbell home ("Masturbation" 83). At the time, it is clear that Portnoy was impressed and attracted by the Campbells' manners and decorum, and that his encounter with them inspires in him great insecurity and awareness of his status as unserious Jew. The retrospective irony is an indication of the sort of linguistic seriousness Portnoy has since attained (as evidenced by his treatment of the Pilgrim and the Monkey), but at the time could only desperately aspire to.

By the time Portnoy dates Sarah Abbott Maulsby, "the Pilgrim," in his mid-20s, his confidence and sense of his own seriousness of purpose are much improved. Flush from his success as a staff member of the House subcommittee investigating the TV quiz show scandals, Portnoy no longer feels so much like a marginalized alien, the son of Jake and Sophie Portnoy of Jewish Newark. Although Sarah has all the credentials of WASP America, Portnoy now has some of the self-assurance and superiority of a serious man with which he can criticize her way of speaking. "Why didn't I marry that girl?", he asks himself, "Well, there was her cutesy-wootsy boarding school argot, for one" (*PC* 233). Whereas, in the Campbell house, Portnoy reacts to gentile speech with amazement and insecurity, with Sarah he is snide and superior. Upon hearing the nicknames Sarah gave to her college friends—"Poody and Pip and Pebble, Shrimp and Brute and Tug"—Portnoy remarks that it was "as though she had gone to Vassar with Donald Duck's nephews" (*PC* 233). No longer so intimidated by gentile speech, Portnoy has begun to judge the seriousness of others, a privilege not accessible to the immigrants' children of his parents' generation. And yet, there is still the bitterness and sense of inferiority that comes from Portnoy's long-held view of himself as a Jewish other. The Pilgrim "could have been a Lindabury, don't you see? A daughter of my father's boss!" (*PC* 237). Still the insurance man's son, Portnoy's sense of superiority is fueled not only by his growing seriousness, but also by the lingering need to take revenge upon those by whom he and his family felt marginalized. Eventually, Portnoy admits that he broke up with the Pilgrim in order to take "[a] little vengeance on Mr. Lindabury for all those nights and Sundays Jack Portnoy spent collecting down in the colored district" (*PC* 240–1). But while Portnoy does extract this vengeance, does do what his father could not have done, it is clear that he is still driven by the insecurity that is the product of what he sees as his father's inferiority. He still sees the Pilgrim as a real American, with the uncontested birthright of the country's spoils, and himself as someone who can't yet take that for granted.

Continuing his development, when Portnoy, in his early thirties, dates Mary Jane Reed, "the Monkey," he exhibits a superiority, an arrogance even, that is a far cry from the adolescent who dreamt of *shikses* while believing that he was unworthy of them. He exhibits no insecurity in the face of this particular gentile. In this relationship, Portnoy is the serious one, and the Monkey is perpetually insecure about her status as the uneducated daughter of a West Virginia coal miner and her suitability as a socially acceptable partner. Again, language plays an important role. Although Portnoy outlaws the words "*like*, and *man*, and *swinger*, and *crazy*, and *a groove*," from her vocabulary, she still doesn't speak well enough to suit him (*PC* 155). He thinks of her speech as a series of "bits" or routines and derides her constantly for her evident lack of eloquence (*PC* 193, 208). But more important even than the way she speaks is the way she writes. Stumbling upon a note that the Monkey has written to her cleaning lady, Portnoy is amazed and infuriated by her low level of literacy. Even her handwriting is unacceptable: "What hopeless calligraphy! It looked like the work of an eight-year-old." Her spelling is no better. "A little word like 'clean' comes out three different ways on the same sheet of paper. [. . .] two out of three times it begins with the letter *k*. K! As in 'Joseph K'" (*PC* 184). The Kafka reference points up just how far the Monkey is from the sort of girlfriend Portnoy, with his ambitions of seriousness, thinks he should have. As the Assistant Commissioner of Human Opportunity, Portnoy aspires to a dignity and public respectability that is perpetually undermined by his fears over the Monkey's low origins. "[W] hat am I doing having an affair with a woman nearly thirty years of age who thinks you spell 'dear' with three letters!" (*PC* 184). The Monkey is a different species of *shikse* from the educated, well-mannered gentile girls Portnoy has been chasing and dating all of his life. Of course, to congenitally confused Portnoy, this problematic lack of seriousness is also part of the attraction. For although he protests over the Monkey's unsuitability, the relationship allows

Portnoy to fulfill his dreams of seriousness, if only in comparison to this distinctly unserious woman.

Portnoy's relationship with the Monkey allows him to cast himself in the role of the serious Jew, and she is often happy to help. She is eager to have someone to "pull her up from [the] abysses of frivolity and waste," and he, of course, has always wanted to be seen as serious. The serious Jew, as played by Portnoy, is a sort of literary critic, "making judgments left and right, advising her what books to read and how to vote, telling her how life should and should not be lived" (*PC* 162). He has a commitment to learning, and understands both the dignity of suffering and the moral imperative of compassion. When he is not belittling her for her slangy speech and her lack of manners, he earnestly takes on the task of educating her, generously attempting to lift her up to his lofty heights. He gives her books to read, edifying books, as part of "Professor Portnoy's 'Humiliated Minorities, an Introduction'" (*PC* 209). Giving her Agee's *Let Us Now Praise Famous Men*, Dos Passos's *U.S.A.* and Du Bois' *The Souls of Black Folk*, Portnoy plays the part of the arbiter and embodiment of seriousness, deciding which books she should read to attain the appropriate level of understanding. His self-declared purpose is "[t]o save the stupid *shikse*, to rid her of her race's ignorance; to make this daughter of the heartless oppressor a student of suffering and oppression" (*PC* 209).

Ultimately, the Monkey is just not serious enough for Portnoy. As he prefers to see himself (at age 33), no amount of education can elevate this girl to the status of an appropriate partner. The teenager who embraced American pop culture as the means to the end that was a *shikse* now disdains the commonness, the tawdriness, of that culture. "This is the kind of girl ordinarily seen hanging from the arm of a Mafioso or a movie star, not the 1950 valedictorian of Weequahic High! Not the editor of the *Columbia Law Review!* Not the highminded civil-libertarian!" (*PC* 200–1). Having attained, by comparison to the Monkey, the seriousness that he has been desiring all his life, Portnoy finds that the Monkey is simply unsuitable. A comment directed to Dr. Spielvogel makes this clear: "Doctor, I had never had anybody like her in my life, she was the fulfillment of my most lascivious adolescent dreams—but marry her, can she be serious?" (*PC* 106).

* * *

What I think emerges from Roth's work between *Goodbye, Columbus* and *Portnoy's Complaint* is a very restricted conception of seriousness. A serious writer must be decorous, high-minded, dignified, and reserved. Highbrow literature is serious; pop culture, the mass media, and the comedic mode are not. Although Portnoy is not Roth, it is interesting to see that, in *Portnoy's Complaint*, the limits of seriousness are widened to such an extent that they almost disappear. For Portnoy, it seems that anything that will take him out of his parochial Jewishness will qualify as serious. The seriousness embodied by bland American culture, with

its unquestioned confidence and polite manners, will do. The seriousness of
highbrow literature, with its bestowal of learned superiority, will do. Even
baseball and roadside diners, with their unquestioned American authenticity,
will do. Anything that can help Portnoy overcome what he sees as a farce of a
household, impossible to be taken seriously by anyone, least of all by *shikses*, will
serve his purpose in his desperate pursuit of some vague idea of seriousness.
The fact that this idea of seriousness is so formless, so flexibly defined, only
adds to Roth's comedy. What we can see here, perhaps, is an example of Roth's
negotiation of inward and outward moves. To contemporary critics of *Portnoy's
Complaint*, the book signaled a great move outward, a break from Roth's earlier
seriousness, a calculated departure from the affiliation with high culture associated with the New York Intellectuals toward the wild frontiers of the late sixties'
"new sensibility." And indeed, as I discuss in Chapter 3, the New York Intellectuals, as represented in the pages of *Commentary* magazine, saw *Portnoy* in much
the same way, with Irving Howe asking,

> who can doubt that Portnoy's cry from the heart—enough of Jewish guilt,
> enough of the burdens of history, enough of inhibition and repression, it is
> time to "let go" and soar to the horizons of pleasure—speaks in some sense
> for Roth? ("Philip Roth Reconsidered" 75)

But in many ways, although *Portnoy* does show Roth seemingly breaking with his
previously restrictive view of seriousness, Portnoy's progress seems to mimic the
cultural negotiations of Jews like the New York Intellectuals, who had their own
"complaints" in their attempts to become Americanized figures on the cultural
scene.

Louis Menand, in his review of *American Pastoral*, makes a similar point,
but suggests that *Portnoy's Complaint* freed Roth to escape the polarity he introduced in "Writing American Fiction," the banal bestsellers set in contemporary
America or the serious books that spurn contemporary reality:

> Roth didn't think that Portnoy represented liberation. He thought that *repre-
> senting* Portnoy represented liberation—liberation from what he regarded as
> the id-less stereotypes of Jewish characters in contemporary fiction, and from
> middlebrow notions of stylistic decorum. Roth didn't think he was escaping
> from Newark. He thought he was escaping from Leon Uris. (94)

Although the nature of seriousness changes with the context—it depends,
inexorably, on who is desired to be taken seriously by—whether it is Portnoy
wanting the *shikses* to take him seriously, or Zuckerman, standing in for the
young Roth, wanting the literary establishment to take him seriously, these pur-
suers of seriousness always embody the radical displacement Roth has claimed
is at the center of his books: "I am not what I am—I am, if anything, what I am
not!" ("Art of Fiction" 240). This paradox—"I am what I am not"—reflects

a typically two-faced strategy from Roth: looking outward to illuminate what is inside, and looking inward to reveal a culture. Portnoy's desperate insistence that he is not who he is is the engine for much of the comedy of *Portnoy's Complaint.* And perhaps the lesson Roth learned from the writing of *Portnoy's Complaint* is that this sort of comedy can be very serious indeed.

Chapter 3

Franz Kafka, Anne Frank, and Roth's "Personal Culture": After *Portnoy* I

Roth invited Kishka to his house*! To* eat*!*
　　　　　"'*I Always Wanted You to Admire My Fasting*'; *or, Looking at Kafka*"

Anne, says my father—the Anne? Oh, how I have misunderstood my son. How mistaken we have been!

The Ghost Writer

Jewish Ghosts

In the Philip Roth Collection at the Library of Congress, among the notes for Roth's 1973 essay-story "'I Always Wanted You to Admire My Fasting'; or, Looking at Kafka," there is a hand-written note page with the heading "Jewish Ghosts." Listed there are six aspects of Kafka's life that Roth would deal with in the piece, including "Last Year," and "Had he lived." Beneath a dividing line at the bottom of the list is written "Anne Frank."[1] There is no mention of Anne Frank in the published Kafka piece, but the presence of her name in the notes is telling. In the decade and a half that followed *Portnoy's Complaint*, Franz Kafka and Anne Frank would become the two "Jewish Ghosts" who most haunted Roth's writing and would appear in perhaps the two most audacious pieces of writing Roth would publish in his entire career.

The first is "Looking at Kafka," probably the most admired short story Roth would ever publish. It is not strictly a short story though—it is divided into two parts: the first an affectionate biographical sketch of Kafka's last year, in which, almost unbelievably, the writer seemed on the cusp of happiness; and the second a fictional memoir in which a surviving Kafka emigrates to America only to become the Hebrew school teacher for one Philip Roth of Newark, New Jersey.

In *The Ghost Writer* (1979), it is Anne Frank who is imagined to have survived her ordeal and made it to America alive. The young writer Nathan Zuckerman, on a pilgrimage to his hero E. I. Lonoff, imagines Amy Bellette, the mysteriously European girl who may or may not be in love with Lonoff, to be Anne Frank, miraculously alive and living incognito. The brilliantly ambiguous narrative does not make clear to the reader that this is Zuckerman's imagining until very late in the novel. Rather, we enter Zuckerman's fiction and Anne Frank comes to life.

As the similar moves of bringing these two figures back to life within fiction may indicate, it is not strictly influence that will be investigated here. It cannot be said that any of Roth's books are written in a Kafkan, or Frankian, style. Rather, Roth has brought Franz Kafka and Anne Frank into a relation with his work through quite conscious, even blatant, moves, inviting the reader (and the critic) to see the connection between Roth and these forebears. It is Roth who is in control here, importing two iconic Jewish writers and deciding upon their meaning within his own work. Consequently, this chapter aims to work toward an understanding of just what Kafka and Anne Frank do for Roth, or, rather, what he makes them do. By looking at the ways in which Roth *uses* these two figures, I hope to illuminate a significant, and interesting, apparent outward move in Roth's career. Characteristically, it is often the case that the presence of Franz Kafka and Anne Frank in Roth's fiction tells us more about Roth himself than about those ostensible subjects.

After *Portnoy*

There is no question that the commercial and artistic success of *Portnoy's Complaint* granted Roth a sort of freedom greater than any he had experienced before in his career. At the very least, the book made Roth a relatively rich man—and although I do not want to suggest that he had tailored any of his earlier books for the demands of a market—he must have felt the freedom which inevitably comes with a secure livelihood which does not depend on the sales of his next book. What's more, the wide sales of *Portnoy*, quite above and beyond merely an intellectual class of readers or a Jewish one, further freed Roth from any demands imposed upon him by a community's mores. If he wanted to be, there was ample evidence that he was now a national writer, one whose books would receive attention on a national, and even international, scale, and there was more than a little commercial curiosity about what *Portnoy's* author would write next.

The three books that Roth wrote in the four years following *Portnoy's* publication can each be described as experimental. There was *Our Gang* (1971), a political satire of Nixon and his administration, *The Breast* (1972), a fantastical tale of a man who is transformed into a breast, and *The Great American Novel* (1973), a wildly comic pastiche of tall tales and parodic storytelling about, of all things, baseball. Each of these books was like nothing Roth had written before, and, for the most part, they bear little resemblance to anything he has written since. These seemed to be the books of a writer who, once he had broken free of any bonds that may have confined him as a young writer, would do anything not to be jailed again. Roth has spoken of the creation of *The Great American*

Novel as an escape from the rigid constraints he placed upon his writing, and *Our Gang* and *The Breast* seem to spring from a similar desire to be playful. "All sorts of impulses that I might once have put down as excessive, frivolous, or exhibitionistic I allowed to surface and proceed to their destination" (*Reading Myself and Others* 96). To many observers Roth, post-*Portnoy*, seemed, if not quite rudderless, unmoored from any consistent subject or direction for his work.[2] After seemingly breaking free of his powerful allegiance to literary seriousness with *Portnoy*, where was he to turn now? Back to the Jewish Newark of his childhood? Back into the arms of Henry James and the New York Intellectuals? Or forward, to what?

These and other questions were raised, and urgently, by Irving Howe in a vicious reassessment of Roth's work published in *Commentary* in 1972. "Philip Roth Reconsidered" is an excoriating, inflammatory piece, and when Roth had Zuckerman explode with rage at a similarly pointed essay by Milton Appel in *The Anatomy Lesson,* many readers saw the latter as Howe, thinly veiled.[3] Howe was among those critics who had heaped praise upon *Goodbye, Columbus* in 1959, but now, in the light of *Portnoy's Complaint, Our Gang,* and *The Breast,* saw Roth's work to date as "in the grip of an imperious will prepared to wrench, twist, and claw at its materials in order to leave upon them the scar of its presence" ("Philip Roth Reconsidered" 69). Much of the essay seems unduly harsh, full of resentment toward Roth's success and the apparent countercultural import of *Portnoy's Complaint.* But one of Howe's points, although still quite ungenerous, is perhaps prophetic in its identification of Roth's "thin personal culture":

> When we speak of a writer's personal culture we have in mind the ways in which a tradition, if absorbed into his work, can both release and control his creative energies. A vital culture can yield a writer those details of manners, customs, and morals which give the illusion of reality to his work. More important, *a vital culture talks back, so to say, within the writer's work,* holding in check his eccentricities, notions, and egocentrisms, providing a dialectic between what he has received and what he has willed. ("Philip Roth Reconsidered" 73)

What Roth lacks, Howe claimed, is a deeply felt and known tradition, Jewish or otherwise, to help him enrich and expand his own personal experience into something larger, something grander, something Howe was increasingly interested in thinking about.[4] It is a severe assessment, but perhaps an understandable one at the time. Roth's two critical and commercial successes, *Goodbye, Columbus* and *Portnoy's Complaint,* each draw on, to a large extent, the Jewish milieu of Roth's youth, the latter book seemingly almost to the point of exhausting the subject. Much of the critical reception of his other books, which draw on a variety of literary traditions and subjects, often claimed that Roth was misguided in pursuing these directions, or even out of his depth. None of the three books that followed *Portnoy's Complaint* would do much to refute such criticism.

Whereas the critical response was not wholly negative, *Our Gang, The Breast,* and *The Great American Novel* offered scant evidence as to where Roth's career was headed. At the time, each seemed like an isolated experiment—and for the most part, they still appear as such today.

Prague

Near the end of this period of experimentation, though, in 1972, Roth travelled to Prague for the first time, and it is tempting to identify this trip as the catalyst for the direction that Roth's career would next take, as he emerged from his experimental phase into a period in which he would write the books that would define the characteristic Rothian voice for years to come. It is as if, in the three books that followed *Portnoy's Complaint*—all, to some extent, moves outward— Roth was casting about to find an outward move that could suitably take him inward as well. He would soon find it. In many ways, *My Life as a Man* (published in 1974, but a book Roth had been working on from as early as 1968), *The Professor of Desire*, and the books that would eventually become *Zuckerman Bound*, still seem like the baseline Roth mode—realistic, comic, seemingly autobiographical novels of American men of a literary bent, with the faint echo (sometimes not so faint) of twentieth-century European history and culture ringing in the background. This echo, more often than not, seemed tied to the "Other Europe" Roth envisioned, of which Prague was the undisputed capital.

"It is Franz Kafka who was responsible for getting me to Prague to begin with." So Roth explained in a short piece he published in the *New York Times Book Review* in 1976, "In Search of Kafka and Other Answers." The essay gives an account of that first trip to Prague and begins by emphasizing the centrality of Kafka in Roth's initial attraction to Prague. Roth spent nearly all of his visit "quite consciously trying to look at whatever Kafka might once have looked at, seeking out the places where he and his family lived, locating the streets and the sites that are mentioned in his letters and diaries, and in Max Brod's biography." In some respects Prague and Kafka were synonymous in Roth's mind, and this instinctive identification of Prague with its most famous literary son would never quite be broken in Roth's writing.

But Roth ended up finding more than just Kafka in Prague, as the essay goes on to disclose. The piece notes two other aspects of the city that would lead Roth to develop a deeper connection to Prague, each having an undeniable effect on his work throughout the following 15 years. The first is the inescapable imprint of the Holocaust on the Czech capital:

> Within the first few hours of walking in these streets between the river and the Old Town Square, I understood that a connection of sorts existed between myself and this place: here was one of those dense corners of Jewish Europe which Hitler had emptied of its Jews, a place which in earlier days must have

been not too unlike those neighborhoods in Austro-Hungarian Lemberg and Czarist Kiev, where the two branches of my own family had lived before their emigration to America at the beginning of the century. Looking for Kafka's landmarks, I had, to my surprise, come upon some landmarks that felt to me like my own. (6)

If this first personal connection had to do with Roth's identity as an American Jew, the second concerned Roth's equally felt identity as an American writer. He met with the Czech publishers of his first two books to discuss with them the possibility of publishing Czech translations of *Portnoy's Complaint* and *Our Gang*, only to find that neither book "was deemed suitable by the authorities for translation." It was the differences between American cultural life, in which political controls hardly existed, and that of Czechoslovakia, where every cultural product had to meet with the approval of "the authorities," that deepened Roth's interest in contemporary Prague.

Upon Roth's return to the United States, he immersed himself in the study of Czech culture. He read all the contemporary Czech writing that he could find in translation. He began attending Antonín Liehm's classes on Czech history, literature, and film at CUNY Staten Island and befriended a number of Czech exiles. In the spring of the following year, 1973, he returned to Prague. It was the absurdly different consequences brought on by writing in Czechoslovakia, rather than America, that spurred on Roth's interest. He explained to Liehm that his Nixon satire, *Our Gang*, was selling well, and "all that can happen to me is that I'll get a little richer." In Czechoslovakia, "writers that do the same thing can count on going to prison. And I have this need to understand why they do it" (Liehm 82). Among the writers he befriended were Ivan Klíma, Miroslav Holub, Ludvík Vaculík, and Milan Kundera, the latter two becoming the first two authors published in Penguin's "Writers from the Other Europe" series, of which Roth was the general editor. From 1974 until 1987, under Roth's guidance, the series brought numerous writers from behind the Iron Curtain to the attention of Western readers. Roth's initial trip to Prague, rather straightforwardly motivated by an earnest, literary love of Kafka, had become the first of many annual visits, his focus shifting to the contemporary literary culture, under constant threat from the totalitarian government. "The purpose of my first visit to Prague had been to see where Franz Kafka had lived. I returned to Prague because I wanted to find out how the writers managed to live there now, working in conditions that were utterly alien to my own writing experience" (Roth, "In Search" 6–7). He would return every spring until 1977, when he was denied an entry visa by the authorities.

The presence of Kafka and Prague in Roth's work of the 1970s almost always reflects this combination of a deeply personal connection and a fascinated awareness of difference. The first aspect is born out of a writer and teacher's love of Kafka's writings, as well as an American Jew's feeling of ancestry. The second stems from a vivid sense of the crucial differences between writing in the West and writing in the East, and the difference between being born a Jew in twentieth-century America or in twentieth-century Europe. In this way, what began as a rather straightforward literary appreciation of Franz Kafka becomes something more, and something more personal for Roth: the conscious use of a significant literary forebear to help define the particular writer Roth wants to be, or cannot help but be. Throughout this era, Roth's use of Kafka is a reaching outward, expanding his fictional worlds to include a very different writer's experience. But although that difference is never forgotten nor denied, Kafka's presence serves to illuminate Roth's characters' particular predicaments—predicaments that seem rooted in Roth's own experience—while Roth keeps them firmly grounded in the experience of the American Jew in the late twentieth century.

"Studies in Guilt and Persecution"

Roth published *My Life as a Man* in 1974, but there are drafts in his archives dated as early as 1968, and Roth himself has said that he began working on it in 1964 ("Art of Fiction" 236). It would eventually present the novelist Peter Tarnopol's anguished attempts to tell the story of his horrible marriage to a woman who essentially tricked him into their union. These attempts dictate the very structure of the book, which consists of two "Useful Fictions"—short stories written by Tarnopol, fictionalizing his plight—and "My True Story," Tarnopol's attempt to achieve some sort of catharsis through autobiography. In 1989, Roth's memoir, *The Facts*, would reveal that the central event of this plot—the outrageous, incredible way in which the protagonist is taken in—had been the one incident from Roth's own life that the writer had not needed to fictionalize, improve upon, or transform before including it in his fiction: Roth himself had been deceived into assenting to a short-lived, unhappy marriage as a young man in exactly the same manner. Margaret Martinson Roth's deception "was a little gem of treacherous invention, economical, lurid, obvious, degrading, deluded, almost comically simple, and best of all, magically effective. To reshape even its smallest facet would have been an aesthetic blunder" (*F* 107). The nearly endless pages of drafts for *My Life as a Man* currently residing in the Roth archive at the Library of Congress are a testimony to the difficulty Roth had finding a suitable fictional home for this obviously powerful and traumatic experience. In fact, the final, published version of *My Life as a Man* can be said to be more concerned with Tarnopol's desperate attempts to find the "correct" way to tell the story of his marriage than with the marriage itself.[5]

Although Roth would, throughout his career, play games with known autobiographical events in his fiction, *My Life as a Man* is a particularly tempting book to look at autobiographically, because the events it mirrors from Roth's life are so well documented (as is *The Ghost Writer*, which I take up below). Just as Peter Tarnopol would, Roth began teaching Kafka's works in the mid-sixties, in one of his courses at the University of Pennsylvania. In a 1969 interview, Roth notes, "When I look back now upon the reading I assigned that year I realize that the course might have been called 'Studies in Guilt and Persecution'" ("Philip Roth's Exact Intent" 2). This period coincided with the stressful breakup of his marriage, and Roth has noted the effect the ordeal had upon his creative life; much like Tarnopol, after Roth's legal separation,

> I was virtually unable to write for three or four years. From 1962 to 1967 is the longest I've gone, since becoming a writer, without publishing a book. Alimony and recurrent court costs had bled me of every penny I could earn by teaching and writing.

He began to think of himself as "a train that had been shunted onto the wrong track" ("Art of Fiction" 227–8).

It was this period of personal anguish that led to a deeper understanding of Kafka's fiction. Writing in 1976, he notes:

> I began reading Kafka seriously in my early thirties at a time when I was enormously dismayed to find myself drifting away, rather than towards, what I had taken to be my goals as a writer and as a man—at a time, in other words, when I was unusually sensitized to Kafka's tales of spiritual disorientation and obstructed energies. ("In Search" 6)

Struggling to find his way again through a difficult period in which the decision to marry the wrong person seemed to have deformed his very identity, Roth found that his predicament allowed him to understand Kafka in a way previously unavailable to him.

> That those trying years provided me with a means of penetrating a great writer whose concerns had previously evaded me, makes me almost willing to be grateful for the obstruction and disorientation I had to experience to begin to get in touch with his fiction. ("In Search" 6)

As Roth's personal struggles would soon become the inspiration for his fiction, he soon discovered that Kafka could provide a correlative for his characters' mystification at the hands life had dealt them.

Kafka is only mentioned a few times in *My Life as a Man*, but looking at those allusions, in addition to further references in the drafts, can shed considerable light on Roth's conception of Kafka in the years before he began visiting Prague. Peter Tarnopol's marriage (like Roth's) would last only a few years before he secured a legal separation, but the back-and-forth recriminations, both in the courtroom and out, would continue until Maureen, the demonized wife, dies in a car accident (just as Roth's wife, Margaret Martinson Roth, did). Until her death, Tarnopol, in turns enraged and unmanned, struggles to produce any fiction worth keeping. He earns his income (and hers) through teaching a couple of courses at Hofstra University. There is a very short passage in "My True Story" in which he describes one seminar he gives and its effect on him. The course, which includes *The Trial, The Brothers Karamazov, Death in Venice* and *Anna Karenina,* "had an unusually powerful hold on me, and I taught the class with a zealousness and vehemence that left me limp at the end of my two hours." At first he cannot understand why teaching this particular course should have such a strange power over him. It is only after some time that he realizes that the choice of works assigned "derived of course from the professor's steadily expanding extracurricular interest in the subject of transgression and punishment" (*MLM* 235).

In an earlier draft, dated 1969–1970, a version of this passage appears, in slightly different form, complete with an imagined course title:

> Studies in Guilt and Persecution. Of Course. [. . .] He had not realized until this moment how, actually he was only giving them a high-class version of his domestic life: he had chosen each and every book for its relevance to his marriage! What a perspective on literature!

In this version, it seems that Kafka plays a bigger role in the course than is intimated in the published book. Not just *The Trial,* but also "In the Penal Colony" and "The Metamorphosis" are on the syllabus, and it is through this last story that the protagonist, here called Abner Reingold (his wife is Lydia Cartwright), sees his fate. "As Abner Reingold awoke one morning from uneasy dreams he found himself transformed in his bed into Lydia Cartwright's husband . . . What has happened to me, he thought. It was no dream." Kafka is used here as a correlative for Reingold's ordeal. Tellingly, it is not just that Kafka illuminates his life; it is his life that illuminates his reading of Kafka. Reingold asks his students why Kafka writes that "it was no dream." None of them can give a satisfactory answer, so Reingold answers himself:

> "Because it wasn't a dream! Because it isn't a dream." [. . .] How could anybody be expected to understand that *it was no dream,* that Kafka meant it, that *Samsa was a cockroach,* who had not the experience of living four years with Lydia?[6]

It is as if it is necessary to go through some horrible personal trauma before being able to understand and fully appreciate Kafka's genius.

Roth's own helplessness in the face of his ordeal seems to have survived in one of Tarnopol's central concerns in *My Life as a Man.* For at the center of his troubles is his utter disbelief that he has such troubles in the first place. Before his marriage, Peter Tarnopol was a literary hotshot, a young man at ease with himself and his chosen vocation. After meeting and marrying Maureen, he is transformed into an impotent, neurotic, failed writer who cannot complete so much as a short story. The significance of Tarnopol's struggle to accept the fact that he is who he has become—not who he thought he would become—is signaled strongly in the book's final line, in which he despairs at "this me who is me being me and none other!" (*MLM* 334). As early as 1968, this focus on the unreckoned consequences of life, and the inability to predict or control those consequences, was to be a part of the book:

> It was comic really to think of the Will working and whittling away at one's character, at Conscience giving orders, and Ambition laying down programs and manifestos, all the while Experience was silently making the man, causing one inevitably to become a creature of a somewhat different order than one's desired, or imagined, self. Wasn't that, in a way, the subject of Kafka's *Metamorphosis*? Things never turn out as you expect, signed Franz Kafka. You become what you become. You happen to yourself.[7]

It is certainly interesting to note that, throughout the many drafts of *My Life as a Man*, nearly every mention of Kafka (and there are quite a few) relates to this particular preoccupation of Roth's—the inevitable and seemingly random ways in which "you happen to yourself."

The Breast, published in 1972, is, at first glance, a recognizably Kafkan fantasy—a man is transformed into 155 pound breast—and Roth's central concerns, and his use of Kafka, seem cut from the same cloth as those in *My Life as a Man*, which he was struggling with while writing *The Breast*. Naturally, turning into a breast is of a different order of catastrophe from entering into a disastrous marriage, but at heart Kepesh is a man confronted with a reality, and truths about himself, that he is hard-pressed to accept and understand. So even though Kepesh suspects at one point that his predicament is the result of having taught too much Kafka—"I have out-Kafkaed Kafka. He could only *imagine* a man turning into a cockroach. But look what I have done"—on the whole his rather unusual situation becomes a stand-in for all of the unusual transformations that life forces us to go through, often against our will (Roth, *Breast* 73). So while Tarnopol cries out repeatedly, "HOW COULD SHE? TO ME!" Kepesh screams, "WHAT DOES IT MEAN? HOW HAS IT COME TO PASS? AND WHY? IN THE ENTIRE HISTORY OF THE HUMAN RACE, WHY DAVID ALAN KEPESH?" (*MLM* 210; *Breast* 23). In the end, all either man can do is accept what has happened to him. Kepesh rather sensibly explains that

> [w]hat had happened to me had happened to me and no one else because it could not happen to anyone else, and even if I did not know why that was so, *it was so*, and there must be reasons to make it so, whether I was ever to know them or not. (*Breast* 28)

Tarnopol, at least until Maureen dies, has no choice but to follow his psychoanalyst, Dr. Spielvogel's, advice: "Tolerate it." For both men, Kafka can serve merely illustrative, or even ironic, purposes, on the way to an understanding that what is happening is happening because it is happening.

Looking at Roth Looking at Kafka

Roth's use of Kafka in these books largely reflects the former's preoccupations with characters astonished and impotent in the face of the inescapability of their particular identities and fates. In "'I Always Wanted You to Admire My Fasting'; or, Looking at Kafka," Roth writes of two escapes for Kafka himself, one real and one imagined, with the latter an escape into the world of Roth's childhood. The implicit collapsing of Kafka's life and work (Roth sees a doomed obsession with entrapment and obstruction in both Kafka's fiction and in his diaries and letters) is characteristic of the way in which Roth writes about Kafka here. The man and his work are one (of course, in the mid-1970s, the same could justifiably be said of Roth). Roth had been teaching some of Kafka's works as a part of a broader course of European masterworks at the University of Pennsylvania since the late 1960s. In 1971 he began teaching a course wholly devoted to Kafka and explained to Antonín Liehm that "for years I told my students that *The Trial* or *The Castle* were written by an author who had really never traveled anywhere, never experienced anything, that everything took place inside him, in his imagination." As might be expected, his first pilgrimage to Kafka's Prague in 1972 had a great effect on his teaching. "After I got back I said to my students: Forget everything I told you. Kafka had no imagination whatsoever. He only had to go downstairs and out onto the street and describe what he saw" (Liehm, 82–3). That Roth at least partly understands Kafka's fiction as a description of "what he saw" on the streets of Prague seems apt for a writer increasingly fascinated by the interaction between his own life and fiction, as the Zuckerman books would soon show.[8] "Looking at Kafka" carries a dedication to the students of Roth's Kafka class, and the first half of the piece, a biographical essay on the last year of Kafka's life, 1924, "as sweet and hopeful a year as he may ever have known as a man, and the year of his death," reads like a university lecture, albeit an elegant, personal, and passionate lecture ("Kafka" 281).

The biographical section of the essay-story is prefaced by a page or so of Roth's musings on Kafka, introducing two motifs that foreshadow the direction the piece will take in its second part. The first is a subtle attempt to tie Kafka to Roth himself. The very first sentence, with its use of the first person and a telling parenthetical comment, suggests that this will be a piece about both Kafka and Roth: "I am looking, as I write of Kafka, at the photograph taken of him at the age of forty (my age)" ("Kafka" 281). In addition, as part of a detailed description of Kafka's features in the photograph, Roth notes that his nose "is long and weighted slightly at the tip—the nose of half the Jewish boys who were my friends in high school." Already, the reader is drawn to the commonalities between the writer and his subject—their age, their Jewish physiognomy. But the very next sentence changes tack, emphasizing a major difference between the two. "Skulls chiseled like this one were shoveled by the thousands from the ovens; had he lived, his would have been among them, along with the skulls of his three younger sisters" ("Kafka" 282). Whatever personal significance Roth finds in Kafka's life for his own, the differences in their milieus cannot be denied. Although Kafka died almost a decade before Hitler's rise to power, the Holocaust necessarily hangs over any imagining of a European Jew in the first half of the twentieth century, casting its shadow both backward and forward in history. Roth was born in the safety of America, avoiding the fate of six million of his fellow Jews, and it is this crucial difference, and the consequent multiplication of differences that spring from it, that will be a significant element of Roth's use of Kafka.[9]

The second motif introduced in this opening is the supposition of alternate fates that Kafka might have met "had he lived." Perhaps, Roth suggests, Kafka might have escaped with his friend Max Brod to Palestine. "But *Kafka* escaping? It seems unlikely for one so fascinated by entrapment and careers that culminate in anguished death" ("Kafka" 282). Or maybe, like the hero of *Amerika*, Karl Rossmann, Kafka could have fled to America and taken up a post at a university. This possibility seems no more likely, and even then, perhaps Kafka would have destroyed his manuscripts, as he famously bid Brod to do. Rather than *the* Kafka, he would have been "just a Jew lucky enough to have escaped with his life" ("Kafka" 283).

But an escape does become the subject of Roth's version of Kafka's last year, in which he finally makes a successful escape from the oppressive environments of his father's house and Prague. He has found love in the arms of Dora Dymant, a 19-year-old Jewish girl with whom he moves in to two rooms in a Berlin suburb. Even though Dora's father forbids her from marrying the tubercular, 40-year-old bachelor—as Irving Malin has pointed out, Kafka can never truly escape Prague because "he carries his family on his back and his illness in his lungs"—Roth is still fascinated by the prospect of such a miraculous escape for a man in whose fiction escape is usually presented as a cruel joke (Malin 273). Roth writes, with some amazement, about this last year of Kafka's life, in which the latter, flush with the love of Dora, finally publishes a volume of his stories, begins to take an earnest interest in the study of Hebrew, and becomes a sort of father to his young companion. This metamorphosis, however brief (for he dies within a year), is perhaps as unlikely as Gregor Samsa's is: "*As Franz Kafka awoke one morning from uneasy dreams he found himself transformed in his bed into a father, a writer, and a Jew*" ("Kafka" 289).

The idea of an escape and transformation for Kafka is taken even further in the second part of "Looking at Kafka," this time through fiction. In this section, Roth takes Kafka and conjures him into the Newark of his childhood, an environment already familiar to the many readers of *Goodbye, Columbus* and *Portnoy's Complaint*. It is 1942. Kafka has survived his illness, escaped the Nazis, and come to America; he is the 59-year-old Hebrew school teacher of Philip Roth, age 9. It is a fantasy of influence, making literal the familiar metaphor of receiving lessons from the masters. It is perhaps the paradigmatic writer's fantasy: "Imagine *me*, Kafka's protégé!" The fact that Roth has Kafka as his Hebrew school teacher suggests that it is a particularly Jewish influence, that Kafka has particularly influenced Roth as a Jewish writer. This idea, though, is quickly made ironic, as Roth and his classmates resent Dr. Kafka for making them "learn an ancient calligraphy at the very hour we should be out screaming our heads off on the ball field." In addition, to the young Roth's embarrassment (for he is essentially a very good boy), the other kids have taken up Philip's nickname for their teacher, "Dr. Kishka." And Philip delights his friends on their walk home "with an imitation of Kishka, his precise and finicky professional manner, his German accent, his cough, his gloom" ("Kafka" 291). Even as Roth conjures Kafka into the world of his formative years, it is the impossibility of such an unproblematic appropriation, the contrast between the boys' vivid American mischief-making and Dr. Kafka's European sobriety, that comes across most clearly.

But if Kafka, as a Hebrew school teacher, doesn't quite become young Philip's mentor, a variation on the fantasy is soon resurrected. As soon as Philip tells his parents that he has heard his teacher lives "in a *room*," they decide to invite him over to dinner, and plans are hatched to fix him up with Philip's Aunt Rhoda. "The massive machinery of matchmaking has been set in motion by my undiscourageable father, and the smooth engines of my proud homemaking mother's hospitality are already purring away" ("Kafka" 293). If Kafka marries Aunt Rhoda, he will almost certainly exert a great influence on Philip's formative years. Young Philip Roth could be Kafka's nephew! But, almost from the moment this idea is conceived, Roth pokes holes through the fantasy, deflating the dreamy idea of being related to Kafka with comic reminders of how alien Kafka is to the world of 1940s America. When Philip, after class, invites Kafka to dinner, "he replies, with a formal bow that turns me scarlet—who has seen a person do such a thing outside of a movie house?—he replies that he would be *honored* to be my family's dinner guest" ("Kafka" 293). Then, to Philip's shock, Kafka writes down the Roths' address in his notebook, "and beneath it, some words *in German*" ("Kafka" 294). Aunt Rhoda, to her nine-year-old nephew, is a thoroughly modern woman, an "interior decorator" at a department store called the "Big Bear," spending "hours in the bathroom every day applying powder and sweeping her stiffish hair up into a dramatic pile on her head." And so, immediately after inviting Kafka to dinner, Philip wonders how he will warn his aunt "about his sour breath, his roomer's pallor, his Old World ways, so at odds with her up-to-dateness" ("Kafka" 294). With echoes of "Eli, the Fanatic," Kafka seems to represent all that these American Jews wished to leave behind.

In the end, it seems that the gaps between Roth's world and Kafka's cannot be bridged even by "the massive machinery of matchmaking." The relationship between Dr. Kafka and Aunt Rhoda is short lived, and ends predictably, with Kafka unable to fulfill his husbandly duties in a hotel room in Atlantic City. This fate allies Kafka with his heroes yet again, another individual doomed to be defeated by forces beyond his control. Here is yet another failed Kafkan escape attempt: Josef K. cannot avoid the tribunal, Gregor Samsa cannot undo his transformation, and Kafka cannot find love and happiness in New Jersey.

As for Philip Roth becoming Kafka's student or nephew, the outcome is similarly unsuccessful, but perhaps not disappointingly so. Roth is ineluctably the product of his own environment, a writer who often draws upon his deeply felt memories of and connections to the Jewish Newark of his upbringing, not the oppressive household of Kafka's Prague. At the end of "Looking at Kafka," Roth tells how he learns, years later, of Dr. Kafka's death. Philip's mother sends him the obituary, for he has stayed on at college over the summer, unwilling to go home where fights with his father have become frequent and maddening. Philip cannot understand it, but he finds himself resenting his father for his love and affection; it is his independence that he so earnestly fights for. "Others are crushed by paternal criticism—I find myself oppressed by his high opinion of me! Can it possibly be true (and can I possibly admit) that I am coming to hate him for loving me so?" ("Kafka" 301). The implicit comparison to Kafka's crushingly critical and actively oppressive father is telling. That the worst family conflicts Philip has had to suffer through were the common arguments of an American adolescence speaks volumes as to the huge gulf that separates Roth's world and Kafka's. But Roth could no more escape his circumstances than Kafka could, and those circumstances would necessarily inform his writing, making him a very different sort of writer than Kafka.

Kepesh in Prague

Roth's 1977 novel, *The Professor of Desire*, is the book in which Roth's visits to Prague first make a deep imprint on his work. It tells the story of David Kepesh, the protagonist of *The Breast*, before he is beset by his fantastical transformation. As Kepesh, a literature professor, sees it, his life has always been a battle between two divergent tendencies. The first is to be the good boy, to do what is respectable, sober, and sane. The second, of course, is to be the bad boy, to pursue his wildest fantasies of erotic desire, to fulfill his taste for adventure, to yield to the temptations of "moral delinquency," as his psychiatrist, Dr. Klinger, calls it. He is seeing Dr. Klinger because, after his divorce from the beautiful, adventuress Helen, he is impotent, depressed, and near-suicidal: "fastened to no one and to nothing, drifting, drifting, sometimes, frighteningly, sinking" (*PD* 103). What's more, he is characteristically unable to decide whether he is adrift because he has yielded too much to temptation, or because he has not yielded enough. For the book's first half, then, this is a familiar tale for Roth: like Tarnopol, Kepesh is a literary Jewish-American man who feels like a train "shunted onto the wrong track"; like Portnoy, Kepesh is unsure whether he is held back by his conscience, or whether he has no conscience at all. And whereas *The Professor of Desire*'s focus on the unreckoned consequences of male desire sets it apart from the earlier books, there is a sense, in the first half, of Roth covering similar ground. These concerns are dispelled, however, with the arrival of Claire Ovington, Kepesh's vitality-restoring new love, and the couple's trip to Prague. The prospect of a satisfying, lasting relationship and the opening up of the setting to include the world behind the Iron Curtain go a long way to making this a different, and in some ways more interesting, book than *My Life as a Man*. The Prague section allows Roth to investigate his long-held fascination with the difference between life in the West and life in the East, and offers yet another opportunity for Kafka to play an active role in the definition of a Roth hero.

Kepesh and Claire spend a few days in Prague as a stopover on the way to Bruges, where Kepesh is to give a paper on "Kafka's preoccupations with spiritual starvation," a telling subject given the way Roth often utilizes Kafka in his fiction (*PD* 165). The account of Kepesh's trip to Prague echoes Roth's account of his own first trip there in 1972. Shown around by a Czech professor of literature, they take the Kafka tour: his school, his father's office, the house in which he wrote, the cemetery in which he is buried. When Kepesh and Claire visit Kafka's grave, Roth executes a rhetorical move that recalls the passage in "Looking at Kafka," in which Roth is looking at Kafka's photo. Just as he does in the earlier work, here Roth moves swiftly from a personal connection, this time between Kepesh and Kafka, to an acknowledgment of massive historical difference:

> The dark rectangular slabs beyond Kafka's grave bear familiar Jewish names. I might be thumbing through my address book, or at the front desk looking over my mother's shoulder at the roster of registered guests at the Hungarian Royale: Levy, Goldshmidt, Schneider, Hirsch. (*PD* 175)

Kepesh places a pebble on the graves of Kafka and his friend Max Brod. "Then for the first time I notice the plaques affixed to the length of the cemetery wall, inscribed to the memory of Jewish citizens of Prague exterminated in Terezin, Auschwitz, Belsen, and Dachau. There are not pebbles enough to go around" (*PD* 176). As in "Looking at Kafka," Roth presents a Kafka with whom he (or his protagonist) shares, at the very least, an undeniable Jewishness. This is the Jewishness of descent, not assent, having nothing to do with either religious practice or Jewish self-identification; rather it is Kafka's physiognomy or the Jewish last names surrounding the writer's grave that usher in feelings of kinship.[10] But the distance between Roth and Kafka is just as immovable. The Holocaust must be acknowledged in any exploration of twentieth-century Jewishness, and the Nazis did not discriminate between those Jews who felt themselves to be Jewish and those who did not.

In addition to the specter of the Holocaust, the differences between contemporary Prague—to which both Roth and Kepesh are drawn to seek out Kafka—and the West become another contextual contrast to be investigated, and illuminated, by Roth's use of Kafka. In *The Professor of Desire*, competing claims on Kafka's resonance become a catalyst to explore Roth's admitted fascination with the way his own experience wildly diverges from that of his Czech counterparts. The Czech professor who shows Kepesh and Claire around Prague was forced into retirement at age 39, when the Russian tanks invaded Prague, crushing the Prague Spring movement of 1968. Kepesh asks him how he survives, how he keeps his sanity, living on a tiny government pension, forbidden to publish anything under the totalitarian regime. He responds: "Kafka, of course."

> Yes, this is true; many of us survive almost solely on Kafka. Including people in the street who have never read a word of his. They look at each other when something happens, and they say, "It's Kafka." Meaning, "That's the way it goes here now." Meaning, "What else did you expect?" (*PD* 169)

In Roth's contemporary Prague, Kafka becomes synonymous with intellectual life behind the Iron Curtain, with Kafka's forever-stymied protagonists the precursors to modern day K.s, faced with the obstructions and absurdities imposed by the Soviets. The Czech professor goes on to explain that, in the months after the Russian invasion, he was tireless in his resistance. He attended secret meetings, passed along petitions, wrote analyses and circulated them in *samizdat*—giving himself an ulcer, but failing, of course, to bring down the all-powerful government.

> What will I do when I stop bleeding? Return to playing K. to their Castle and their Court? This can all go on interminably, as Kafka and his readers so well know. Those pathetic, hopeful, striving K.'s of his, running madly up and down all those stairwells looking for their solution, feverishly traversing the city contemplating the new development that will lead to, of all things, their success. (*PD* 170)

Fearing that a life of futile, Kafkan striving will lead to no less than physical disintegration, the professor now spends his days translating *Moby Dick* into Czech, a project that is perhaps equally futile, as there already exists a fine translation and nothing the professor writes is allowed to be published anyway. Nonetheless, he continues on, drawn to the fierce ambition, and the rage, of Melville's protagonist: "The appetite to set things right, to emerge at the top, to be declared a 'champ'" (*PD* 170). It is this sustained appetite, in the face of an unbeatable adversary, that separates Ahab from Kafka's disillusioned protagonists, and that, one suspects, attracts the professor to the translation.

Naturally, after talking to Kepesh about his personal connection to Kafka, the Czech professor asks Kepesh what drew him to the writer. It was not "political hopelessness," Kepesh explains, but rather, "sexual despair, [. . .] vows of chastity that seem somehow to have been taken by me behind my back, and which I lived with against my will." (*PD* 171). Again, like Roth, and like Tarnopol, here is a man who turns to Kafka when his life seems to have been "shunted onto the wrong track." For Kepesh, Kafka's stories furnish a correlative for his despair and disbelief at failing to reach what seems to be an ordinary, yet thoroughly unattainable, goal.

> What I started to say about Kafka, about reading Kafka, is that stories of obstructed, thwarted K.'s [sic] banging their heads against invisible walls, well, they suddenly had a disturbing new resonance for me. It was all a little less remote, suddenly, than the Kafka I'd read in college. (*PD* 172)

What is interesting is that, in addition to associating his sexual troubles with Kafka's protagonists, he also takes the Czech professor's experience with totalitarianism as an analogy for his predicament.

> I can only compare the body's utter singlemindedness, its cold indifference and absolute contempt for the well-being of the spirit, to some unyielding, authoritarian regime. And you can petition it all you like, offer up the most heartfelt and dignified and logical sort of appeal—and get no response at all. (*PD* 172)

We are certainly meant to take seriously Kepesh's ordeal with impotence, the unmanning, mystifying battle against an unwilling body. Yes, it is understandable that Kepesh sees his body as an authoritarian regime. But juxtaposed, through their differing claims on Kafkan experience, with the Czech professor's impoverished life under an actual authoritarian regime, Kepesh's predicament pales a little by comparison. Kepesh himself can't quite avoid slipping into a tummler's patter in describing his difficulties to the Czech: "You think poor K. is clever—you should have heard me trying to outfox impotence" (*PD* 172).

What I think we see coming into Roth's work here is a complex, yet unapologetic, defense of his own concerns as a writer. Kepesh's impotence may not compare in significance or misery to the suffering of the Czechs, but it is a subject for fictional representation nonetheless, and it is a subject that Roth is much more qualified to explore. By placing these two very personal readings of Kafka side by side, Roth seems to find room for both.[11] In a 1984 interview, Roth spoke of American writers working in a society in which "everything goes and nothing matters," whereas in Czech society, "nothing goes and everything matters." Nonetheless, he did not envy the Czech writers their political oppression and weighty topics. Harking back to his perennial interest in seriousness, he contends:

> To write a serious book that doesn't signal its seriousness with the rhetorical cues or thematic gravity that's traditionally associated with seriousness is a

worthy undertaking too. To do justice to a spiritual predicament that is *not* blatantly shocking and monstrously horrible, that does *not* elicit universal compassion, or occur on a large historical stage, or on the grandest scale of twentieth-century suffering—well, that's the lot that has fallen to those who write where everything goes and nothing matters. ("Art of Fiction" 244)

In this way, Kafka serves Roth's purpose of investigating, and legitimizing, his own particular concerns as a Jewish writer, born and bred in America and living in a free society without oppressive political constraints. Whereas the claustrophobic atmosphere and personal paranoia of Kafka's fictional world can easily be seen as a precursor to life under the totalitarianism of the twentieth century, Roth's work in the 1970s demonstrates that Kafka is perhaps equally evocative when used to illustrate smaller-scale—yet no less maddening—problems of powerlessness and bewilderment in the face of a personal reality.[12]

The Ghost Writer

As Roth's 1979 novella, *The Ghost Writer*, begins, Nathan Zuckerman, a serious and talented young Jewish writer, arrives at the isolated home of one of his literary idols, E. I. Lonoff, way up in the Berkshire mountains. Zuckerman has come to "submit myself for candidacy as nothing less than E. I. Lonoff's spiritual son, to petition for his moral sponsorship and to win, if I could, the magical protection of his advocacy and his love" (*GW* 7).[13] In the very first sentence of the book, Zuckerman compares himself to a bildungsroman hero, and he rather self-consciously sees this visit as part of his literary education, the young apprentice seeking knowledge and wisdom at the foot of the master. But, as his ambition to be Lonoff's "spiritual son" suggests, he is also looking for a more personal sort of father figure, as, in the book's first chapter, he hints at a wounding dispute with his own father from which he is fleeing. But before he can tell the reader more about this quarrel, he is immediately distracted by the girl he sees sitting in the next room when Lonoff's wife opens the door. She has a strange and enchanting beauty, with a head that seemed "conceived on a much grander and more ambitious scale than the torso," and Zuckerman wonders "where I had seen that severe dark beauty before" (*GW* 17, 12). Is she Lonoff's daughter? His *grand*daughter? His concubine? All of these thoughts pass through Zuckerman's head before Lonoff introduces them. She is Amy Bellette, a former student of Lonoff's, attempting to sort through Lonoff's manuscripts to give them to the Harvard library.

After agreeing to stay over for the night in Lonoff's study, Zuckerman finds he cannot sleep. His head is swimming from Lonoff's praise for his literary potential and from the presence of the mysterious and bewitching Amy. Upon hearing voices in the room above him, he stands up on the bed to be able to make out the words. Still not close enough to the ceiling to hear, he gets up on

Lonoff's desk, but finds he needs to get a few inches closer. Without making a sound, he inserts between his feet and the desk a volume of short stories by Henry James. Zuckerman can now make out the voices in the room above. It is Lonoff and Amy. She is crying and begging him to leave his wife for her. She calls him Dad-da, he imitates Jimmy Durante for her—there is a history here that Zuckerman can only guess at. In the end, despite her best efforts, Lonoff shows the restraint that Zuckerman so admires in the great man's writing, and refuses her. "Oh," Zuckerman thinks, after getting down from the desk, "if only I could have imagined the scene I'd overheard! If only I could invent as presumptuously as real life! If one day I could just *approach* the originality and excitement of what actually goes on!" (*GW* 87). It is with Zuckerman's astonishment over what he has heard and his desperate desire to prove himself as a writer of great fiction that the chapter ends.

The next chapter begins: "It was only a year earlier that Amy had told Lonoff her whole story" (*GW* 88). "Her whole story" is that she is Anne Frank, the famous diarist of the Second World War. She did not die at Belsen, as is commonly believed. Instead, in the chaos that followed the liberation of the camps, she made her way to England, and after writing to Lonoff, gained his sponsorship to come study at Athene, the small liberal arts college where he teaches. There she has lived for more than five years as Amy Bellette, keeping her secret from everyone, most torturously from her father, who, in the years since the war, has labored to keep her diary and her memory alive in the public imagination. It is only in 1955, after taking the bus to New York and seeing the Broadway production of the play adapted from her diary, that she finally breaks down and tells Lonoff her secret. The whole of this, the third chapter of *The Ghost Writer*, is devoted to telling Anne's story. It is only afterwards, in the next chapter, that we learn that this section is a figment of Zuckerman's imagination, his attempt to "invent as presumptuously as real life," spurred on by his own personal turmoil and the conversation he overheard. Amy Bellette is really Amy Bellette, and Anne Frank is dead.

Goodbye, Columbus Revisited

To begin to understand why and how Zuckerman imagines Amy as Anne Frank, we must first look at the situation that Roth puts Zuckerman in at the beginning of *The Ghost Writer*. Nathan Zuckerman, full of earnest literary ambitions, has published a handful of short stories in prominent magazines, and, at 23, has just completed his longest, most ambitious story to date. Entitled "Higher Education," it retells an old family dispute, in which two of Zuckerman's relatives fought over their mother's inheritance money. As he has with each of his previous stories, he sends a manuscript to his father, expecting praise and admiration in return. Instead, his father expresses anger and surprise that Nathan would portray the family in such a bad light, engaging in a vicious, petty squabble. What's more, there is also the matter of how gentiles will read the story. In the midst of their big argument, Nathan's father tells him, "your story, as far as Gentiles are concerned, is about one thing and one thing only. [. . .] It is about kikes. Kikes and their love of money" (*GW* 68).

In the ensuing weeks, while Zuckerman is staying at a writer's colony, his father gives the story to Judge Leopold Wapter, one of Newark's most esteemed and respected Jewish figures, to elicit his opinion. Judge Wapter sends a letter to Zuckerman, explaining that he understands that great artists throughout history have been persecuted by their communities for their idiosyncratic work. Nonetheless, he goes on, an artist does have "a responsibility to his fellow man," and to "the cause of truth and justice." With that in mind, the judge has enclosed with the letter a questionnaire—"serious and difficult questions to which Mrs. Wapter and I would like you to give just one hour of your time." Among the ten questions included are the following:

> If you had been living in Nazi Germany in the thirties, would you have written such a story? [. . .] What in your character makes you associate so much of life's ugliness with Jewish people? [. . .]Can you honestly say that there is anything in your short story that would not warm the heart of a Julius Streicher or a Joseph Goebbels?" (*GW* 74–5)

As a postscript to the letter, Judge Wapter has added this seemingly benign remark:

> If you have not yet seen the Broadway production of *The Diary of Anne Frank*, I strongly advise that you do so. Mrs. Wapter and I were in the audience on opening night; we wish that Nathan Zuckerman could have been with us to benefit from that unforgettable experience. (*GW* 74)

Almost needless to say, Judge Wapter's letter does nothing to bridge the gap between Nathan and his father, and Nathan is restlessly going over their fight, and their estrangement, in his mind in the hours before he overhears Lonoff and Amy in the room above him.

Speaking of the Zuckerman trilogy, of which *The Ghost Writer* is the first book, John Updike has stated that "Roth's inventing what looks like a *roman-à-clef* but is not" (quoted in Roth, "Interview with Philip Roth" 2). Zuckerman is Roth's alter ego, and by placing him in situations from his own biography, as he does throughout the trilogy, Roth can alter and refine those situations for better fictional effect. Reading *The Ghost Writer* upon its publication in 1979, many readers could be expected to be aware of the autobiographical source material of Zuckerman's ordeal. The controversy that sprung up around the publication of the stories of *Goodbye, Columbus*, the angry letters that rolled in to Roth and the publications that first printed the stories, and the denouncing rabbis all contributed to the defining event of Roth's early career. Although Roth vigorously defended his work and motives in "Writing About Jews," in subsequent interviews he let on just how surprised and taken aback he had been by the angry Jewish critics of his early work. He explained that he had "imagined fiction to be something like a religious calling, and literature a kind of sacrament." Having decided that he would be a serious artist in the vein of Tolstoy, James, and Flaubert, he didn't imagine that his motives, and particularly his attitude toward Jews, would be called into question:

> I had gravitated to the genre that constituted the most thoroughgoing investigation of conscience that I knew of—only to be told by more than a few Jews that I was a conscienceless young man holding attitudes uncomfortably close to those promulgated by the Nazis. ("Reading Myself" 406)

It is this situation from his own biography that Roth takes as the starting point for *The Ghost Writer*. Nathan Zuckerman is a young American Jewish writer with serious literary ambitions who, upon writing a story about American Jews, finds, to his surprise, that some American Jewish readers are more sensitive about the subject than expected. But whereas, for Roth, criticism came from leaders of the Jewish community and ordinary readers, in the fictional version, Roth increases the force of the blow by putting the objections into the mouth of Zuckerman's own father.

This sharpening and refining of Roth's own experience for his fiction can also be seen in the role the Holocaust plays in Judge Wapter's letter to Zuckerman. For, although scarcely mentioned in any of the angry letters and rabbi's sermons, it was clear to Roth that it was the Holocaust which hung over the impassioned response from Jewish readers of his early stories. Roth has written that the attacks on his work seemed to "imply that the sufferings of the Jews throughout history, culminating in the murder of six million by the Nazis, have made certain criticisms of Jewish life insulting and trivial" ("Writing About Jews" 446). This position is concretized in Judge Wapter's questionnaire for Nathan, with its questioning of whether he would write such a story in Nazi Germany and the insinuating mention of Streicher and Goebbels.[14] It is further emphasized by the Judge's recommendation that Zuckerman go see the Broadway adaptation of the diary of Anne Frank. By implication, the Judge is suggesting that, after seeing the play, Nathan will think twice before writing such things about Jews. Anne Frank, in her Broadway incarnation, is invoked here as a constant reminder of the need to be careful, not to give Gentiles any more reason to hate or persecute Jews. It is this suggestion that triggers Zuckerman's imagining of Amy Bellette as Anne Frank, and *his* version of Anne competes with that proposed by Judge Wapter (and, it is implied, Zuckerman's father) in the book's central conflict.

The battle dramatized in *The Ghost Writer*, a fictional version of the battle over Roth's early work, centers on a difficult question: in the wake of the Holocaust, how do you write about Jews? That this battle rests on differing interpretations of Anne Frank is a reflection of just how central a figure she was in postwar American apprehension of the Holocaust. In a 1984 interview, Roth stated that, in his early career, "I knew less about anti-Semitic repression from personal experience than I did about the repressions Jews practiced upon themselves, and upon one another, as a consequence of the history of anti-Semitism" ("Art of Fiction" 238–9). Anne Frank's presence in *The Ghost Writer*, imaginary though it is, is Roth's way of retrospectively offering up to his younger self the realities of the Holocaust, or at least concretizing the complicated history and issues that lay behind his detractors' objections.

Bringing Anne Home

The Anne Frank chapter of *The Ghost Writer*, entitled "Femme Fatale," is written in the third person, but filtered through Amy/Anne's point of view. In a long interview with *The Paris Review*, Roth has said that when he started writing the section,

> I was somehow *revering* the material. I was taking a high elegiac tone in telling the story of Anne Frank surviving and coming to America. I didn't know where I was going so I began by doing what you're supposed to do when writing the life of a saint. It was the tone appropriate to hagiography.

It was only after struggling with the draft for some time that he realized that he was going about it all wrong. "The victim wasn't herself going to talk about her plight in the voice of 'The March of Time.' She hadn't in the *Diary*, so why should she in life?" It is telling that Roth also adds that "[i]n retrospect, my difficulties look somewhat bizarre, because just what Zuckerman was fighting against, I was in fact succumbing to—the officially authorized and most consoling legend" ("Art of Fiction" 242). Indeed, it is the fact that Zuckerman imagines Anne Frank as a fully, and particularly, human character, not as a saint out of Jewish history to be piously worshipped, that sets him apart from his critics in the ideological landscape of the book. Zuckerman's Anne Frank is nothing like the saint that Roth describes writing about in his early drafts. She is fiercely independent, determined to succeed in life on her own merits, often angry with the world, and unafraid of sexual desire. Reinvented as Amy Bellette, she becomes an aspiring writer much like Zuckerman; when she finally rereads her diary once it is published, she reads it calmly and critically, as if it were just another piece of juvenilia. She has come to America because "after Belsen, she figured it might be best to put an ocean the size of the Atlantic between herself and what she needed to forget" (*GW* 91). In Zuckerman's imagining, Amy's need to forget overpowers even her need to see her father again, and she is determined to live with her choice.

It is the Broadway play that finally triggers her breakdown; only then does it become horribly clear to her that she can never see her father again. After seeing the play, she takes a hotel room and calls Lonoff, weeping uncontrollably until he drives down to New York to see her. When he arrives, she tells him that "of course it happened. It had to happen. It's what happens there. The women cried. Everyone around me was in tears. Then, at the end, in a row behind me, a woman screamed, 'Oh, no.' That's why I came running here" (*GW* 88). She realizes that it is too late now to be Anne Frank ever again; Anne Frank must be dead for the world to have her and her powerful story. She imagines an actor coming out onto the stage after each performance and announcing, "But she is really alive. You needn't worry, she survived, she is twenty-six now, and doing very well" (*GW* 89). Even if she could convince her father to keep her survival a secret, what if he were found out? She has become an icon, a symbol of the six million murdered, a figure invested with so much cultural weight that asserting her continued existence is unthinkable. Anne Frank will forever be the 15-year-old girl whom the world knows from the remarkable diary she kept, and from the enormously successful play and movie adapted from that diary.

> "They wept for me," said Amy; "they pitied me; they prayed for me; they begged my forgiveness. I was the incarnation of the millions of unlived years robbed from the murdered Jews. It was too late to be alive now. I was a saint." (*GW* 107–8)

Around the breakfast table on the morning after Zuckerman's imaginative night are Zuckerman, Lonoff, his wife, and Amy. But initially, Zuckerman cannot keep from seeing Amy as he has imagined her, as Anne Frank. As he narrates the rather uneventful breakfast conversation, he keeps slipping into an unruly internal monologue, in which the fantasy is taken even further:

> I kept seeing myself coming back to New Jersey and saying to my family, "I met a marvelous young woman while I was up in New England. I love her and she loves me. We are going to be married." "Married? But so fast? Nathan, is she Jewish?" "Yes, she is." "But who is she?" "Anne Frank." (*GW* 112–13)

He imagines the looks on his parents' faces when they comprehend just who Zuckerman's young love really is. He sees himself instantly forgiven for his literary sins. "*Anne, says my father—the Anne? Oh, how I have misunderstood my son. How mistaken we have been!*" (*GW* 114). This suggests that Zuckerman's imagining of Amy as Anne is part of a fantasy in which he proves to his father that he is a good Jewish boy after all.[15]

As Michael Rothberg convincingly argues, "Nathan's absurd fantasy reveals how the Holocaust, far from evoking anxiety, as it did in the Jews of Woodenton [in "Eli, the Fanatic"], has come to fortify an acceptable Jewish identity" (59).

Seen this way, the similarities between Zuckerman's Anne and Zuckerman him-self take on new resonance. In some ways, Zuckerman has imagined Anne Frank to be his double, a Jewish writer much like himself. Like Zuckerman, literature is more truly her religion than Judaism; while her sister Margot dreamt of becoming a midwife in Palestine, she read Goethe and Dickens and dreamt of growing up to be a writer. Both Zuckerman and Anne look to Lonoff as a surrogate father, one who will nurture their literary talents. And, late in the book, when Zuckerman acknowledges, finally, that Amy could no more be Anne Frank than he could be, he draws a parallel between her relationship with her father and his: "No, the loving father who must be relinquished for the sake of a child's art was not hers; he was mine" (*GW* 120). While the fantasy is alive, it is implied that Anne's similarities to Zuckerman will help him appease his father. His imagined Anne is the impossible ideal that would suit both Zuckerman's and his father's ideas of what a Jewish writer should be: at once an ambitious artist in thrall to the great books as well as a noble, suffering Jew whose very experience speaks of the gravity of twentieth-century Jewish history. It is a mix-ture that would allow Nathan, if he could marry her, to be true to his vocation while still pleasing his parents, and it is an impossibility. For Amy is not Anne, and Nathan cannot be the writer his father wants him to be.

America's Anne Frank

The Ghost Writer is set in 1956, whereas Roth's own conflicts with his Jewish crit-ics occurred in 1959. This is not autobiography, and a number of other facts have been changed to suit Roth's fictional aims, but the change of date is not arbitrary. Frances Goodrich and Albert Hackett's adaptation of *The Diary of Anne Frank* opened at the Cort Theatre on Broadway in October of 1955, and by setting the book in 1956, when the play was still running, Roth can incorpo-rate it into his story. The Broadway adaptation of the *Diary* looms large in *The Ghost Writer*, both as the event that finally convinces Amy that she can never reclaim her original identity in Zuckerman's fantasy, and as the prescriptive work of art that Judge Wapter, and by extension Zuckerman's father, recom-mends that Zuckerman partake of to cure his unacceptable fictional approach to portraying Jews. The play opened to almost unanimously positive reviews and a packed house every night. It went on to win the Critics' Circle Award and the Pulitzer Prize. It is a result of the play's success, and the Hollywood film adapted from the play that followed in 1959, that Anne Frank's diary became perhaps the primary symbol of the Holocaust for Americans. But the adaptation of the diary into a play was specifically tailored for American audiences of the 1950s, and the nature of that tailoring, much discussed in recent years, can shed further light on *The Ghost Writer*.

In 1950, Meyer Levin, a moderately successful Jewish-American novelist living in Paris, was given a copy of *The Diary of a Young Girl* in its French translation.

As a war reporter in 1945, he had been one of the first to witness, and report back to the world, the horrific details of the concentration camps. After reading the *Diary*, he became convinced that it was a hugely significant book and could fully communicate the human side of the atrocity if made into a powerful play. He contacted Otto Frank and volunteered to help him find an American publisher. In exchange, he asked that Frank allow him to attempt a dramatization of the *Diary*. Levin did play some part in securing the book's American publication in 1952 and contributed enormously to its commercial success with a front-page rave review in the *New York Times Book Review* on the weekend before it was published. But Frank could not guarantee that a Broadway producer would take on Levin's adaptation, and the eventual producer, Kermit Bloomgarden, decided to commission Albert Hackett and Frances Goodrich Hackett, a husband-and-wife screenwriting team, whose credits included *It's a Wonderful Life* and *Seven Brides for Seven Brothers*, to write the play's script. Levin, for his part, protested the decision through all means possible—the media, the courts, petitions—and fighting to produce what he saw as an adaptation truer to the spirit of the *Diary* would become an obsession that dominated his life until his death in 1981. Although I do not want to spend a lot of time on the Levin case, much of the recent scholarship on the adaptation of the *Diary* has used the controversy as a starting point to a fuller investigation of the universalizing aspects of the adaptation.[16] Levin's central claim over the years was that his play was rejected because it was too Jewish; he continually maintained that the Hacketts were brought in because they would downplay the Jewishness of the attic's inhabitants in the pursuit of a more universal "message" to attract a bigger audience. And while the Hacketts' sincerity and good faith in approaching the adaptation is well documented, it is clear that, in many instances, they opted for the universal instead of the particular (and particularly Jewish) in adapting the *Diary*.

The pursuit of a truly universal appeal in adapting the play seemed to be endorsed by all of the players involved in the production, including Otto Frank. The Hacketts' play went through a series of drafts, and after each one they would give it to a number of people for their input. These people included Frank, the producer Bloomgarden, and the American playwright Lillian Hellman, who Levin was convinced led the charge to erase Anne's Jewishness from the play. After receiving the Hacketts' fourth draft, Otto Frank communicated his criticisms back to them in a letter:

> Having read thousands of reviews and hundreds of personal letters about Anne's book from different countries in the world, I know what creates the impression of it on people and their impressions ought to be conveyed by the play to the public. Young people identify themselves very frequently with Anne in their struggle during puberty and the problems of the relations mother-daughter are existing all over the world. These and the love affair with Peter attract young people, whereas parents, teachers and psychologists learn about the inner feelings of the young generation.[17]

With the encouragement of Frank, in addition to Hellman and the play's producers, the Hacketts eventually produced a play that has much in common with many conventional Broadway plays of the 1950s. Scenes of tension and distress are mixed in with comedic incidents, a romance blossoms between two adolescents, and there is little explicit mention of precisely why these people are in hiding. A comparison between the Hacketts' play and the *Diary* shows that the Hacketts excised or changed the emphasis of much of the book's Jewish content in an attempt to increase the (presumably Gentile) audience's identification with the characters.

On April 11, 1944, after a burglary downstairs caused the inhabitants of the attic to fear that they would be discovered, Anne Frank famously wrote in her diary:

> Who has inflicted this upon us? Who has made us Jews different from all other people? Who has allowed us to suffer so terribly up till now? It is God that has made us as we are, but it will be God, too, who will raise us up again. If we bear all this suffering and if there are still Jews left, when it is over, then Jews, instead of being doomed, will be held up as an example. Who knows, it might even be our religion from which the world and all people learn good, and for that reason only do we suffer now. (261)

This passage, in the Hacketts' play, became: "We're not the only people that've had to suffer. There've always been people that've had to—sometimes one race—sometimes another—and yet . . ." (Goodrich and Hackett 88). Instead of an anguished attempt to understand why the Jews have suffered so, the play has Anne actually playing down the suffering of the Jews and essentially equating European Jews in the Holocaust with all persecuted groups throughout history. The play's director, Garson Kanin, defending the above change, is on record as calling Anne's passage "an embarrassing piece of special pleading. [. . .] The fact that in this play the symbols of persecution and oppression are Jews is incidental, and Anne, in stating the argument so, reduces her magnificent stature" (Ozick, "Who Owns" 96). Suffering is suffering, the new passage implies, and throughout the play, such vague ideas of tolerance and understanding trump historical specificity.

In keeping with such an approach, the play also radiates an optimism that is surprising for a story with so grim an ending. This was reflected in many of the play's contemporary reviews; it was called "a moving document about the durability of the young in spirit," or "a story of the gallant human spirit" (Graver 94). Perhaps the most famous contributor to this sense of optimism is the play's final scene. After the families are discovered by the Nazis and taken away to the camps, the play jumps forward to after the war, when Otto Frank returns to Amsterdam and learns that his daughter's diary has been found. He opens the diary, and the audience hears Anne's disembodied voice speaking: "In spite of everything, I still believe that people are really good at heart" (Goodrich and

Hackett 91). As the curtain falls, the audience is left with this inspiring, and reassuring, image: even right up to her doom, Anne maintained her innocent belief in the basic goodness of humanity. The line is indeed in the *Diary*, but the play lifts it out of its complicating and ambiguous context. Anne follows that line with an impassioned acknowledgment of the horror that awaits her and her fellow Jews upon discovery:

> It's a wonder I haven't abandoned all my ideals, they seem so absurd and impractical. Yet I cling to them because I still believe, in spite of everything, that people are truly good at heart. It's utterly impossible for me to build my life on a foundation of chaos, suffering and death. I see the world being slowly transformed into a wilderness, I hear the approaching thunder that, one day, will destroy us too. I feel the suffering of millions. (332)

Lawrence Graver has reported that the play has made such an impact that both the Oxford and Cambridge reference books on American theater, at least in 1995, still mistakenly stated that the play's last line is also the closing line of the diary (95). Tellingly, in *The Ghost Writer*, Zuckerman's Anne comments on this famously optimistic sentiment. After reading and rereading the diary, she reflects upon the differences between her younger self and who she has become, after the horrors of the concentration camps.

> She was not, after all, the fifteen-year-old who could, while hiding from a holocaust, tell Kitty, *I still believe that people are really good at heart.* Her youthful ideals had suffered no less than she had in the windowless freight car from Westerbork and in the barracks at Auschwitz and on the Belsen heath. She had not come to hate the human race for what it was—what could it be but what it was?—but she did not feel seemly any more singing its praises. (*GW* 105)

This passage illustrates the willful reorientation being performed by the placing of the line at the end of the play; by emphasizing Anne's optimism while scarcely mentioning just how that optimism was snuffed out, the play turns a blind eye to the horrors of the Nazis' final solution.

In a letter to Otto Frank, explaining why they did not want the song in the play's Hanukkah scene to be sung in Hebrew, the Hacketts wrote,

> It would set the characters in the play apart from the people watching them [. . .] for the majority of our audience is not Jewish. And the thing that we have striven for, toiled for, fought for throughout the whole play is to make the audience understand and identify themselves [. . .] to make them feel "that, but for the grace of God, might have been I."[18]

But the problem with this perhaps admirable ambition is, as Judith Doneson has pointed out, that "it was not by chance that Anne was hiding but by Nazi design—and, specifically, because she was Jewish" (70–1). And, Zuckerman might add, it was not just because she was Jewish, but because she was a Jew born in Europe in 1929, not in Newark, New Jersey, in 1933. The play's tendency to universalize aspects of Anne Frank's story is reflected in Judge Wapter's invocation of the play in *The Ghost Writer*. For he is engaging in another sort of universalization, one that downplays the specific historical milieu from which Anne and her family were hiding. In the wake of the charges against him in 1959, Roth argued that

> [t]he success of the struggle against the defamation of Jewish character in [America] has itself made more pressing the need for a Jewish self-consciousness that is relevant to this time and place, where neither defamation nor persecution are what they were in the past. For those Jews who choose to continue to call themselves Jews, and find reason to do so, there are courses to follow to prevent it from ever being 1933 again that are more direct, reasonable, and dignified than beginning to act as though it already is 1933—*or as though it always is.* ("Writing About Jews" 451)

The Judge seems to suggest that the lesson to be taken from the Holocaust is that American Jews must always be fearful, must always be careful, for the smallest mistake on their part might precipitate another such catastrophe. When Nathan's mother tries to explain Judge Wapter's invocation of Streicher and Goebbels by pointing out what Jews had only recently suffered through, Nathan is not as sober and articulate as Roth was: "In Europe—not in Newark! We are not the wretched victims of Belsen! We were not the victims of that crime!" (*GW* 77). Throughout the book, and especially in his imagining of Anne Frank, Zuckerman counters the approach to Jewish writing suggested by his father and Judge Wapter by always emphasizing the particular context that is relevant.[19]

Cynthia Ozick and Zuckerman's Anne

In 1997, on the occasion of a revival of the Hacketts' *Diary of Anne Frank* on Broadway, Cynthia Ozick wrote a scathing essay in the *New Yorker*, entitled "Who Owns Anne Frank?" In her impassioned summary of, and repudiation of, all of the ways in which Anne Frank's diary has been put to use over the years, Ozick is tireless in her insistence on the diary's utter singularity as a historical document. She argues that, because Anne's diary ends before she is discovered, because it could not record the events that led to her doom, the diary has lent itself to appropriation:

> The diary in itself, richly crammed though it is with incident and passion, cannot count as Anne Frank's story. A story may not be said to be a story if the

end is missing. And because the end is missing, the story of Anne Frank in the fifty years since *The Diary of a Young Girl* was first published has been bowdlerized, distorted, transmuted, traduced, reduced; it has been infantilized, Americanized, homogenized, sentimentalized; falsified, kitschified, and, in fact, blatantly and arrogantly denied. [. . .] Almost every hand that has approached the diary with the well-meaning intention of publicizing it has contributed to the subversion of history.

And every hand that has approached the diary is met here with Ozick's fiercely argued disdain: the Hacketts, Meyer Levin, even Otto Frank. She criticizes the perceived optimism and hope embodied in Anne Frank's story as "nonsensical," calling the diary "a story of fear" (77–8). The adapted play and film have created the world's Anne Frank, transforming her into something that does a great disservice to her memory. The Anne Frank industry has made of her perhaps the primary conduit through which Americans understand the Holocaust, magnifying the damage done by these appropriations. But mostly, it is the fact of appropriation, any appropriation, that Ozick condemns. These, "whether cheaply personal or densely ideological, whether seen as exalting or denigrating, have contributed to the conversion of Anne Frank into usable goods. There is no authorized version other than the diary itself." It is not for us, the living, to tell Anne Frank's story, and perhaps we should not have been given the temptation to do so. Ozick closes the essay with this dramatic and emotional response:

> It may be shocking to think this (I am shocked as I think it), but one can imagine a still more salvational outcome: Anne Frank's diary burned, vanished, lost—saved from a world that made of it all things, some of them true, while floating lightly over the heavier truth of named and inhabited evil. (100, 102)

Ozick's wish is for an Anne Frank who is allowed to maintain her particularity, a specific and circumscribed individual vanquished by a very real and unalterable force of evil. In some ways, although Zuckerman himself (and Roth) is engaging in an appropriation of Anne Frank, imagining her so as to prove his legitimacy as a Jewish writer, his Anne dramatizes Ozick's passionately argued plea. The reason Zuckerman's Anne breaks down after seeing the play that has been made of her diary is that she has been robbed of her particularity, of her individuality. Aimee Pozorski has drawn parallels between the question of the representation of Anne Frank and the argument over Zuckerman's story, "Higher Education," seeing both as concerned with "the conflict of idealization versus reality." Zuckerman's father is sure that all gentile readers will see in his son's story is "Kikes and their love of money," rather than "the scientists and teachers and lawyers they become and the things such people accomplish for others" (*GW* 68). As a barrier against anti-Semitism, he wants an idealized picture of Jews put across, much as the dramatization of Anne Frank's diary was intended to universalize and idealize her story, seemingly for the sake of gentile theatergoers. Pozorski continues:

> Although Nathan's family and community criticize him for not considering the history of the Jews and its vexed relation to "Higher Education," Nathan's position, like Ozick's, is actually more historical than the ideal representations of Jews advanced by his father, Doc Zuckerman, and the heartened readers of *The Diary of Anne Frank.* (90)

Zuckerman, in both the writing of his story and in his imagining of Amy Bellette as Anne Frank, reasserts particularity in the face of this idealizing instinct. Allegiance to the particular nature of reality is portrayed as a significant part of Zuckerman's newfound literary principles.[20] In his fantasy, the production and great success of the Hacketts' play effectively means that Anne Frank can no longer be Anne Frank; American culture has usurped her identity and made of it something determined by its own need to draw certain lessons from the Holocaust.[21] And yet, that need, particularly in American Jews, is entirely understandable and perhaps even necessary.

The difficulties and crises of identity facing American Jewry after the Holocaust were complex and manifold; the problem of how to continue writing about Jews in this changed landscape was an aspect with particular resonance for Roth as a young Jewish writer. In an honest appraisal of his early battles, Roth expressed his understanding of the complexity of postwar American Jewish experience:

> What makes [writing about Jews] problematical is that Jews who register objections to what they see as damaging fictional portrayals of Jews are not necessarily philistine or paranoid. If their nerve endings are frayed, it is not without cause or justification. They don't want books that will wound the feelings of Jews already victimized, if not by anti-Semitic persecution in one form or another, by the distaste for Jews still endemic in pockets of our society. (*Reading Myself and Others* 108–9)

For the members of Roth's generation, who were born in America, and came of age in the aftermath of the Holocaust, the need to move forward and forge a collective identity appropriate to the present was always informed by the utter inescapability of the past, of the devastating collective trauma suffered only recently. Without this understanding, the objections expressed by Zuckerman's father and Judge Wapter in *The Ghost Writer* would carry no dramatic weight; they would be mere paper tigers, philistine arguments to be easily rebuked by Zuckerman, the hero in pursuit of truth and justice. As it is, the conflict is much more nuanced and complicated; Zuckerman's fantasy of Anne Frank is not mere one-upmanship, it is a fantasy in which he himself becomes implicated,

drawn into the tortured and irresolvable questions that the Holocaust has left
for all surviving Jews. By appropriating Anne Frank into his life, he demonstrates that she, and the catastrophe in which she perished, are as inescapable
for him as they are for his elders.[22]

In addition to her condemnation of the appropriations of Anne Frank,
Cynthia Ozick has stated in many forums her opposition to fictional representations of the horrors of the Holocaust. She argues that the overwhelming supply
of documentary evidence and memoirs are the only morally justifiable way we
should comprehend the atrocities; all else is a sort of deformation of the
truth.[23] And yet, one of the best known of her fictions is the short story "The
Shawl," itself a fictional tale of a woman whose baby is thrown by a concentration camp guard against an electrified barbed-wire fence. She has said that she
regrets having written the story, but "the idea came over me, and it wrote itself"
(Ben-David 10). A similar sentiment was expressed by Roth when asked if he
took the Holocaust as a subject in the Zuckerman books: "For most reflective
American Jews, I would think, [the Holocaust] is simply there, hidden, sub-
merged, emerging, disappearing, unforgotten. You don't make use of it—it
makes use of you" ("Interview with *The London Sunday Times*" 118). For American
Jewish writers such as Ozick, Roth and Zuckerman, the choice to deal with the
Holocaust in their fiction is no choice at all—it is always there, informing their
very identities and literary sensibilities. In this sense, Anne Frank can truly be
seen as a ghost writer haunting these authors' pages, a Jewish writer whose masterpiece will forever be defined by the cataclysm that extinguished her life and
continues to haunt ours.

Although, on the surface, it appears that Roth's use of Anne Frank and his
most notable use of Kafka employ very similar mechanisms of imagined return,
it is clear that these two figures have served Roth's work in different ways. Roth
seems to have been drawn to Kafka's work first, finding something intriguing
and haunting in the Czech writer's life and fiction that rang particularly true in
the light of his early struggles to define himself as a writer and as a man. He
seems less drawn to Anne Frank by choice; rather, her story is one that inescap-
ably comes with being an American Jew in the twentieth century. As perhaps the
central American Holocaust narrative, Anne's diary becomes a metonym for
the catastrophic event with which all Jews, and in particular Jewish writers, must
grapple. But as figures from the recent past against whom Roth defines his
protagonists, and, in turn, himself, as a particular writer with a particular
history, writing in a particular time and place, Kafka and Anne Frank can be
seen as doing similar work in Roth's fiction. Perhaps, in the end, these two
monumental Jewish writers serve as part of the "personal culture" that Irving
Howe claimed Roth was lacking:

> When we speak of a writer's personal culture we have in mind the ways in
> which a tradition, if absorbed into his work, can both release and control his
> creative energies. [. . .] *A vital culture talks back, so to say, within the writer's work,*

[. . .] providing a dialectic between what he has received and what he has willed. ("Philip Roth Reconsidered" 73)

It is difficult to say whether Roth's use of these two figures would have satisfied Howe's requirements for a vital personal culture. But by allowing both Kafka and Anne Frank to talk back within his work, and by talking back to them, Roth has turned outward in order to better explain his own circumstances, the endless series of influences that go in to making a person, and a person's world, what it is. In doing so, Roth places himself within a tradition that is bigger, and more unwieldy, than he could have merely willed into being.

Chapter 4

The Freudian Lock: After *Portnoy* II

Man is tied to the weight of his own past, and even by a great therapeutic labor little more can be accomplished than a shifting of the burden.

Philip Rieff

I should myself be glad to know whether the primal scene in my present patient's case was a phantasy or a real experience; but, taking other similar cases into account, I must admit that the answer to this question is not in fact a matter of very great importance.

Sigmund Freud

The experience of psychoanalysis was probably more useful to me as a writer than as a neurotic, although there may be a false distinction there.

Philip Roth

In the last chapter, we saw how Roth's readerly connection to Kafka, apparently borne out of his sense of dislocation and rudderlessness in the mid-1960s, came to color much of his fiction throughout the 1970s as it grew into a fascination with "the other Europe." The 1960s also saw Roth enter into psychoanalysis, an experience which provided him with another rich body of ideas that would immeasurably inform his fiction over the next decade and a half. Of course, the most noticeable, and most immediate fictional product of this experience was *Portnoy's Complaint*. In a 1974 essay entitled "In Response to Those Who Have Asked Me: 'How Did You Come to Write That Book, Anyway?'" Roth details the circuitous path that eventually led to the writing of *Portnoy*. The novel famously portrays Alexander Portnoy's struggle to reconcile his rebellious, outlandish sexual urges with his repressive Jewish conscience. But, as the essay explains, between 1962 and 1967, Roth went through a struggle of his own, writing drafts that were either overly fantastical (a tone well suited to the protagonist's acting out) or overly realistic (which suited the stereotypically obedient child-hood), failing to find a form that could simultaneously express the two poles of Portnoy's predicament. It was only when Roth took inspiration from a crucial element of his own 1960s experience—his psychoanalysis—that the correct presentation of the problem became clear to him:

> The psychoanalytic monologue—a narrative technique whose rhetorical possibilities I'd been availing myself for years, only not on paper—was to furnish the means by which I thought I might convincingly draw together the fantastic element [. . .] and the realistic documentation. (Roth, *Reading Myself and Others* 36)

This formulation, offering a conception of psychoanalysis as a form ripe for exploitation by the writer of fiction, provides a key to *Portnoy's Complaint*, as well as a large part of the fiction Roth would write over the ensuing 16 years.

This chapter will explore the many ways in which Roth has taken advantage of Freud's theories for his own ends in the books written from *Portnoy's Complaint*, published in 1969, up until the conclusion of *Zuckerman Bound* (which brought together in one volume *The Ghost Writer, Zuckerman Unbound, The Anatomy Lesson*, and *The Prague Orgy*) in 1985.[1] I hope to show that, apart from being a commercial and creative breakthrough in unleashing Roth's comic talents into his fiction, *Portnoy's Complaint* also signals the beginning of a period of Roth's career in which an understanding of psychoanalysis becomes almost essential to an understanding of the fiction.[2] As evidenced mainly in *Portnoy's Complaint, My Life as a Man*, and *The Anatomy Lesson*, Freud seems to have served Roth's work in three important ways. First, Roth has taken advantage of the narrative possibilities inherent in the psychoanalytic therapy session as a site of self-storytelling. This is most clearly apparent in *Portnoy's Complaint*, for which the importance of the central conceit (a Jewish analysand's monologue) cannot be overstated, but Peter Tarnopol's attempts to tell his self's story in *My Life as a Man* also demonstrate this strategy. Secondly, most significantly in *My Life as a Man*, the first of Roth's many books to feature a novelist as a protagonist, Roth explores the idea that the particular introspection called for in psychoanalysis is comparable to, and perhaps a catalyst for, the act of writing fiction. Finally, the extensively defined, immutable self that Freud proposes provides an assumption that conflicts with Roth's characters, most notably in *The Anatomy Lesson*. Throughout this period, Freud's reality principle could be said to be the ultimate problem for each of Roth's protagonists, who characteristically move toward a resignation to the utter immutability of the self.

This constricting aspect of the Freudian conception of the self becomes more and more apparent in Roth's work as the Zuckerman saga moves toward its conclusion. Whereas at the beginning of this period, Roth tends to focus on the possibilities for comedy (in *Portnoy's Complaint*) or creativity (in *My Life as a Man*) that Freudian self-interpretation provides, by the time of *The Anatomy Lesson* and *The Prague Orgy*, it is the restrictions of a Freudian mindset that are most emphasized. As Roth's alter ego Nathan Zuckerman outlandishly attempts to escape his identity as a writer chained to mining his own self, Roth himself seems to be straining at the limits that a Freudian conception of the self imposes on his characters. This suspicion is strengthened by the book that follows *Zuckerman Bound, The Counterlife*, in which Zuckerman is not granted the impossibility of a new self, but instead a new way of conceiving of the self, seemingly breaking with a Freudian sensibility. The specific nature of that break, and the ways in which psychoanalysis may actually sow the seeds for such a change, gestures toward the adventurous path that Roth's work would take following *The Counterlife*.

The Story of the Self: *Portnoy* and *My Life as a Man*

Freud famously called his most central developmental mechanism the Oedipus complex, taking its name from Sophocles's play *Oedipus Rex*. This literary analogue is hardly incidental to Freud's overall work; he points out that the play's gradual revealing of climactic events is "a process that can be likened to the work of a psychoanalysis" (*Interpretation* 262). Indeed, psychoanalysis can be seen as a process in which stories of the self are told. Just as Sophocles artfully reveals to the audience the true account of Oedipus's past, so the analyst suggests the stories that may lie behind a patients' dreams, symptoms, or even choice of words. To pursue this parallel between a work of literature and the therapeutic process of psychoanalysis, one must focus on the ways in which Freudian interpretation proceeds: it is always retrospective, working backward from a symptom (or any psychical production) to its proposed causes or antecedents. A patient's verbal tics, for example, are not symptomatic of anything until, through the process of analysis, their hidden sources are revealed. Likewise, in the Freudian conception, dreams do not communicate meaning in themselves, but must be elucidated, their meaning created by the analyst. It is the fact that dreams and symptoms are theoretically construed as inscrutable to the dreamer or the sufferer that necessitates the analyst's interpretation.

In this sense, the analyst plays the role of the storyteller, fashioning new tales of the patients' self. But, as Philip Rieff points out, the analyst is not the only storyteller. First, the patient must tell his own story:

> [M]eaning does not emerge out of the raw material of incident and language in a piece, at once. [. . .] the patient offers the dream (or fantasy or random number or name), and is then asked by the analyst to associate around it, and thereby make it symptomatic. (118)

The process of free association, one way in which the analyst procures the patient's story, replaced hypnosis in Freud's fundamental revision of Josef Breuer's cathartic treatment of hysteria. Whereas, for Breuer, the patient can hardly be said to be the author of his own stories (they emerge only in a hypnotic state, prompted by the analyst's suggestion), Freud emphasizes the patient's freedom and authority to express anything, whether he thinks it relevant or not:

> [H]e [the analyst] admonishes them to relate everything that passes through their minds, even if they think it unimportant or irrelevant or nonsensical; he lays special stress on their not omitting any thought or idea from their story because to relate it might be embarrassing or painful to them. ("Freud's Psycho-Analytic Method" 267)

Although it must be emphasized that Freud privileges the analyst's story over the patient's (he claims that a patient cannot analyze himself), psychoanalysis nonetheless grants the patient the freedom to tell his own story. It is this freedom and the absolute candor that this freedom entails that appeals to Roth and can account for his use of psychoanalysis as the template for *Portnoy's Complaint*.

An investigation of Freud's presence in Roth's work naturally begins with *Portnoy's Complaint*. The novel takes the form of an extended comic monologue delivered, in therapy, by a psychoanalytic patient. Alexander Portnoy's "disorder," defined in a mock encyclopedia entry on the book's opening page, is a condition "in which strongly-felt ethical and altruistic impulses are perpetually warring with extreme sexual longings, often of a perverse nature" (*PC* 1). The reader is, from this point onward, in a Freudian world, populated by its language, theories, and therapeutic practice.

In the psychoanalytic process, in its inherent potential for storytelling, Roth sees a ready-made structure to be exploited for its literary possibilities. To take full advantage of these possibilities, especially for their comic effects, Roth creates Portnoy, who seems an exaggeratedly imagined ideal for Freud's therapeutic measures. Portnoy certainly seizes upon the opportunity for the patient to tell his story; his monologue goes on for close to 300 pages, detailing, in chronologically erratic anecdotes appropriate to the psychoanalytic process, his various problems. An unquenchable id warring with an authoritarian superego; a fixation on his mother compounded by an emasculated father; early sexual experience that seems the root of all of his behavior: Portnoy has it all. That these neuroses are evident to the reader is perhaps unexpected, for, until the novel's final line, the analyst remains silent. As Freud states, the analyst is necessary to unearth such buried tales of the patient's self; "the situation of analysis involves a superior and a subordinate" ("On the History" 337). Without any interaction between the subordinate patient and the superior analyst, how does Roth take advantage of the particular storytelling opportunities granted by psychoanalysis?

Roth fills this absence in two main ways. First, Portnoy is a patient with an obvious knowledge of Freud's writings and theories. As an explanation of his perpetual desire for sexual adventure, he remarks that "all the unconscious can do anyway, so Freud tells us, is *want. And* want! *And* WANT! Oh Freud, do I know!" (*PC* 103). Likewise, when ranting about the feelings of guilt he has inherited from his overbearing parents, he singles out the representative of parental authority in Freud's conception of the mind as "[t]hat tyrant, my superego" (*PC* 160). And, like any good student of Freud, when he realizes that most of his girlfriends have had small breasts, he asks, "is there an essay somewhere I can read on that?" (*PC* 216). Portnoy, though at times seemingly desperate for the psychoanalyst's help, essentially diagnoses himself. In addition, as David Brauner has argued, "Portnoy uses Freudian ideas as a means of anticipating and deconstructing possible interpretations of his own behavior" ("Getting in" 46). His knowledge of psychoanalysis is a protective weapon, allowing him both to sing of his suffering and to ridicule the way it fits into a psychoanalytic pattern, essentially preempting any interpretation from the analyst. Although Freud may have argued with Roth's conception of a man who can detect the processes that formulate his self, Freud's theories have permeated the culture to such an extent that the reader does not doubt Portnoy's analysis. Philip Rieff, writing in 1959, noted that Freud's "insistence that the unconscious has its own laws, and that no psychic product is without meaning, tends to make analysts of us all" (103). Roth, by giving Portnoy the analytical tools that Freud insisted could only be wielded by a trained analyst, is using Freud for his own purposes, but in a way that pays tribute to the pervasive cultural influence of Freud's theories. This influence allows Roth to fully exploit psychoanalysis as a site of stories of the self while skirting Freud's credo of the analyst as necessary for interpretation. Throughout his work, Roth gives his characters these Freud-derived interpretive tools to analyze themselves, to tell their own versions of the stories of their selves.[3]

The second way in which Roth succeeds in making Portnoy a recognizable psychoanalytic case without the benefit of the analyst's interpretation is made clear in an assertion Portnoy makes toward the end of the book. Remarking on yet another ridiculous turn of events in his exasperating life, he remarks: "Doctor, maybe other patients dream—with me, *everything happens.* I have a life *without* latent content" (*PC* 257). Indeed, part of the book's comedy stems from the way Roth makes manifest that which Freud proposes lies beneath the surface. Whereas Freud theorizes an implicit fear of castration that drives the individual from the Oedipal stage, Portnoy's mother actually threatens her young son with a knife when he doesn't want to eat his dinner (*PC* 16–17). A classic Freudian might suggest that a man, such as Portnoy, with an inability to settle down with one woman, has an incestuous fixation on his mother. But in Portnoy's case, the analyst is not necessary to make such a claim, not with Portnoy's mother greeting her son on the phone: "Well, how's my lover?" (*PC* 97). When Portnoy, after years and years of rebelling against his overbearing Jewish parents by pursuing gentile women, finally seduces a Jewish one, and in Israel no less, it seems only Freudian that he finds himself sexually impotent (*PC* 256–7). These examples give a sense of how Roth can allow Portnoy, the analysand, to so completely dominate his own therapeutic sessions. Roth's prerogative as a novelist allows him to create a character in which Freud's buried motives are plainly apparent. This also serves to create a satire of Freud, as "Portnoy implicitly criticizes the tendency of psychoanalysis to incorporate all events into a phallocentric narrative. Once Portnoy has preempted a Freudian reading of his psyche [. . .] such a reading loses its potency and immediately seems reductive and redundant" (Brauner, "Getting in" 46). With no latent content to uncover, what is left for the analyst to do?

If Portnoy analyzes himself, leaving the reader wondering what, if anything, the analyst will have to say about his case, at least his monologue appropriately takes place in psychotherapy. To take advantage of the idea that all of us, after Freud, are in some way psychoanalysts, Roth isolates this interpretive mindset from the therapeutic setting in one of the stories embedded within *My Life as a Man*. The novel has an idiosyncratic make-up, beginning with two "Useful Fictions," short stories written by Peter Tarnopol, followed by Tarnopol's attempted autobiography. The second story, "Courting Disaster (or, Serious in the Fifties)," recounts the unexpected troubles that greet Nathan Zuckerman, a budding writer and literature instructor, in his twenties.[4] Included in these troubles are the terrible migraine headaches that lead him to be granted medical discharge from the army. Unable to find any explanation from doctors, Zuckerman obsesses over finding the cause of the debilitating headaches, suspecting that they may be the unconscious product of his desire to leave the army. His neurologist mentions to him that he may want to enter himself into a study in psychosomatic medicine, as he seemed to have a "'Freudian Orientation' in the questions I asked him and in the manner in which I had gone about presenting the history of the disorder" (*MLM* 55).

Zuckerman himself doesn't see his approach as particularly Freudian, but rather a product of his literary mindset. He is analyzing himself like he would analyze one of the characters in the books he studies:

> Whereas an ordinary man might complain, "I get these damn headaches" (and have been content to leave it at that), I tended, like a student of high literature or a savage who paints his body blue, to see the migraines as *standing for something*, as a disclosure or "epiphany," isolated or accidental or inexplicable only to one who was blind to the design of a life or a book. What did my migraines *signify*? (*MLM* 55)

This suggestion, that there is a great similarity between a Freudian mindset and a literary one, has important implications for Zuckerman, for all of *My Life as a Man*, and for much of Roth's work. It is reinforced by Zuckerman's account of the change in his writing that accompanies his migraines. Whereas previously he had only written critical articles, he now begins working on what becomes his first published short story. "[I]n the hospital, where in six weeks' time I had written my second and third stories, I could not help wondering if for me illness was not a necessary catalyst to activate the imagination" (*MLM* 55). It is his headaches or, more accurately, his search for the meaning underlying his headaches, that initially sparks his creativity as a writer of fiction.[5] This realization, coming as it does in a story written by Tarnopol, prefigures the way in which psychoanalysis is set up as an alternative to writing in his "autobiographical" portion of *My Life as a Man.*

"My True Story," Peter Tarnopol's "nonfictional" text that follows his two "Useful Fictions" in *My Life as a Man*, begins with a short, italicized blurb, mimicking (and parodying) the concise authorial biographies found on book jackets. Written by Tarnopol, it briefly describes his early literary success, before detailing the seven years of personal tumult that followed, in which he struggled with a nightmarish marriage, an unsuccessful love affair, and an extended period of therapy at the hands of the psychoanalyst Dr. Otto Spielvogel. Still lost and confused, unable to overcome his problems by channeling them through his fiction, Tarnopol turns to autobiographical writing in an attempt to come to terms with the disastrous marriage that seemingly wrecked his secure sense of self. The blurb closes with this telling disclaimer: "*It remains to be seen whether his candor, such as it is, can serve any better than his art (or Dr. Spielvogel's therapeutic devices) to demystify the past and mitigate his admittedly uncommendable sense of defeat*" (*MLM* 100–1). This formulation, placing autobiographical writing, fiction writing, and psychoanalysis on the same level as tools to help better understand the self, further illuminates Roth's frequent use of Freud. Psychoanalysis, as a process that attempts to verbalize the stories of the self, seems a parallel structure to the writing life that Roth, beginning with *My Life as a Man*, takes as his main subject of investigation in his work over the next decade. Tarnopol's account of his time in therapy, and especially the event that eventually leads to his abandonment of his treatment, further reinforces this parallel.

The event in question is Dr. Spielvogel's publication of an article which includes a thinly veiled depiction of Tarnopol's case, an article that sends Tarnopol into a fury.[6] It is not so much that Spielvogel has betrayed Tarnopol's confidence by revealing so much of his case (although that certainly irks him as well), but that Spielvogel has gotten so much of his case wrong. It is not Tarnopol's sensibilities as a patient that are offended as much as his sensibilities as a writer. "I could not read a sentence in which it did not seem to me that the observation was off, the point missed, the nuance blurred" (*MLM* 243). The ensuing argument between writer and doctor points to one of the integral features of the novel, and highlights one of Roth's stated obsessions throughout his career: "the relationship between the written and the unwritten world" (*Reading Myself and Others* xiii). What they are arguing about, essentially, is the correct telling of the story of Tarnopol's self—the crux of the novel itself, in which fiction, autobiography, and psychoanalysis are placed in the balance to see which is best suited to represent the "unwritten world." As Mark Shechner has written, Tarnopol had given "Spielvogel his best lines and Spielvogel had botched them." After giving up on his analysis, he retreats to Quasay, a writer's colony, where he embarks upon the composition of his autobiography, which becomes the bulk of *My Life as a Man*. Shechner claims that Tarnopol "takes his lines back and takes charge of his own story, laboring to show how, with sensitivity, imagination, and a flair for *le mot juste*, it might properly be told" (*After the Revolution* 221–2).[7] Unfortunately (for Tarnopol), at the end of the novel, it is not at all clear that this project—properly telling his own story so that he can comprehend what has happened to him and move on—has succeeded. Rather, Roth leaves unresolved whether fiction, nonfiction, or psychoanalysis are adequate on their own to fully exorcise his demons.

The Heavy Self: *The Anatomy Lesson*

When, in *The Anatomy Lesson*, the more fully formed Nathan Zuckerman is confronted with chronic, unexplainable pain just as Tarnopol's Zuckerman is, he casts about for psychosomatic interpretations in much the same way. Far from igniting his creativity, however, this Zuckerman's search for the meaning that may or may not underlie his pain is accompanied by an inability to write, a drying up of his creative capacities. His exasperation with his condition leads to a disavowal of interpretation that, in its contrast to the younger Zuckerman's attitude, suggests that Roth's attitude toward Freudianism has significantly changed from 1974 to 1983:

> Everybody wants to make pain interesting—first the religions, then the poets, then, not to be left behind, even the doctors getting in on the act with their psychosomatic obsession. They want to give it *significance*. What does it mean? What are you hiding? What are you showing? What are you betraying? It's impossible just to suffer the pain, you have to suffer its meaning. But it's not interesting and it has no meaning—it's just plain stupid pain. (*AL* 439)

The connection of the younger Zuckerman's search for the meaning of his pain with the birth of his career as a writer suggests that the revelations of the self that Freudian interpretation provides have great value for the writer of fiction. What does it mean then, when the Zuckerman of *The Anatomy Lesson*, himself a writer who has built his career upon the fictionalization of his self, renounces such interpretation?

Zuckerman's chronic pain in *The Anatomy Lesson* does not occur within a vacuum. It is merely the final (he hopes) blow to his already reeling self-confidence as a man, and, more significantly, as a writer. The death of his parents, combined with a falling out with his brother, has cut him off from his identity as a son and a brother, aspects of his self central to his writing. Similarly, mining the fictional possibilities of his childhood in the Jewish Weequahic section of Newark, New Jersey, now seems irrelevant, with Newark almost completely transformed into an African-American city, the Jews nearly all gone. He feels as if the story of his self, which he has continually relied upon as a starting point for his fiction, has dried up:

> Zuckerman had lost his subject. His health, his hair, and his subject. Just as well he couldn't find a posture for writing. [. . .] Everything that galvanized him had been extinguished, leaving nothing unmistakably his and nobody else's to claim, exploit, enlarge and reconstruct. (*AL* 323)

This Zuckerman offers a stark contrast to Tarnopol's younger Zuckerman, so eager to delve into the unexplored regions of his self for imaginative inspiration. The latter is at the start of his career as a writer and believes that his self will provide him with ample material for his life's writing. The elder Zuckerman is in quite a different place. He feels he has no more self to explore, that self-interpretation does not lead anywhere, that, in fact, he has exhausted his self.[8] He desires to escape his self, prompting a decision to enter medical school and become a doctor. This decision, following from his suffering from this unexplained pain, seems an acknowledgment, by an older, more jaded Zuckerman, of the tyranny of the body, and the often paltry resources that the mind can muster to combat that tyranny. Debra Shostak, in her discussion of Roth's focus on embodiment, writes that Zuckerman's pain "gives the lie to the possibility of pure, unfleshed consciousness and therefore to the myth of a subject or self as divisible from the body as object" (42). The idea of the self as subject that can be isolated and profitably mined seems a necessary one for Zuckerman's sense of himself as a writer. "If you get out of yourself you can't be a writer because the personal ingredient is what gets you going, and if you hang on to the personal ingredient any longer you'll disappear right up your asshole" (*AL* 399). Zuckerman desires to leave behind the writing life because it necessitates a self-interpretation that he feels he can no longer practice.

The contrast between the two Zuckermans highlights an important aspect of Freud's work. That there are many benefits to Freud's psychoanalytic process of interpretation of the self cannot be denied. In uncovering those aspects of identity that the individual cannot know (or is unwilling, or unable, to acknowledge) on his own, the ultimate aim of psychoanalysis is a more complete self-knowledge. With this new knowledge, it is hoped, the patient can better manage his psychical resources. Ricoeur emphasizes the modesty of this aim, stating that "what Freud desires is that the one who is analyzed, by making his own the meaning that was foreign to him, enlarge his field of consciousness, live better, and finally be a little freer and, if possible, a little happier" (35). Likewise, for a young writer such as Tarnopol's Zuckerman, Freudian interpretation can open up the self, exposing its possibilities for fictional transformation. But a focus on these benefits of the interpretive process can obscure the ultimate resignation to reality that is at the center of Freud's great project.

The central function that the resolution of the Oedipal complex serves is that it dictates that the ego "no longer lets itself be governed by the pleasure principle, but obeys the *reality principle*" (Freud, *Complete* 357). Neuroses result when this process is incompletely resolved, when the individual fails to wholly submit to the unalterable limitations of reality. Similarly, Freud insisted throughout his life that although psychoanalysis can illuminate the self, it cannot fundamentally change it. The implicit product of Freud's demystification of "false consciousness" is the acknowledgment of underlying reality and of man's obligation to live with that reality. "Over against illusion and the fable-making function, demystifying hermeneutics [like Freud's] sets up the rude discipline of necessity" (Ricoeur 35). In other words, according to Freud, we must not delude ourselves into thinking that we are the authors of our selves or that we can ever escape our selves. All we can hope for is a better understanding of our selves, and a sober consciousness with which to interact with the world. As Philip Rieff argues, for Freud, "man is tied to the weight of his own past, and even by a great therapeutic labor little more can be accomplished than a shifting of the burden" (xi). Zuckerman comes to a realization that Freudian interpretation of the self, which has been so important to his creativity, cannot help him in his current situation, in which he feels he knows his self all too well and desires to escape it.

Roth concludes *The Anatomy Lesson* on a note of resignation. Zuckerman, having broken his jaw in a drug- and alcohol-fueled fall in a Jewish cemetery, now roams the halls of the hospital as a patient, following the doctors around, dreaming of becoming a doctor himself. His desire to escape his self and create a new one—to enter medical school and leave the writing life behind—is still alive at the end of the book, but Roth's final sentence indicates the ultimate hopelessness of this enterprise. Zuckerman wanders through the hospital, "as though he still believed that he could unchain himself from a future as a man apart and escape the corpus that was his" (*AL* 505). The dual connotation of "corpus"—suggesting both body and body of work—reinforces the fact that Zuckerman is as tied to his identity as a writer as he is tied to his own humanity, and as tied to his unreasoning body as well. But whereas, in "Courting Disaster," Roth suggests that Freudian self-interpretation could be a great boon to a writer's creativity (a suggestion confirmed by the many ways Roth has used Freud throughout this period), now, in *The Anatomy Lesson*, he suggests its limitations. Zuckerman cannot escape his identity as a writer, but, as a writer, he cannot write without some method of self-reflection. What Roth seems to be rejecting is not self-interpretation in itself—since without that, a writer cannot be a writer—but the Freudian framework for that interpretation. Zuckerman cannot escape his self, yet feels that he has exhausted it of its fictional possibilities. What is needed, therefore, is not the impossibility of a new self, but a new way of conceiving of the self, a way to grant the self new possibilities for fictional transformation.

In *The Prague Orgy*, the epilogue to *Zuckerman Bound* which continues Zuckerman's story after *The Anatomy Lesson*, similar themes of the desire to escape the self are present. Zuckerman sees, in the literary reclamation project that sends him to Prague, a chance to break away from "the narrative encasing me," only to realize, again, that "one's story isn't a skin to be shed—it's inescapable, one's own body and blood" (568). This vision of the self as a story is an interesting conception, one that hints at the new directions that Roth soon takes, but, keeping within an essentially Freudian worldview, it is the story that authors Zuckerman, rather than the other way around. It is not until *The Counterlife* (which follows *The Prague Orgy*) that Roth finds a way for Zuckerman to escape the strictures of the self as Freud conceives it: unified, unchangeable, forever tied to the events of the past.

The Counterlife

Zuckerman Bound follows Nathan Zuckerman's path, from his young idealism in *The Ghost Writer*, to his disillusioning brush with fame in *Zuckerman Unbound*, to his exhaustion with his self in *The Anatomy Lesson*, concluding with his ultimately fruitless search for a different story in Prague in *The Prague Orgy*. It is not surprising, then, that *The Counterlife* features characters attempting to radically change their lives, to change the essence of what was thought to be their selves. Both Nathan and his brother Henry decide to risk their lives for their sexual potency. Henry leaves his comfortable New Jersey existence to become a Zionist militant in the West Bank. Nathan, who has never been able to settle down with a woman for more than a few years, and depends upon America for the subject of his fiction, decides to marry Maria, have a child with her, and move to London. He explains that his desire to finally start a family is an extension of his general desire to escape his self:

> As a writer I'd mined my past to its limits, exhausted my private culture and personal memories [. . .] I wanted [. . .] to break away and take upon myself a responsibility unlike any bound up with writing or with the writer's tedious burden of being his own cause. (*C* 287–8)

This explanation sounds as if it could have been voiced by Zuckerman to justify his desire to become a doctor in *The Anatomy Lesson*. But whereas that book ends with the implicit resignation that Zuckerman cannot unchain himself from his identity as a writer, here Roth has Zuckerman follow through on his desire to escape his self, and explores the consequences thereof. Zuckerman will still have a self, of course, but he will no longer be professionally required to endlessly interpret it for his fiction. Instead, he looks to the twinned hope of a new love and a new family to draw his attention away from his self alone.

Similarly, Henry's new identity in the West Bank (or Judea) seems to represent the opposite of everything he was in New Jersey. Nathan travels to Israel to talk to Henry, prompted by brotherly concern, but also by a writerly curiosity in Henry's transformation. Most of his time in Israel is spent trying to understand just how his brother has so completely altered his life story. "I could not grasp this overnight change so against the grain of what I and everyone took to be the very essence of Henry's Henryness" (*C* 122–3). Henry, never before religious, has now taken the Hebrew name of Hanoch and refuses to talk with Nathan about anything not related to Israel and his new life. The Zionist fight seems infinitely more tied up with the sweep of history than his dentist's office and calls for a near total selflessness in the service of the cause. In response to Nathan's questions about the motives for his remarkable reinvention, Henry tellingly replies: "The hell with *me*, forget *me*. *Me* is somebody *I* have forgotten. *Me* no longer exists out here. There isn't time for *me*, there isn't need of *me*— here Judea counts, not *me*!" (*C* 109). Henry's emphatic statement seems to be a denial of his self, but it is more accurately a rejection of self-reflection, of time and energy spent trying to figure out what the self is. He is more interested in how his self can be useful for the Zionist cause than in the nature of his self.

The Counterlife's preoccupation with radical change, with characters in flight from the long-accepted versions of their selves, signals an important change in the way Roth conceives of his characters. Portnoy's fundamental predicament is that he desires to break free of the restrictions imposed upon him by his parents: "to be bad—and to enjoy it!" (*PC* 124). But he never quite succeeds at this project, hemmed in as he is by continual feelings of guilt. Similarly, Tarnopol cannot break free from his obsession over his disastrous marriage. Far from moving on, he cannot even decide upon an acceptable version of what has happened to him. And Zuckerman, in *The Anatomy Lesson*, can no longer stand to be chained to the writer's life of self-reflection, but cannot be anything else either. For each character there is a sort of reality principle: the essentially unchangeable facts of himself from which he feels he cannot escape. The action of these books consists of these characters pushing up against these facts, straining to defy them, but ultimately, necessarily, accepting them.

This acceptance is underlined in the last line of *The Anatomy Lesson*, indicating the fruitlessness of Zuckerman's desire to become a doctor. It is similarly highlighted in the final line of *My Life as a Man*, in which Tarnopol realizes the fact that he is "this me who is me being me and none other!" (*MLM* 330). This statement is rooted in a particularly pessimistic version of Freud's conception of the self, essentially unchangeable and determined by the past. Each character in *The Counterlife*, by contrast, could very well exclaim that he is "this me who is being me *and another*!" signaling that Roth has exchanged Freud's model of the self for something more fluid, more easily changed. One psychotherapeutic approach that may shed some light on what Roth has adopted is referred to as narrative therapy.

Narrative Therapy and the Self as Narrative

Narrative therapy is a psychotherapeutic approach that, although dependent on the work of many earlier theorists and therapists, was first outlined in its entirety in Michael White and David Epston's 1990 book *Narrative Means to Therapeutic Ends*. White and Epston recognize that, in psychoanalysis and, in fact, all methods of psychotherapy, what is being interpreted is not actually the self, but the necessary representation of the self in language. Thus, "in order to make sense of our lives and to express ourselves, experience must be 'storied' and it is this storying that determines the meaning ascribed to experience." Whereas, for Freud, the stories of the self told in therapy are a necessary means to uncover the "true" self that underlies them, for White and Epston, unconvinced of any objective knowledge of the self beyond its representation in language, the stories *are* the self:

> If we accept that persons organize and give meaning to their experience through the storying of experience, and that in the performance of these stories they express selected aspects of their lived experience, then it follows that these stories are constitutive—shaping lives and relationships. [. . .] Thus, the text analogy is distinct from those analogies that would propose an underlying structure or pathology in families and persons that is constitutive or shaping of their lives and relationships. (9–10, 12)

Freud conceives of the self as an undeniable entity, shrouded in the shadows of the patient's often illogically coded stories, that, even when uncovered by a trained analyst, cannot be fundamentally altered. White and Epston, by contrast, posit a much more apparent, fluid self, made up of the stories the patient tells about herself. It follows, then, that narrative therapy is much more optimistic in its efforts to effect change in the patient. By working with the patient, the narrative therapist attempts to restory her experience, shaping the story of her self into one better suited to her current situation. "The core of the therapeutic technique they [White and Epston] describe consists of composing written interventions that tell different stories about their clients' lives and their future course" (Crossley 60). *The Counterlife* can be read as a series of such "written interventions" about the lives and future course of Nathan and Henry Zuckerman. It is almost a natural progression for Roth, who has made so much use of the opportunities for self-storytelling within the Freudian model, to be drawn to a conception of the self similar to that put forth by narrative therapy, which privileges such storytelling above all other explanations of the self.

Narrative Means to Therapeutic Ends was published in 1990, three years after *The Counterlife*, making it difficult to claim that Roth was familiar with the practices of narrative therapy while writing his novel. It is certainly possible, however, that Roth was familiar with many of the theorists that White and Epston cite as forerunners to the ideas that fuel narrative therapy, such as Michel Foucault, Jacques Derrida, and the anthropologist Edward Bruner.[9] Regardless of Roth's familiarity with its methods, in delineating a practical therapeutic approach that uses a model of the self as narrative, the theories of narrative therapy can provide a contrast to psychoanalysis, which so permeated Roth's previous work.

Keeping the ideas of narrative therapy in mind, it is notable how often the self is conceived of as a text or a narrative in *The Counterlife*. At Henry's funeral in "Basel," Henry's wife Carol delivers a eulogy in which she states that "Henry died to recover the fullness and richness of married love" (*C* 30). Nathan, who knows that Henry's surgery was prompted by his desire to continue his extramarital affair with his assistant, wonders if Carol believes what she is saying, or whether she is "a subtle and persuasive writer of domestic fiction, who had cunningly reimagined a decent, ordinary, adulterous humanist as a heroic martyr to the connubial bed" (*C* 52). Comparing Henry's flight to Israel with his earlier love affair for which he nearly left his wife, Nathan is forced to admit: "Certainly the rebellious script he had tried following ten years back could hardly touch this one for originality" (*C* 85). And Maria, questioning Nathan's intentions to marry her and start a family in England, tells him,

> You *do* want to make a narrative out of it, with progress and momentum and dramatic peaks and then a resolution. You seem to see life as having a beginning, a middle, and an ending, all of them linked together with something bearing your name. (*C* 195)

Domestic fiction, a script, a narrative: each character's actions are depicted in textual terms, pointing to their willful origins. Throughout the novel, the self is conceived of as a narrative, and each character becomes the author of his or her own story. In his previous work, Roth had often depended upon Freudian language and theories for the formulation of his characters' selves. But in *The Counterlife*, along with a newfound freedom to change one's self, Roth has granted his characters a new way of thinking about the self. As narrative therapy claims, these two concepts go hand in hand; a conception of the self as narrative lends itself more easily to practical change—changing the self becomes as easy as revising a story. As Maria seems to imply, seeing the self as a narrative is an all too appropriate concept for a writer like Zuckerman, or like Roth. Ignoring Freud's vision of man tied to the weight of his past, the characters in *The Counterlife* all act like novelists, writing the stories of their selves as they choose to.

The five chapters of *The Counterlife*, a series of often contradictory variations, constitute Roth's exploration of the consequences of the various narratives that these characters might choose to enact. Thus, in "Basel," Henry attributes the cause of his heart disease to the stress caused by his failure to pursue what he desired ten years earlier: to leave his wife and move to Switzerland with his mistress, Maria. "*It was the consequence of failing to find the ruthlessness to take what he wanted instead of capitulating to what he should do*" (*C* 15). In "Judea," by contrast, his account of his disease is just the opposite—it was brought on by his adulterous desire itself, "the original Jewish dream of escape [. . .] Switzerland with the beloved shiksa" (*C* 115).

Although the fact of Henry's heart disease is undeniable in each case—the body is reality for Roth—its meaning is determined by the particular story that Henry chooses to tell about himself.[10] Rather than utilizing a Freudian mindset, in which events have a definite significance that the analyst can reveal, here the meaning of past events can change as the individual's story of his self changes. In "Basel," distraught because his impotence condemns him to a life without adultery, Henry construes his heart disease as a product of his submission to the responsibilities of a good husband and father. In "Judea," however, with Henry eager to see himself as a devout Jew fighting for the noble cause of his religion, the disease becomes a product of the infidelities themselves, his failure to submit to his responsibilities as a good Jew.

Although Roth explores many alternative stories of the self in *My Life as a Man*, Tarnopol, in that book, is confined to relative inaction due to Roth's conception of his self along Freudian lines and Tarnopol's reliance on psychoanalysis for one of those stories. In *The Counterlife*, having abandoned Freud and adopted a more fluid, narrative form, Roth pursues these various stories with all of their ramifications for the self. This is similar to the process pursued by narrative therapists. They start with the assumption that "one's past events cannot be changed. [. . .] However, the interpretation and significance of those events can change if a different plot is used to configure them" (Polkinghorne 182). Working with the patient, they hope to tell a new story, in line with how the patient would like to see himself, that necessarily alters the meaning of some past events. Thus, the meaning of Henry's heart disease changes completely as he creates, as Nathan observes, "the sense of himself he would now prefer to effect" (*C* 117).

Narrative Freud

In *Reading for the Plot*, his landmark study of the narrative workings of fiction, Peter Brooks evokes Freud as a model that can illuminate the way plots proceed and function. He explains:

> If we turn toward Freud, it is not in the attempt to psychoanalyze authors or readers or characters in narrative, but rather to suggest that by attempting to superimpose psychic functioning on textual functioning, we may discover something about how textual dynamics work and something about their psychic equivalences. (90)

Like Brooks, my intention in this chapter has been to psychoanalyze neither Roth, nor his readers or characters. Rather, I am more interested in how Roth makes use of Freud, how concepts of psychoanalysis have seeped into his work, coloring how he creates his characters and how those characters make sense of their lives. I see this reliance on psychoanalytic thinking waning in *The Counterlife*, but it would be a mistake to suggest that Roth's new conception of his characters' selves is a complete abandonment or refutation of psychoanalytic thought. Rather, it might be better to think of it as an extension of, or supplement to, this long period of immersion in Freud's theories of the self and its analysis. Whereas the radical mutability of the self implied by the chaotic narratives of *The Counterlife* seemingly contradicts Freud's ultimate resignation to his vision of man tied to the weight of his past, it is possible to see the seeds of narrative therapy—the transformative possibilities of narrative and interpretation—within Freud's writing.

One strand of what we might call the interpretive possibilities of Freud's psychoanalysis can be elucidated through reference to his famous case history of the "Wolf Man." Freud traced the origins of the Wolf Man's neuroses to a childhood dream, in which the patient saw six or seven white wolves perched in a tree outside of his window, staring at him. He awoke terrified from the dream, and quickly developed a fear of animals that lasted for years. Freud theorized that this dream, and the resulting phobia, was the result of the patient seeing his parents having sex when he was a year and a half old—an event that the patient did not remember. From all of the various recollections, associations, and symptoms the Wolf Man exhibited to Freud, this early event was posited as the primal scene, the initiating and motivating incident that set the patient's entire narrative in motion. Freud stakes the entire analysis on the truth value of this particular construction; after reviewing the case, he states: "either the analysis based on the neurosis in his childhood is all a piece of nonsense from start to finish, or everything took place just as I have described it above" ("From the History" 56).

The Wolf Man's first course of treatment, which is the subject of the case history "From the History of an Infantile Neurosis," concluded in July 1914. Freud finished the piece in November of that year, but did not publish it until 1918. The published piece remains unchanged from its 1914 version, except for two long passages that Freud has inserted, in brackets in order for the reader to see what has been added. In what Brooks calls "one of the most daring moments of Freud's thought, and one of his most heroic gestures as a writer," Freud allows for the possibility that the patient did not witness his parents having sex after all; perhaps he merely saw two animals copulating and subsequently constructed a fantasy about his parents (Brooks 277). As many commentators have noted, this is a significant moment in the evolution of Freud's thought. It suggests that the actual occurrence of events constructed within the analysis need not have taken place to retain their explanatory and persuasive power. Keeping in mind the absolute necessity that Freud assigns to the primal scene in the original draft, it is astonishing to read in the second bracketed passage,

I should myself be glad to know whether the primal scene in my present patient's case was a phantasy or a real experience; but, taking other similar cases into account, I must admit that the answer to this question is not in fact a matter of very great importance. ("From the History" 97)

The implication of this addition is that narratives can retrospectively create meanings for past events (or nonevents), rather than merely following from significant events in a fixed and causative sequence. The past no longer necessarily determines succeeding events; sometimes the meaning of past events can be determined by the present—of course, this is essentially the guiding principle of narrative therapy.

But this apparently substantial change in Freud's thinking did not compel him to go back and revise his conclusions about the Wolf Man's early experience in the piece. Rather, Freud leaves everything in and supplements his original case history with the bracketed material—leaving both his certainty and his doubts in the finished product. D. P. Polkinghorne argues that that the apparent contradiction left for the reader is indicative of a new complexity in Freud's thought. "He maintained that the two logics—one which insists on the causal efficacy of origins and the other which treats events as the products of meanings—must exist side by side" (121). Brooks, ever on the lookout for implications within Freud's thought for the ways in which narratives work, sees in the Wolf Man case history similarities to the open-ended narratives found within modernist and post-modernist fictions:

A narrative account that allows the inception of its story to be either event or fiction [. . .] perilously destabilizes belief in explanatory histories as exhaustive accounts whose authority derives from the force of closure, from the capacity to say: here is where it began, here is what it became. (277)

This sounds very much like the "narrative account" offered within *The Counterlife*— the reader is never sure which set of events "actually happened," and Roth continually refuses the satisfaction that comes from the neat solutions and definite conclusions of traditional realist narratives. In an interview just before the book's publication, Roth posed questions from an imagined reader to himself to illustrate the strategies at work here: "Which is real and which is false? All are equally real or equally false. Which are you asking me to believe in? All/none" ("Interview with Philip Roth" 11). Whatever his motivations for doing so, Freud's inclusion of the bracketed material creates a narrative in which the relationship between origins and subsequent events are called into question, undermining the assumption that there is always a definite motive or starting point to be uncovered. A belief in such uncertainty would eventually become one of the central tenets of narrative therapy.

The American psychoanalyst Donald Spence, in his *Narrative Truth and Historical Truth*, offers up a critique of Freud that nonetheless argues that the "narrative tradition" has always been a part of psychoanalysis. Spence distinguishes between narrative truth, "the persuasive power of a coherent narrative," and historical truth, a set of events that actually happened (21). He argues that Freud's insistence, until the end of his life, that the analyst is a sort of archaeologist, uncovering buried pieces of the patient's past, was very often a necessary bulwark against the charges of charlatanism that plagued psycho-analysis in its early years. "To function in this tradition was, as we shall see, not only to function as a dispassionate scientist; it also provided the best protection against the charge of suggestion and the best defense against the doubts of the incredulous nonbelievers" (32). But Freud's desire to portray psychoanalysis as a scientific pursuit led him to confuse and conflate narrative truth with histori-cal truth, overlooking the ways in which the particular context of interpretation within analysis necessarily dictates the ways in which the patient's history is constructed, and overlooking the fact that a successful interpretation may have more to do with its persuasiveness as a good story with explanatory power than with its status as historical truth. "Interpretations are persuasive, as we shall see, not because of their evidential value but because of their rhetorical appeal; conviction emerges because the fit is good, not because we have necessarily made contact with the past" (32). Spence's argument is that psychoanalysts have always been engaged in the construction of narrative truth, going all the way back to Freud. What is important is that analysts understand the difference between narrative truth and historical truth, and keep in mind the necessary work that is done in putting a patient's experiences, dreams, and memories into language—work that is always colored by the particular desires and motiva-tions of both the analyst and the patient, and by the particular context of the "analytic space." It is no surprise that Spence's book is one of a very few psycho-analytic texts to be referenced in some of the seminal works of narrative ther-apy; he seems to provide a valuable link between the two practices.[11]

The Freudian Lock

Serge Viderman, the French psychoanalyst, expresses similar views in his skepti-cism of the definite, historical truth that can be interpolated from any one interpretation. After considering an interpretation in a case study by Melanie Klein, Viderman responds:

> [T]his is a perfectly likely interpretation but [. . .] it conforms to a model that is only one among other possible interpretations, a model chosen according to the Kleinian system of interpretation for tactical reasons; and it cannot lay claim to any other truth than the one created for it in the analytic space by the speech which formulates it. (263)

It is the confidence in the rightness of an interpretation that can never be proven, a confidence assumed to be inherent in psychoanalysis, that sets

Henry off on a scathing denunciation of his brother Nathan's psychoanalytic worldview in the second chapter of *The Counterlife*. Nathan has come to Israel to try to understand why Henry has given up his respectable, conventional life in New Jersey for the life of a pious warrior in the West Bank; Henry seems to resent any assumption of, or search for, his motives:

> [L]et me tell you something—you can't explain away what I've done by motives any more than I can explain away what you've done. Beyond all your profundities, beyond the Freudian lock you put on every single person's life, there is another world, a larger world, a world of ideology, of politics, of history—a world of things larger than the kitchen table! [. . .] There's a world outside the Oedipal swamp, Nathan, where what matters isn't what made you do it *but what it is you do*. (*C* 144)

It is the idea of a "Freudian lock" that Henry protests most—that Freudian interpretation's assumption of historical truth is reductive, and restrictive of the ways in which people shape their lives. He is drawn to "another world," in which motives cannot always be pinned down, or explained in a logical, consequential way. Any interpretation that Nathan may offer up is only one interpretation and can never fully exist as an objective explanation of why Henry has done what he has done. In having Henry deliver this critique of a psychoanalytic, archaeological view to his novelist brother, Roth is doing more than merely "giv[ing] the other guy the best lines," as he has said he is wont to do ("Interview with *The London Sunday Times*" 113). It is perhaps a message to himself, informing Roth the writer that there are, and always have been, many ways of telling a story, of creating character, plot, possibility, and consequence. The Roth who had always given his characters firm and fixed (if sometimes unknown) motivations becomes a Roth who would continually emphasize the essentially mysterious and unknowable nature of human behavior.

I'd argue that it is this "Freudian lock," the rigidity of the Freudian explanation of the self, that can account for Roth's apparent break with psychoanalysis in *The Counterlife*. Jeffrey Berman, writing about the psychoanalysts in Roth's fiction, has noted that Roth does not understand psychoanalysis "as a narrative strategy similar to fiction making, with both the analyst and the fiction writer creating as opposed to discovering truth." Roth's version of psychoanalysis is "frozen in time, imprisoned by a rigid Freudian ideology that most analysts have long ago abandoned or sharply revised." Unable to say whether "psychoanalysis failed Roth or whether he failed psychoanalysis," Berman nonetheless identifies an important aspect of Roth's Freudian thinking (106). Unlike Brooks, Spence, and Viderman, Roth does not envision psychoanalysis as a body of knowledge that can create truths about the self. Rather, Freud becomes something of a straw man for Roth to fight against, a rigid structure constricting his characters, as they attempt to conceive of the self as something freer. In the end, this became too much of a straightjacket for Roth's enduring need to make of his career a "self-conscious and deliberate zig-zag." A new sense of the self was needed. As he has Zuckerman say in *The Counterlife,*

> The burden isn't either/or, consciously choosing from possibilities equally difficult and regrettable—it's and/and/and/and/and as well. Life *is* and: the accidental and the immutable, the elusive and the graspable, the bizarre and the predictable, the actual and the potential. (*C* 310)

* * *

I do not want to suggest that *The Counterlife* shows Roth's characters escaping the inflexibility of the Freudian self for some sort of ultimate freedom from the determining forces of their own pasts, their bodies, history, or ethnicity. Despite the characters' seeming freedom to write new stories for themselves, none of the new directions can be said to end well. In particular, the conclusion of the novel's final chapter, "Christendom," in which Zuckerman sets off for a new life in England with his new wife, Maria, pregnant with his child, points to a caveat to *The Counterlife*'s abandonment of a rigid Freudian model. It is the specter of anti-Semitism, in the guise of Maria's unhinged sister, her prejudiced mother, and a rude woman in a restaurant, that fuels a vicious quarrel that threatens to undo their happy future together. Less shocked by the continued existence of anti-Semitism in England than by his own sensitivity to the issue, Zuckerman sees the eruption of marital strife as the intrusion of history and ethnic identity into their idyll. Even though he is "[a] Jew without Jews, without Judaism, without Zionism, without Jewishness," Zuckerman is a Jew nonetheless, and there is no escaping the historical inheritance, however figured, that marks him from birth (*C* 328). In an imagined letter to Maria, Zuckerman makes the case for the circumcision of their impending child, arguing that the act is the ultimate reminder that the dream of life as an idyll—the pastoral—is a dangerous and unattainable goal:

> Circumcision makes it clear as can be that you are here and not there, that you are out and not in—also that you're mine and not theirs. There is no way around it: you enter history through my history and me. Circumcision is everything that the pastoral is not and, to my mind, reinforces what the world is about, which isn't strifeless unity. Quite convincingly, circumcision gives the lie to the womb-dream of life in the beautiful state of innocent prehistory, the appealing idyll of living "naturally," unencumbered by man-made ritual. (*C* 327)

The dream that Zuckerman and Maria pursued, an idyllic ascent into the untroubled happiness of true love, is deflated here, refigured as an unattainable delusion of "strifeless unity." "We couldn't just be 'us' and say the hell with 'them' any more than we could say to hell with the twentieth century when it intruded upon our idyll" (*C* 312). Zuckerman's critique of the pastoral, a fiercely argued reminder of all that we cannot control, offers a balancing restriction to the psychological freedom Roth grants his characters in the novel. Explaining the lack of a single, unified reality in *The Counterlife*, Roth stated that the book's unusual form is intended to emphasize the ways in which people construct their selves, and their reality, out of narrative. He claims: "We are writing fictitious versions of our lives all the time, contradictory but mutually entangling stories that, however subtly or grossly falsified, constitute our hold on reality and are the closest thing we have to the truth" ("Interview with Philip Roth" 10–11). But these "fictitious versions" do not take place within a vacuum, and Zuckerman's realization at the end of *The Counterlife* is that the reality of the world continually works to restrict and impede the stories we might tell. As many critics have noted, this stance colors much of Roth's work after *The Counterlife*, as Roth "examines the seduction, delusion, and power of antitragic 'utopian thinking'" (Posnock 103).[12] Indeed, Roth's "American Trilogy" in many ways investigates the tragedies of men whose failures are tied to pastoral dreams of innocence and individuality, as they try in vain to set their own course amid the turmoil of American history. In some ways, the four books that immediately followed *The Counterlife*, books that I take up in the next chapter, each can be seen to work to undermine a sort of pastoral version of autobiography, one that proposes that one can write truthfully about the self without writing about, and thus exposing, other people.

The Counterlife explores a series of imaginative possibilities for Roth's characters, and, considering his work thereafter, seemingly opened up a range of possibilities for Roth as a writer. The increasingly adventurous narrative strategies of *The Facts*, *Deception*, and *Operation Shylock*, calling into question any accurate representation of reality as well as anything like an authentic self, are testaments to *The Counterlife* as a watershed in Roth's career. And Nathan Zuckerman's reappearance in *American Pastoral*, *I Married a Communist*, and *The Human Stain*, this time a storyteller on the sidelines of the action, signals that Roth has moved beyond the problem of Zuckerman's exhaustion with his self with great success. These books almost seem to be the product of a different writer than the Roth so conspicuously aligned with the Freudian view of the self. It is certainly tempting, from this vantage point, to commit the sin of confusing Roth with Zuckerman, and to imagine a writer, exhausted with his tried and true fictional methods, who granted himself a counterlife as a novelist who keenly appreciates his life and his self as a series of fictional possibilities.

Chapter 5

Nonfiction Writings

I am a thief and a thief is not to be trusted.

Philip, Deception

In 1989, thirty years into a career that had already been characterized by its willfulness, its urge to subvert expectations, and the range of its preoccupations, Philip Roth published what must have seemed a truly strange book: an autobiography. Titled *The Facts: A Novelist's Autobiography,* this was a memoir of Roth's life up to the publication of *Portnoy's Complaint* in 1969. It's a rather prosaic and straightforward look back on the author's coming of age in America: his upbringing, his college days, his disastrous first marriage. It would have seemed quite a conventional, almost boring, book from such a notoriously adventurous writer, had it not been for its prologue and epilogue. The book is prefaced by a brief letter from Roth to his most recent fictional protagonist, Nathan Zuckerman, asking him to read the ensuing memoir and let him know what he thinks of it. Naturally, the book's epilogue is Zuckerman's response to Roth, a 35-page excoriation of the book we've just read, urging Roth not to publish it: "you are far better off writing about me than 'accurately' reporting your own life" (*F* 161). These bracketing letters throw a wrench into the seemingly clear logic of Roth's apparent autobiographical move. It's as if, even when he's abandoning fiction, it refuses to abandon him. The presence of the letters, especially Zuckerman's concluding riposte, serves to make autobiography itself a subject of inquiry, as Roth's alter ego calls into question the genre's veracity, literary merit, and usefulness. The subject would preoccupy Roth for some time, as *The Facts* was the first of four books, published consecutively, each of which contained, at least in part, nonfictional accounts of the author's life. *Deception* (1990) is subtitled "A Novel," but it is in the form of the notebooks of an author named Philip, one who, in all personal details, resembles Philip Roth. *Patrimony* (1991) is a memoir of Roth's father's final two years, as he suffered through the illnesses which would take his life. And *Operation Shylock* (1993) is subtitled "A Confession," with Roth telling the "true," though outlandish and generally regarded as fictional, story of an impostor calling himself "Philip Roth," wreaking havoc in Israel with Roth's identity.

Although *The Facts* marks the first extended work of autobiography in Roth's oeuvre, he has, of course, played with known biographical facts about himself in many of his novels. Roth has thrived for decades upon playing with the temptation of readers to read his protagonists as thinly veiled autobiographical portraits of himself. John Updike's characterization of Roth's Zuckerman books as a project that "looks like a *roman-à-clef* but is not," hits upon what is certainly one of the most intriguing aspects of those books, and of much of Roth's written output (Roth, "Interview with Philip Roth" 2). Neil Klugman, Alex Portnoy, David Kepesh, Peter Tarnopol, and Zuckerman all share a certain amount of biographical detail with their creator, and, since Roth became an established literary figure, with more and more known about his own biography, he has, as Joe Moran has claimed, "created a kind of 'hall of mirrors' effect which has only added to the public confusion about the relationship between the author and his characters" (104). For many critics, these four "autobiographical" books continue and extend Roth's interest in this "hall of mirrors" effect: probing the permeability of the borders between fact and fiction, exploring the ways in which nonfiction may be just as unreliable a representation of reality as fiction, and playing games with readers' expectations of divulgence. And while I do agree with Debra Shostak's assertion that these books continue Roth's project of making "capital out of his readers' inclinations toward biographical interpretations of his work," this is not the area on which I will focus here (158–9).[1] There have been sufficient inquiries into Roth's puncturing of the myth of nonfictional transparency (not least by Roth himself), and there is no need for yet another look at the ways in which Roth plays with "the facts," or generic distinctions, or his readers' beliefs about him.

In addition to this common academic reading, the popular press unsurprisingly cast these four books as the continuation—perhaps the culmination—of a popular critical narrative: Roth is always writing about himself. Justin Kaplan wrote that Zuckerman's critical skewering of Roth in *The Facts* "suggests that for Roth his life and his work, his 'facts' and his 'fiction,' are virtually identical," and hoped that the book would be "a final turn of the screw to his proprietary materials, the Philip Roth megillah." In a review of *Deception*, Christopher Lehmann-Haupt mused that Roth's readers "must surely be growing impatient for the author to stop analyzing his imagination and start exercising it, if he hasn't dissected it beyond repair by now." The reviews of *Operation Shylock* mostly stuck to the same script, seeing the book caught in "the centrifugal force of its narrator's self-absorption." Hillel Halkin summed up what seemed a common sentiment, writing that "some men are naturally monogamous, and Roth is naturally monographous; the only subject that has ever genuinely interested him as an author is the self that he is trapped in" (54). It is worth questioning the simplified reading that equates autobiographical reference with solipsism. In an early draft of *Operation Shylock* (then called *Duality*) from 1990, found in Roth's archive in the Library of Congress, there is evidence that Roth played with the idea of publishing these four books in one volume; there is a title page for just such a potential collection:

TWO-FACED
An Autobiography in Four Acts
   1. *The Facts*, a Novelist's Autobiography
   2. *Deception*, a Novel
   3. *Patrimony*, a True Story
   4. *Duality*, a Novelist's Fantasy ("*Operation Shylock*; Drafts" 1)

Two-Faced would be a wholly appropriate title for the series, if it indeed were a series, for it suggests Roth's simultaneous inward and outward gaze, of which these four books provide a particularly good example. While Roth is ostensibly writing about himself, this chapter will argue, he finds himself inevitably writing about other people, and the consequent ethical dilemmas lend these books a significant shared concern. This concern has, for the most part, been over-looked in recent works of Roth scholarship. *Two-Faced* also suggests deception and betrayal, the attendant accusations always tempted by writing nonfictional depictions of other people. I find in Roth's investigation into autobiography in *The Facts*, *Deception*, *Patrimony*, and *Operation Shylock* not a solipsistic exercise of self-absorption, but instead evidence of a renewed concern with the responsi-bilities of writing about others and with the differing, and often conflicting, claims that aesthetics and ethics can exert upon the writer.

Patrimony and the "Unseemliness" of Writing

I begin with *Patrimony*, Roth's memoir of his dying father's final year, because, in contrast to the other three books discussed here, its status—whether it is nonfiction, or fiction, or some admixture—is never in question. There are no games being played here, no teasing hints that the author should not be trusted, no web of textual reference to penetrate: it is, very simply, a faithful account of a father's illness and death by a loving and loyal son. That Roth should leave aside, for the moment, the self-conscious courting of generic con-fusion seems appropriate given the subject matter. As Mark Shechner points out, "Dissolving reality and speaking only through masks is fine, when the sub-ject is yourself, [. . .] but your father is *your father*, and postmodernism and magic realism simply won't do" (*Up Society's Ass* 127). *Patrimony* stands apart from the other "autobiographical" books in its seemingly unquestioned belief in the transparency of nonfiction writing; nowhere does Roth raise doubts as to whether his version of the events narrated here is trustworthy. Clearly, the shock and significance of a father's death trumps all such writerly games (for one book, at least).

In addition, *Patrimony* differs from the other books of the period in that its central subject is someone other than Philip Roth. The book's first words are "My father," and its focus is trained upon Herman Roth throughout:

> My father had lost most of the sight in his right eye by the time he'd reached eighty-six, but otherwise he seemed in phenomenal health for a man his age when he came down with what the Florida doctor diagnosed, incorrectly, as Bell's palsy, a viral infection that causes paralysis, usually temporary, to one side of the face. (*P* 9)

It turns out that the facial paralysis has been caused by a "massive tumor" in Herman's brain, and the book details the nearly two years between this diagnosis and his death, in October 1989. Philip is with his father through most of the hellish ordeal; the book is both an account of those two years and an appraisal of his father's whole life. It is a loving, clear-eyed portrait of a man as stubborn and uncompromising as he was devoted and generous. Roth writes, with equal parts admiration and criticism, "He could never understand that a capacity for renunciation and iron self-discipline like his own was extraordinary and not an endowment shared by all" (*P* 79). But as well as paying tribute to the father, the book is also, inevitably, a picture of the son. In her study of memoirs of the deaths of parents, *Bequest and Betrayal*, Nancy K. Miller notes that: "Producing an account of another's life normally belongs to the domain of biography [. . .] But when the biographical subject is a member of one's own family, the line between genres blurs" (2). *Patrimony* is not a biography of Herman Roth, but then again, it is not just another installment in Philip Roth's autobiography either. It tells readers something about both of them, often at the same time. Naturally, a son's portrait of his father will tend to highlight those aspects of the father that have influenced and formed the son's character; this book is no different. Throughout his life, Herman Roth drew from a seemingly inexhaustible well of stories about Newark's past, telling anyone who would listen the tales of the community that used to thrive there. Philip is undoubtedly appreciative of this urge to narrate, telling a friend, "*He's* the bard of Newark. That really rich Newark stuff isn't my story—it's his" (*P* 125). And yet Philip—not Herman—is the Roth whose name is on *Patrimony*'s cover, reminding us that, as Paul John Eakin has pointed out, "the signature on the title page [. . .] reflects the necessarily unequal distribution of power in situations of this kind" (176).[2]

Eakin, in his work on life writing, has discussed a "relational concept of selfhood," in which the self cannot be conceived as completely autonomous, self-determining, or free from encroachment on, and by, others' selves. If we accept that our lives are inevitably tied up with those of others, writing truthfully about oneself will always require writing truthfully about others. "Because our own lives never stand free of the lives of others, we are faced with our responsibility to those others whenever we write about ourselves. There is no escaping this responsibility" (Eakin 161, 159). Writing nonfiction, especially autobiographical writing, therefore inevitably invites ethical considerations that do not apply to fiction. When an author purports to tell the truth, and that true story involves people other than himself, he takes it upon himself to expose others in ways of his choosing. This exposure can, of course, be benign, and no one would deny a writer's right to tell a story from his perspective. This right, however, must be weighed against the rights of those exposed, who have no control over the way that they are portrayed. As Richard Freadman has remarked, "Writers have a right to write. But how far into the privacy of others does that right extend?" (123). These considerations figure in all four of the books discussed in this chapter, but *Patrimony*, perhaps because Philip's and his father's selves are so clearly interconnected, provides a particularly provocative illustration of the ethical issues which must be faced when writing nonfiction.

Both Eakin and Miller have written about *Patrimony* in their discussions of the ethics of life writing; for each of them, one scene in particular stands out (Eakin 182–6; Miller 24–9). After a stint in the hospital for a biopsy on his tumor that has left him weakened and constipated, Herman excuses himself from a lunch with Philip, Claire Bloom, and Philip's nephew and niece to try to move his bowels again. After some time passes with Herman still upstairs, Philip goes up to check on his father. Detecting the "overwhelming" smell halfway up the stairs, Philip finds his father naked, stepping out of the shower, and near tears. "In a voice as forlorn as any I had ever heard, from him or from anyone, he told me what it hadn't been difficult to surmise. 'I beshat myself' ":

> The shit was everywhere, smeared underfoot on the bathmat, running over the toilet bowl edge and, at the foot of the bowl, in a pile on the floor. It was splattered across the glass of the shower stall from which he'd just emerged, and the clothes discarded in the hallway were clotted with it. (*P* 171–2)

After helping his father back into the shower, bagging up the soiled clothes, and drying him off with a clean towel, Philip gets him into bed.

> "Don't tell the children," he said, looking up at me from the bed with his one sighted eye.
> "I won't tell anyone," I said. "I'll say you're taking a rest."
> "Don't tell Claire."
> "Nobody," I said. (*P* 173)

The scene is important for Eakin and Miller because "it poses so starkly the ethical dilemmas of life writing" (Eakin 185). Herman is mortified by his "accident," and is absolutely clear in telling his son that this is an event he wishes no one to ever know about. And yet, even as he portrays his father's shame, as well as his own promise not to tell, Roth includes it in his book, making of it, in fact, a central scene. Roth's disobedience of his father's wishes is blatant—as Adam Phillips points out, "it is the novelist-son, not the father, who demands, by promising, the larger reticence"—as he exposes his father's most private embarrassment to an audience that numbers in the thousands ("Philip Roth's Patrimony" 167). On what grounds can this exposure—this betrayal—be justified?

Roth, for his part, seems to justify the scene's inclusion by making it central to the book's narrative. The idea of patrimony, what a child inherits from a father, as the title suggests, looms large in the book. As it becomes clearer that the tumor in his father's brain will soon kill him, Philip considers what his patrimony ultimately is. Some years earlier, Philip had told his father to cut him out of his will, reasoning that he had enough money and that the inheritance could really help his brother Sandy's children if it were to be divided among a smaller number of beneficiaries. As his father nears death, however, Philip realizes that he regrets his earlier decision: "I wanted it because it was, if not an authentic chunk of his hard-working hide, something like the embodiment of all that he had overcome or outlasted" (*P* 104–5). Unable to swallow his pride and admit to his father that he did, in fact, want to be included in the will, Philip does not mention it. After hearing that his father, in a fit of unburdening, has left his tefillin—the trappings of Orthodox Jewish prayer—in an unused locker at the YMHA, Philip wonders why he didn't give them to one of his sons: "I wouldn't have prayed with them, but I might well have cherished them, especially after his death" (*P* 96). Instead, his father gives him his own father's shaving mug, which Philip had been fascinated by since he was a child. These potential inheritances are on his mind as he cleans up the bathroom after his father's accident there: "There was my patrimony: not the money, not the tefillin, not the shaving mug, but the shit." Cleaning up the shit becomes Philip's patrimony, he claims, "not because cleaning it up was symbolic of something else but because it wasn't, because it was nothing less or more than the lived reality that it was" (*P* 176). Roth sees significance in this scene because it is free of the sentimental, mediated ideas of what a son gets from his father—he critiques his own imagining of the tefillin as patrimony as "a scene out of some Jewish parody of *Wild Strawberries*" (*P* 94). Cleaning up after your father when he can no longer do it himself is a son's duty; being able to take care of the parent who raised him is perhaps all he can ever hope for by way of repayment. Of course, claiming that "the shit" is the patrimony because it isn't symbolic paradoxically makes it symbolic; making the incident part of a book, instead of merely part of his life, allows Roth to grant it narrative meaning. It is this narrative meaning that Roth trades his father's privacy for.

Although, in the narration of the "shit" scene, Roth gives no indication of the discomfort that may have accompanied his betrayal of his father's privacy, the closing pages of the book point to the unavoidability of these issues. About six weeks after his father's death, Roth dreams that his father, dressed in a white shroud, reproaches him: "I should have been dressed in a suit. You did the wrong thing" (*P* 237). Some pages earlier, Roth describes how he and his brother had decided to bury their father in a shroud—the traditional Jewish burial garb—instead of his insurance man's suit. After he wakes from the dream, however, Roth realizes that it had nothing to do with his father's apparel in the grave: "he had been alluding to this book, which, in keeping with the unseemliness of my profession, I had been writing all the while he was ill and dying" (*P* 237). This is the first mention of the necessary "unseemliness" that goes into the making of a book like this: writing everything down, thinking about a book while thinking about your father, "mak[ing] autobiographical literature out of a parent's intimate suffering" (Miller 24). Roth reports that he had misgivings about burying his father in the shroud, even before the dream, but "I hadn't the audacity to say, 'Bury him naked'" (*P* 234). In the book, which Roth takes his dream-father's protest to be about, Roth *is* audacious enough to leave his father naked—he depicts him naked, near tears, and exceedingly vulnerable after having "beshat" himself. Suffering his father's condemnation in a dream is the reckoning Roth must face for leaving the realm of fiction and entering the ethical and moral dimensions of nonfiction.

What's Left Out of *The Facts*

Whereas *Patrimony*, through its focus on Roth's father's life and death, blurs the distinction between biography and autobiography, *The Facts*, published two years earlier, seems to want to be read as a traditional, conventional autobiography. This sense only holds, however, if we consider the opening letter from Roth to Zuckerman, and Zuckerman's response at the end of the book, to be mere brackets—supertextual additions pasted onto the "real" book that resides in between. The letters' form and content encourages such a reading; the correspondence is prompted by, and discusses, "the book" itself. Roth writes to Zuckerman to ask him what he thinks of the manuscript he has enclosed, and Zuckerman responds, having "read the manuscript twice," urging Roth not to publish it (*F* 161). The conceit serves to privilege the chapters that separate the two letters as the primary text, reducing the letters to the status of commentary. It is a mistake, however, to assume that this is the case, especially when one remembers that Zuckerman's lines, which make up the final 35 pages of the book, are written by Roth. Whatever Roth's motivation for their inclusion was, the letters are a significant part of the book and make Roth's autobiography distinctively discursive and doubly self-reflexive: "two-faced," to use his own term. If we read the letters as carrying equal weight as the autobiographical "manuscript," the book becomes a critical text, often highlighting the inescapable intrusion of ethical dilemmas into life writing.

The letter to Zuckerman with which Roth begins the book works mainly to justify the writing of an autobiography. Roth explains that he has written the "manuscript" for the most part as a sort of self-therapy, to recover from a series of medical misfortunes and a mental breakdown, "so as to fall back into my former life, to retrieve my vitality, to transform myself into *myself* (*F*5). Briefly, near the end of the letter, Roth notes that writing an autobiography for the first time led him to consider the effect the published text would have upon those written about, "the problem of exposing others":

> While writing, when I began to feel increasingly squeamish about confessing intimate affairs of mine to *everybody*, I went back and changed the real names of some of those with whom I'd been involved, as well as a few identifying details. This was not because I believed that the rerendering would furnish complete anonymity (it couldn't make those people anonymous to their friends and mine) but because it might afford at least a little protection from their being pawed over by perfect strangers. (*F*9–10)

This is all Roth says on the matter before getting on with the "true story" of the autobiography. The passage reads as a relatively familiar sort of disclaimer, and I think, for most readers, makes little difference in the apprehension of the book. The chapters that follow give an interesting, if a bit prosaic, account of Roth's upbringing, marriage, and early notoriety as a writer, and few would argue that, by changing the names of a few private individuals, Roth is telling less than the whole truth. But this is precisely Zuckerman's protest after reading Roth's manuscript; he doesn't like the book—"this isn't you at your most interesting"—and the reason the book fails, in Zuckerman's opinion, has its roots in Roth's changing of names to protect the innocent (*F*162).

It is something of a joke that Zuckerman, a character whose existence depends upon Roth writing fiction, would self-interestedly try to convince his creator that nonfiction is not his forte: "I owe everything to you," he admits, "while you, however, owe me nothing less than the freedom to write freely" (*F*161). But it is telling that this "freedom to write freely," or the lack thereof, is the fulcrum on which Zuckerman's argument—given to him by Roth—rests. Why is Roth better off impersonating Zuckerman than impersonating himself? Because "I am your permission, your indiscretion, the key to disclosure" (*F*161–2). It is precisely because, when writing the story of an alter ego, "a being whose experience [is] comparable to my own and yet register[s] a more powerful valence," Roth does not need to worry about exposing others, nor about exposing himself (*F*6). In Zuckerman's view, in *The Facts*, Roth is worrying far too much about both, crippling his ability to write interestingly, to see others clearly and to depict himself fully. "[T]o tell what you tell best is forbidden to you here by a decorous, citizenly, filial conscience. With this book you've tied your hands behind your back and tried to write it with your toes" (*F*169). Zuckerman doesn't let Roth off the hook and suggest that perhaps he's more comfortable writing fiction simply because he is well-practiced at it; no, the freedom from the ethical considerations that we must ordinarily shoulder is a central ingredient in Roth's fiction-making process: "kind, discreet, careful—changing people's names because you're worried about hurting their feelings—no this isn't you at your most interesting. In the fiction you can be so much more truthful without worrying all the time about causing direct pain" (*F* 162). Roth's decision to include the scene depicting his father's shame in *Patrimony*, published two years later, would invite criticism over the ethics of his decision to violate his father's explicit wish for privacy. Here, Roth has Zuckerman criticize his writing for precisely the opposite reason: that Roth is so aware of the effects of nonfiction writing that he has handicapped himself aesthetically, instead of ethically, thus preventing himself from giving a true sense of his life.

One specific example Zuckerman gives is Roth's depiction of May Aldridge (whose real name Zuckerman assumes has been changed), who, as Roth's lover in the late 1960s, offered comfort, tenderness, and calm to the writer in the wake of his disastrous marriage. In *The Facts*, she by no means plays a large part, but is depicted as a balm to Roth, "the loveliest-looking woman I'd ever known, [. . .] sweet-tempered [. . .] accommodating" (*F* 131–5). Zuckerman, in his anger, takes umbrage at this portrayal of May. It's simply too pretty a picture, too admiring, too romanticized to be true. He suggests that because May is still alive, Roth cannot bring himself to show all sides of her, not wanting to hurt or expose her. "You [. . .] don't begin to give a proper portrait of her. You don't appear to have the heart—the gall, the guts—to do in autobiography what you consider absolutely essential in a novel" (*F* 183). What's more, Zuckerman implies, Roth may not even be aware that he is not telling the whole story. If he were, he might have reported the reason for his reticence to the reader:

> You won't even say here, as you might so easily, in a footnote or just in passing, "I find it inhibiting to write about May. Even though her name has been changed, she's still alive and I don't want to hurt her, and so her portrait will have an idealized cast to it. It is not a false portrait but it is only half a portrait." Even that is beyond you, if it has even occurred to you. She is so vulnerable, this May, that even saying that might wound her horribly. (*F* 183)

This is surely one point at which the reader is particularly aware that Zuckerman is a fictional character; for even as Roth has his alter ego chastise him for not being able to insert a disclaimer attesting to his inhibition, he is inserting the disclaimer nonetheless. And so Roth gets to have it both ways, it seems, presenting an idealized portrait of "May Aldridge" (and thus protecting the real woman who might read the book), while apologizing to his other readers (and perhaps to his conscience), explaining that he is too hemmed in by restraint and decorum to tell the whole story.

But the issue of May Aldridge is not left at that. Zuckerman goes further, asking Roth, "what *didn't* you like about May?" (*F* 181). He then guesses at some of the things Roth may have left out of his portrait. Responding to Roth's description of May's apartment as reflecting "the traditional tastes of her class," Zuckerman interjects, "The *awful* tastes of her class. There is nothing *worse* than the taste of the American WASP upper class" (*F* 134, 181). Philip comes off as too taken with her background, especially for a son of the proudly liberal, working-class Herman Roth: "I suspect a lot about her class and her background and her taste, far from impressing you, positively disgusted you." What's more, Zuckerman wonders if she was a drug addict: "Was she a pill popper like Susan McCall, her obvious embodiment in *My Life as a Man*? Surely Susan's pill popping is meant to stand for some addiction, if it isn't simply the flat-out truth." The relationship must have ended, Zuckerman infers, because "you didn't want another broken woman" (*F* 182). Again, it is instructive to remember that Roth is writing Zuckerman's lines. If, as Zuckerman has argued, Roth is too concerned with not hurting May to include the bad with the good in his depiction of her, why would he put these words into Zuckerman's mouth? The reader, who is aware that Zuckerman is a fictional character, can surely be forgiven for thinking that Roth wants it to be known that May's background *did* disgust him, that she was an addict, that she was a broken woman.

And so, what is the point of all of this? If Roth really is inhibited by his concern for May, why include what can be seen as pretty hurtful accusations? If Roth wants to give a full portrait of May, regardless of whether she's hurt by it, why not paint that picture in the first place? Regardless of Roth's intentions, what the bizarre treatment of May Aldridge does, I think, is dramatize the ethical conflict that arises when entering into life writing. *The Facts*, with its two versions of May Aldridge, enacts what might be thought of as two voices inside the writer's head: one that argues for ethical consideration of those written about, even at the expense of the full truth, and one arguing that the writer of an autobiography must tell the story of his life as truthfully, or at least as fittingly, as possible, damn the consequences. It certainly seems possible that the struggle between Roth and his character over the correct presentation of May Aldridge reflects Roth's discovery, once he set himself to writing an autobiography, of the very different considerations that a memoirist must face.

The Drama of *Deception*

Deception is the book Roth published between *The Facts* and *Patrimony*, and although it is subtitled "a novel," it is by no means the return to straightforward fiction that that might suggest. Its oblique strategies of tempting the reader to read this work of fiction as nonfiction eventually culminate in a dramatic rendering of battles fought over the ethics of writing, making it very much of a piece with the works published before and after it.

Deception reads like a writer's notebook. More specifically, it reads like the transcriptions of conversations between a writer named Philip—one who seems to be, by all given details, Philip Roth—and his British mistress, who comes to visit him in his writer's studio in London. Interspersed with these conversations are more conversations between Philip and other, mostly Eastern European, women, who also come to his studio. There is little in the way of exposition, description, or attribution of dialogue; the book is almost entirely made up of dialogue between Philip and these women. As far as plot goes, there isn't much of one; the affair waxes and wanes—she wants to leave her husband, she wants to stay with him and make it work; sometimes they have sex, sometimes they just talk.

As interesting as some of the writing is, the book's dramatic interest—and relevance to this discussion—doesn't really take hold until after the first 170 pages. The final 30 pages of the book are taken up by two long conversations that essentially justify the existence of the work as a novel, giving shape to what is, up to that point, quite a shapeless, seemingly artless series of conversations, the equivalent of an extended glimpse through a keyhole. The first of these final conversations is between Philip and his unnamed wife, who has found his notebook—what we have been reading up to now—and accuses him of cheating on her with the women depicted therein. She guesses that the British woman is the model for the British female character in the novel Philip has been working on (although it is not named, this novel is very clearly meant to be Roth's book of 1986, *The Counterlife*). He tells her that what she has read is all fiction, that he has been "imagining myself, outside of my novel, having a love affair with a character inside my novel" (*D* 176). She is not exactly convinced, but the argument swiftly moves on to the question of whether or not Philip will publish the notebook as it is. In some ways, Philip and his wife replay the conflict between Roth and Zuckerman over May Aldridge sketched above, except here Philip is the one arguing against discretion while his wife tries to convince him to at least change some names: "Because what you've got a portrait of is adulterous love, and consequently, it might be advisable to take your name out—don't you think? 'Philip, do you have an ashtray?' You would change that to 'Nathan,' would you not?" (*D* 183). But it's not Nathan, Philip claims, it's an imagined version of himself, not a character. In what must be read as a prospective justification for *Deception* itself, Philip explains his need to insert himself into his writing:

> I portray myself as implicated because it is not enough just to be present. That's not the way I go about it. To compromise some "character" doesn't get me where I want to be. What heats things up is compromising me. It kind of makes the indictment juicier, besmirching myself. (*D* 177–8)

The legalistic language is reminiscent of remarks Roth gave in an interview in 1984, when speaking of the writerly skill of impersonation. He speaks admiringly of Witold Gombrowicz who, in *Pornografia*, "introduces himself as a character, using his own name—the better to implicate himself in certain highly dubious proceedings and bring the moral terror to life" ("Art of Fiction" 223).[3] But while readers of Gombrowicz and Roth may be intrigued and excited by the implication of the author in his books, what Philip seems unconcerned by are the other people who may be implicated as well. This is Philip's wife's concern, naturally, especially as she suspects that the notebook is not as fictional as Philip is claiming.

"What about humiliating me?" she asks, clearly worried that readers will take Philip for his word and believe that he is cheating on his wife (*D* 184). She begs him to, at the very least, change his name to make the book seem more like fiction. He refuses, claiming that, "somebody telling me what to write happens to drive me absolutely nuts" (*D* 185). By apparently writing a work of fiction that aims to resemble nonfiction, Philip finds himself caught between the differing considerations that guide the two modes. His adamant rejection of his wife's protests demonstrates clearly which side he is on: "I cannot and do not live in the world of discretion, not as a writer, anyway. I would prefer to, I assure you— it would make life easier. But discretion is, unfortunately, not for novelists" (*D* 184). The extremity of this statement, the absolute refusal to even entertain the possibility of being discreet, points up the centrality of these issues to the novel. And as *Deception*'s final conversation shows, concerns over exposure and betrayal are not confined to books in which the names are left unchanged.

This conversation takes place some time later, after "the novel"—*The Counterlife*—has been published. It is between Philip and his British mistress again, after he has moved back to America and some time since they have last spoken. The novel, and her place in it, dominates their discussion:

> "Ever since I read your book I haven't known whether to call or not. I thought about it a lot."
> "I'll bet you did. I thought about it too. I thought about its effect on your marriage."
> "Oh, well, he didn't read it."
> Laughing. "Wonderful. Of course. All that worrying for nothing." (*D* 188)

Immediately we see that Philip's wife's initial accusations—that his notebook records his affair with the woman who inspired the British character in his novel—are in fact correct, highlighting perhaps the central deception referred to by the book's title. We also begin to see clearly the overall method of the book, that the first 170 pages of endless conversation exist primarily to provide the central piece of material evidence to be taken up in the book's final 30 pages. (Of course, this is but one interpretation; these final conversations may be further fictional sketches imagined in Philip's notebook.) The recognizable character in "the novel" has not ruined Philip's mistress's marriage, but the potential effect of exposing someone in a published work—no matter how fictionalized—is still the matter at stake both here and in Philip's conversation with his wife. The unnamed mistress expresses mixed feelings over having recognized herself in the novel, first professing bafflement over Philip's cavalier exposure of what was, naturally, a secret affair: "why, why do you *do* that? Why do you take life like that? [. . .] Why did you then write a book which she, I'm sure, can't help but think is based on a real person?"

Philip's answer is much like the justification he gives his wife for the potential publication of his notebook: "Because it's what I do" (*D* 193). She threatens, half-jokingly, to write and publish a book of her own, titled *Kiss and Tell*, potentially exposing him in the same way that he has exposed her. He tells her that he is in no position to stop her, especially as he may write another book about her, presumably the book we hold in our hands now. *Deception* ends on this note, with both final conversations portraying Philip as resolute in his belief in the writer's right to write what he wants, regardless of whether his books expose real people with no control over their entrance into public view. But an earlier version of the book, with a different ending, shows a more conflicted protagonist, again suggesting that these issues were not so easy to resolve.

In the second draft of *Deception*, dated February 1989, the closing conversation between Philip and his mistress is present almost exactly as it would be in the published version. But whereas, in the final version, that conversation closes the book, here it is followed by a further seven handwritten pages, with an indication that they be "italicized throughout." The passage begins: "What he did not tell her was that much had happened to him too and much of it painful. He had—there wasn't any better expression for it—hit bottom" ("*Deception*; Drafts" 83a). What had happened to him was a breakdown exactly like the one Roth suffered, a breakdown recounted in the prefatory letter in *The Facts*, and eventually further fleshed out in *Operation Shylock*. Minor surgery gone wrong, and extreme side effects from sleeping pills, led to something akin to mental dissolution. As Philip tells it here, however, in the depths of his breakdown, he attributes this catastrophe to his use of his mistress in his novel:

> [E]ven though he felt his mind disintegrating, whirling itself into a chaos of mental rubble, he was able to understand with the utmost clarity that his suffering was a punishment for having betrayed her. He could imagine how her presence in his novel, however disguised, had been recognized by her husband and had ruined her marriage once and for all, leaving her the adulteress, alone and destitute with her child. ("*Deception*; Drafts" 83d–83e)

In this version of *Deception*, the consequences of writing about others, and the questions around the ethics of writing in general, take on an even more significant role. The sense of the notebook as a series of transcriptions ("Listen, you can't take down everything someone says like that," Philip's mistress tells him at one point), the personal biographical details left intact that might expose a couple's privacy, the recognizable flaunting of a secret affair in a published novel: the book is concerned with the transfer of words and deeds from the unwritten to the written world (*D* 195). The fallout from this transfer is explored over the book's final 30 pages, and, in this early draft, pursued even further. Philip's anguish is the result of some sort of divine retribution for exposing another through his writing. This is reminiscent of one of the many explanations Zuckerman entertains for his chronic pain in *The Anatomy Lesson*: that he is being punished for the sin of having written his *Portnoy*-like *Carnovsky*, for exposing his family and "his tribe":

> Zuckerman was taking "pain" back to its root in *poena*, the Latin word for punishment: poena for the family portrait the whole country had assumed to be his, for the tastelessness that had affronted millions and the shamelessness that had enraged his tribe. (319)

As far as Philip's remorse over exposing his mistress goes, it lasts only as long as his debilitating ordeal does. After his recovery, when he begins to write again, he discovers that he is soon able to leave discretion and inhibition behind. "Divulging, exposing—as she saw it, betraying—that's how he knew that the terrible interruption was finally over and that, at least for now, he was fully recovered" ("*Deception*; Drafts" 83f–83g). Although this section was not included in the published version of *Deception*, it is striking that Philip's understanding of how to recover from his debilitating breakdown—by reentering the amoral arena of fiction-making—is exactly the opposite of the strategy with which Roth apparently begins this period, in *The Facts*. There, he explains, he turns to non-fiction writing "to transform myself into *myself*": "out of fuel, back to tank up on the magic blood" (*F* 6). Here, it is fiction—especially figured as an escape from ethics—that is understood as having magical powers.

Operation Shylock: Whose Story Is It?

Operation Shylock is subtitled "A Confession," and the first line of its preface places the book firmly within the conventions of nonfiction, as well as immediately introducing issues concerning the ethical treatment of those real people written about within: "For legal reasons, I have had to alter a number of facts in this book" (*OS* 13). Both the subtitle and the opening of the preface indicate that Roth is working very hard here to convince; this is meant to be read as nonfiction, and the first-person narrator throughout is manifestly identical with the book's author. And yet the plot of the book is so wild, so ridiculous, so contrived even, as to defy belief in its basis in fact.

While Philip Roth is in New York, still shaky after surviving the mental break-down touched upon in *The Facts*, another man is in Israel, promoting a bizarre political program he calls "Diasporism," calling for the return of Israel's Ashkenazi Jews to Europe, in order to prevent a "second Holocaust" at the hands of Israel's Arab enemies (*OS* 43). What's more, this man—an American who happens to resemble Roth—claims to be Philip Roth, and is using the author's fame to advance his cause. Already planning to travel to Israel to interview the novelist Aharon Appelfeld, the "real" Philip finds himself caught up in a reality consistently proving to be stranger than fiction. In between confrontations with the impostor—whom he names Moishe Pipik, a Yiddish nickname from his childhood—Philip attends the trial of John Demjanjuk, the man accused of being Treblinka's Ivan the Terrible; meets and eventually sleeps with Pipik's girlfriend, a vivacious nurse and a "recovering anti-Semite"; runs into an old friend from college, who is now an outspoken anti-Zionist in Palestine; is entrusted with the diaries of Leon Klinghoffer, the Jewish pensioner killed during the Palestinian hijacking of the *Achille Lauro*; and apparently goes on a top-secret mission to Athens for the Israeli secret service, the Mossad.[4] Many commentators have focused on the book's excesses—its litany of exhaustively talkative characters, endless monologues and shouted disputes, and proliferation of doubles—as elements of a work that seems to be playing familiar postmodern games.[5] Whereas I agree that *Operation Shylock* extends Roth's inquiry into the performative and divided nature of the self, as well as enacting "a blurring of artifice and life that permanently fractures any reliable boundary between the two," what is often overlooked in studies of this text are the ways in which *Operation Shylock* continues Roth's investigation of the potential costs and conflicts that arise from nonfiction writing (Posnock 144). Seen this way, Pipik's "plot," rather than a representation of the divided self of "Philip Roth," becomes a dramatization of a text claiming to be factual, thus implicating, exposing, and invading the privacy of Philip Roth.

Almost from the first appearance of Pipik in the book's pages, he is figured as a text. When Appelfeld tells Philip the details of Pipik's plan to resettle more than a million Ashkenazi Jews on the continent from which they fled to Israel, he adds, "Philip, I feel that I'm reading to you out of a story you wrote" (*OS* 31). Philip, trying to get a handle on the situation, has similar thoughts on the matter: "It's Zuckerman, I thought, whimsically, stupidly, escapistly, it's Kepesh, it's Tarnopol and Portnoy—it's all of them in one, broken free of print and mockingly reconstituted as a single satirical facsimile of me" (*OS* 34). Throughout Philip's bizarre time in Israel, as he tries to get to the bottom of the ludicrous events set in motion by his impostor, he continually refers to those events as a plot, and seems more affronted by the plot's poor construction and lack of literary merit than anything else. He speaks of wanting to escape the plot "on the grounds of its general implausibility, its total lack of gravity, its reliance on unlikely coincidence, the absence of inner coherence, and of anything resembling a serious meaning or purpose" (*OS* 317). But, as Philip's qualifiers above— "whimsically, stupidly, escapistly"—suggest, if Pipik's plot is a text, it is not a fictional one, nor is it one written by Philip Roth. In fact, the very threat of Pipik's plot stems from his claim that he is telling the truth, that he *is* Philip Roth—this is precisely the root of Philip's fears; he worries that people will believe these claims and confuse the "Diasporist" with the author.

Just as the claim to, or appearance of, nonfiction opens up the possibilities that *Deception* could expose Philip's wife, that *The Facts* could expose "May Aldridge," and that *Patrimony* could expose Herman Roth, Pipik's assertion that his narrative is nothing other than the truth threatens to expose, to implicate, and to invade the privacy of Philip Roth. Roth, who, in his past three books, had examined the consequences of this sort of exposure from the position of the writer, now finds himself on the other side of the conflict, powerless to determine the way his story is told. His concerns, at first, are clear. After Pipik's girlfriend comes to Philip, begging him to avoid legal action, to have some sympathy for Pipik, who is in remission from cancer, and "whose thoughts are only for saving others," Philip responds that his only interest is "his entangling our two lives and confusing people about who is who. What I cannot permit and what I will not permit is his encouraging people to believe that he is me" (*OS* 98–9). Philippe Lejeune, one of the foremost theorists on autobiography, identifies a central, and basic, issue in thinking about the ethics of life writing: "Everyone thinks he is more or less the owner of his name, of his person, of his own story (and even of his image)" (quoted in Eakin 142). When your name, story, or image is included in somebody else's nonfiction work, it can easily feel like a theft, like an infringement upon your rights of ownership. Summing up the history of legal conceptions of privacy, Paul John Eakin notes that privacy has often been equated with nothing less than the fact of personhood, and so "when privacy is abridged, [. . .] the result [is] that the integrity of the person is breached or violated" (161). Philip threatens Pipik at their first meeting, appealing to "[t]he law that says that a person's identity is his private property and can't be appropriated by somebody else" (*OS* 75).

Although Philip never does take legal action against Pipik, the question of who shall have the right to tell the story of Philip Roth underlies their struggle over authorial power. Appelfeld, whom Philip meets with after his initial confrontation with Pipik, sees the nature of the conflict right away. "It's perfect [. . .] You are going to rewrite him" (*OS* 107). After a few days in Jerusalem, contending with the utter absurdity of Pipik's plot, Philip explicitly conceives of the conflict with his impostor as a "narrative contest," one that, considering his profession, he should expect to win:

> It would be comforting, it would be only natural, to assume that in a narrative contest (in the realistic mode) with this impostor, the real writer would easily emerge as inventive champion, scoring overwhelming victories in Sophistication of Means, Subtlety of Effects, Cunningness of Structure, Ironic Complexity, Intellectual Interest, Psychological Credibility, Verbal Precision, and Overall Verisimilitude [. . .] (*OS* 246–7)

Instead, Philip finds himself undone in Jerusalem as the one written about, "without the least control over this narrative Ping-Pong in which I appear as the little white ball," rather than his usual role as the man composing the narrative at his typewriter (*OS* 358). He longs for the power to rewrite the story—a longing especially maddening as it is *his* story—which leads him eventually to impersonate his impersonator, spewing out long monologues for whomever will listen about the urgently necessary repatriation of the Jews in Europe. "[I]nstead of disowning the doctrine of Diasporism, he becomes its advocate, out-Pipiking

Pipik. By shifting the battleground from the personal to the professional, the question becomes not 'who is the real Philip Roth?' but 'who is the more persuasive author?'" (Brauner, *Philip Roth* 103). This tack, however, rather than rewriting Pipik's plot, merely ventriloquizes what Pipik has already written, leading Philip to wonder if it is not the product of a mind "too unhinged by the paranoid threat to be able to think out an effective counterplot in which to subsume the Pipikesque imbecility" (*OS* 246). If only Philip's considerable powers of narrative composition could defeat this very real adversary. At one point, when Philip and Pipik are together in Philip's hotel room, the former, in an attempt to interrupt Pipik's narrative, tells the latter a story of his Great Aunt Gitcha, which calms down the exasperated impostor, who soon falls asleep:

> I had put my sonny boy to sleep, with my story anesthetized him. I remained in the chair by the window wishing that it had killed him. When I was younger my Jewish betters used to accuse me of writing short stories that endangered Jewish lives—would that I could! A narrative as deadly as a gun! (*OS* 186)

Here, as he longs for the authorial power to take back his story, Philip connects this conflict with his earliest battles with Jewish readers over his initial published work; this connection will be further highlighted in the book's denouement.

Evil Speech

About halfway through the book, Pipik, somewhat implausibly (in the already implausible world of this book), disappears from the plot, and the focus shifts to a different ethical conundrum, one that restores Philip to the position of author, as it centers on the contents of *Operation Shylock* itself.[6] After Pipik and Jinx disappear from Israel, but not from Philip's mind, Philip is abducted and taken to an abandoned schoolhouse, in the classroom of which he sits and waits, not knowing what new calamity awaits him. This new situation is more frightening than the mere worry about an impostor smearing his good name: "Would that I were still a ludicrous character in his lousy book!" (*OS* 317). With Pipik gone, Philip eases back into the role of the writer, and for that task, continuing the book's seemingly endless succession of impassioned monologues, he finds himself lectured on the writer's ethical responsibilities. Enter Louis B. Smilesburger, an elderly agent for the Mossad, Israel's secret service, who had previously masqueraded as a Holocaust survivor wishing to contribute to the cause of Diasporism. Before telling Philip why he has been abducted, why he has been *chosen*, Smilesburger launches into an extended monologue—a seeming non sequitur—on the Chofetz Chaim and *loshon hora*. The Chofetz Chaim, of whom Smilesburger claims to be a disciple, was a Polish rabbi and scholar who devoted his life to the eradication of *loshon hora*, or "evil speech."

"The Chofetz Chaim formulated [. . .] the laws that forbid Jews' making derogatory or damaging remarks about their fellow Jews, even if they are true" (*OS* 333). As Smilesburger continues, it becomes clear that this prohibition extends far and wide, and that few utterances, unless wholly positive, can be deemed acceptable:

> There is nothing about *loshon hora* that the Chofetz Chaim did not clarify and regulate: *loshon hora* said in jest, *loshon hora* without mentioning names, *loshon hora* that is common knowledge, *loshon hora* about relatives, about in-laws, about children, about the dead, about heretics and ignoramuses and known transgressors, even about merchandise—all forbidden. (*OS* 333–4)

Josh Cohen, writing about the convolution of these prohibitions, notes that "this intricacy stems from the difficulty of containing the unintended effects of even the most minimal of speech" (85). It is an attempt to formulate an ethics of speaking that eventually comes to the conclusion that it is better, in the end, to keep your mouth shut. What's more, the prohibition of *loshon hora* even extends to "evil speech" directed at yourself, for, in the parable that Smilesburger tells to illustrate this wrinkle, even denigrating only yourself can end up hurting others (*OS* 338–9). What Smilesburger's monologue seems to outline is a set of religious injunctions that stem from an adoption of something very close to Eakin's "relational concept of selfhood."

Smilesburger's lecture turns out to be the preface to an argument that should be familiar to readers of *The Facts* and *Deception*: the argument centers on what is ethical for the writer to put in or leave out of the book itself. Just as Zuckerman argues with Roth in *The Facts* over whether to include the whole truth about "May Aldridge," and Philip argues with his wife about the revelations of *Deception*, here Philip and Smilesburger grapple over how much Roth puts in or leaves out about his adventures in *Operation Shylock*. Philip describes how, when he finished writing the book, some years after the events described, he sends the manuscript to Smilesburger, even though he was under no obligation to do so. The question of obligation is raised, we learn, because of what Philip recounts in the manuscript's final chapter, which has been ultimately cut out of the published version of *Operation Shylock*:

> I have elected to delete my final chapter, twelve thousand words describing the people I convened with in Athens, the circumstances that brought us together, and the subsequent expedition, to a second European capital, that developed out of that educational Athens weekend. (*OS* 359)

His trip to Athens was, presumably, as an operative for the Mossad, on a mission to identify Jewish traitors to Israel—contributors to the PLO—so that they can be assassinated. He is able to perform this mission by posing as Moishe Pipik (who, of course, had been posing as him), whose proposed program of exporting Israel's Jews back to Europe makes him an ally of the anti-Zionists. Under the oversight of Smilesburger, "I undertook to give the most extreme performance of my life and seriously to mislead others in something more drastic than a mere book" (*OS* 359). But Smilesburger, who meets Philip in New York after reading the manuscript, indicates to Philip that the matter of a "mere book" is not as trifling as Philip seems to think. Claiming to have retired from the Mossad, Smilesburger advises Philip out of personal concern, but nonetheless is unwavering in his message: Philip must not publish his account of his secret mission, for the sake of the integrity of the Israeli state, and for his own safety. Naturally, Philip has no intention of bowing to Smilesburger's arguments: "I went where I went, did what I did, met whom I met, saw what I saw, learned what I learned—and nothing that occurred in Athens, absolutely nothing, is interchangeable with something else" (*OS* 383). Here, Philip is absolutely committed to telling the whole truth of what happened to him, regardless of the effect his published work might have on the security of the Jewish state—or on his own security. And yet, *Operation Shylock*, as it is, contains no chapter detailing Philip's mission for the Mossad.

* * *

Ross Posnock has noted a tension inherent in what he calls Roth's "assault on purity," his urge to expose as a lie "the American myth of the natural" (50, 20). This assault, as many critics have identified, has been an increasingly central aspect of Roth's fiction as he has aged: *The Counterlife, American Pastoral*, and *The Human Stain* all take pains to show the dangers in the very human instinct toward blinkered nostalgia, idealism and the pastoral. But such an antagonistic stance, Posnock points out, "can't escape the inflated selfhood of the alienated intellectual, a posture that is symptomatic of the American reflex to heroicize, hence to simplify and purify" (50). This pose is a familiar one to readers of Roth's early essays "Writing American Fiction" and "Writing About Jews," or indeed any of the Zuckerman books. As Posnock astutely notes, it carries its own dangers of naïve belief in the salvational power of the lone artist. It is a pose that shows up in *Deception*, when Philip, reminding his wife that "discretion is, unfortunately, not for novelists," informs her that "I write what I write the way I write it, and if and when it should ever happen, I will publish however I want to publish and I'm not going to start worrying at this late date what people misunderstand or get wrong!" (*D* 184–6). A similar vision of the author is put forward by Zuckerman in *The Facts*, when he suggests that writing with a concern for the others who may be affected by your words is akin to tying "your hands behind your back and [trying] to write [. . .] with your toes" (*F* 169). One of the things the conclusion of *Operation Shylock* suggests is that the hallowed autonomy of the author mooted here—his apparent immunity from the ethics that handicap others—may be precisely the target of these four books' tangled representations of the ethical dilemmas of writing.

Philip is deliberately ambiguous about why he excises the chapter on his Athens mission from *Operation Shylock*. The book ends, after Philip has categorically refused Smilesburger's entreaties, with the latter advising Philip to "Let your Jewish conscience be your guide" (*OS* 398). It is natural to assume, considering the makeup of the published book, that Philip's "Jewish conscience" is behind his decision to bow to Smilesburger's pressure and consider the effects of his proposed candor. Of course, Roth's "Jewish conscience" was called into question from the very beginning of his career, and references to the battles between Roth and the Jewish critics of *Goodbye, Columbus* are made frequently in the epilogue, reminding readers of the birth of his stubborn insistence on writing as he will write, damn the consequences. As he drives down to New York to meet Smilesburger, Philip reflects that "Never in my life had I submitted a manuscript to any inspector anywhere for this sort of scrutiny."[7] He continues, narrating the familiar construction of his adversarial defense of the writer's rights:

> To be degenerating into an acquiescent Jewish boy pleasing his law-giving elders when, whether I liked it or not, I had myself acquired all the markings of a Jewish elder was more than a little regressive. Jews who found me guilty of the crime of "informing" had been calling for me to be "responsible" from the time I began publishing in my middle twenties, but my youthful scorn had been plentiful and so were my untested artistic convictions, and [. . .] I had been able to hold my ground. I hadn't chosen to be a writer, I announced, only to be told by others what was permissible to write. (*OS* 377)

This illuminating passage, sketching the outline of the "oppositional high modernism" that Posnock identifies as Roth's prevailing mode, reveals the connection between the ethical considerations confronted in Roth's "autobiographical period" and the considerations Roth was accused of disregarding in his earliest fiction about Jews (Posnock 50). In both cases the choice is figured as between being "acquiescent" to what others define as "permissible," and "holding your ground" and standing by your "artistic convictions." In both of these specific situations, the Jewish community makes up these "others," ostensibly asking Roth to consider the effects his writing may have on the community's interests and security—remember that many of Roth's early detractors claimed that his work would give succor to enemies of the Jews. Whereas, in the wake of the controversy over *Goodbye, Columbus*, Roth resolutely stood by his principles, here, in the last book of a series that stirs up the ethical conundrums attendant to writing, Philip seems to yield to the warnings to watch what he says.

In those earliest battles, Philip claims, he was armed with "untested artistic convictions"; he tests them here. Nonfictional writing becomes a magnifying glass through which the time-tested instincts and artistic decisions of an established writer come in for close examination. Writing truthfully about his life and the lives of those around him, a project initially conceived of as a path back to sanity and stability, leads Roth to uncharted territory, and, if we are to believe *Operation Shylock*, to the edge of madness. Whether it be "May Aldridge," Herman Roth, Philip's wife and mistress, or Roth himself that are threatened with exposure, the consequences of the written word are examined in these four books as they had never before been in his fiction; this inquiry would continue in *I Married a Communist* and *The Human Stain*, both of which feature memoirs that threaten or enact exposure and betrayal. Near the end of *Operation Shylock*, Philip tells the reader that one of his early adopted "artistic convictions" was the belief that "nothing need hide itself in fiction," that literature is a realm apart from the moral and ethical demands imposed by others. But as he drives down to New York to meet the Mossad agent for whom he risked his life, Philip asks himself a question that haunts all four of the books of this period: "Nothing need hide itself in fiction but are there no limits where there's no disguise?" (*OS* 377).

Chapter 6

The American Experience: *American Pastoral,*
I Married a Communist, and *The Human Stain*

*Isn't that what this country's all about? I want to be where I want to be and I don't
want to be where I don't want to be. That's what being an American is—isn't it?*

Seymour Levov, American Pastoral

*You finally leave home, the Ur of we, and you find another we? Another place that's just
like that, the substitute for that?*

Coleman Silk, The Human Stain

You flood into America and America floods into you.

Nathan Zuckerman, I Married a Communist

It is now a critical commonplace that with the publication of *American Pastoral*
(1997), *I Married a Communist* (1998), and *The Human Stain* (2000), known as
the "American Trilogy," Roth began a "career resurgence" that ushered in a late
period of productivity and significance that now rivals that of Henry James.[1] For
many critics, the trilogy's situation of its three protagonists in three different
eras of American history, with Roth interrogating the historical forces that bring
each man down, showed Roth indisputably moving into the ranks of the major
novelists, no longer "bogged down in self-indulgent game playing," but instead
investigating "the larger ironies and tragedies of the American communal experience" (Cryer 4K). This polarity invokes the long-running critical narrative
that Roth has for much of his career been concerned mostly with himself, writing solipsistic riffs on his autobiography that forsake the wider world in favor of
an unremitting inward focus, endless variations that tell us more about Philip
Roth than anything else. In this formulation, the trilogy represents the long-
wished-for break, its foregrounded historical focus signaling Roth's move
beyond self-absorbed game-playing, finally doing what novelists should do:
engaging with the culture around them. "What happened?" Ken Gordon asked
facetiously, "The new books seem to recognize the existence of *other people*. Or,
rather, the fact that other people can be as endlessly fascinating and unknowable

as Nathan Zuckerman." Of course, it has long been assumed by many that Nathan Zuckerman is merely a version of Philip Roth, and many critics have echoed Gordon in their assessments of the trilogy. Michiko Kakutani saw the trilogy as an abandonment of Roth's "long obsession with alter egos and mirror games," his "narcissistic pyrotechnics," and a move beyond "the solipsistic presentations of self he had been practicing for years to create a capacious chronicle of American innocence and disillusion" ("Postwar Paradise" C11; "Confronting the Failures" E1). With a similarly clear value judgement, Christopher Tayler noted that, before the trilogy, "there was definitely a feeling that he'd staked out his territory and settled down for good. The territory in question was the land of novelistic self-scrutiny." The trilogy, in contrast, "turned the received wisdom inside out and catapulted their ageing author well beyond the first rank of American novelists" (11).

The novels that make up the trilogy do indeed seem a monumental achievement, with their self-conscious wide-angle lenses turned upon three important American eras, but it is worth countering this critical consensus. As I have argued throughout this book, Roth has consistently balanced inward and outward moves, always resisting the choice between one or the other. I would argue that, far from breaking with his previous work, the "American Trilogy" shows many continuities with the rest of Roth's work, exhibiting preoccupations that have drawn Roth's scrutiny for more than 40 years. Zuckerman's role as observer in the trilogy, the imaginer of other people's stories, for example, continues the movement that runs through *Zuckerman Bound* and *The Counterlife*, with Nathan seemingly moving from a Freudian concept of the self as rigidly defined, to a more fluid sense of the self as narrative, to, finally, something of a renunciation of his own self's story (which turns out to be, as we will see, ultimately futile). Zuckerman's uncertainty as to how much or how little he should involve himself in the lives of others shows a concern first taken up in *Letting Go. The Counterlife*'s introduction of the dangers of a pastoral vision of the world is continued here as well, with all three books dangling pastoral dreams in front of their protagonists.[2] Both *I Married a Communist* and *The Human Stain* feature memoirs that threaten or enact exposure and betrayal, echoing a central concern of Roth's "autobiographical" books of the late 1980s and early 1990s. And the trilogy's focus on the validity of ever accurately putting a life into words continues a preoccupation that Roth has mined since *My Life as a Man*. Perhaps most significantly, though, one of the central concerns of the "American Trilogy" is the interaction between self and society, between the individual and his community, between self-determination and social determination, issues first explored by Roth in his debut collection, *Goodbye, Columbus*, and it is this connection that will be my subject in this chapter. For all that the trilogy seems a new chapter in Roth's long and varied career, I hope to show that, rather than breaking with what has come before, the series continues and deepens Roth's investigation into one of his most enduring concerns.

In this book's first chapter, I discussed *Goodbye, Columbus* in the context of the changing terrain of postwar liberal thought. Roth's early stories were informed by the dominant liberal discourse of the 1950s, in which the individual was esteemed instead of the mass, which offered a seemingly chastened, realistic view of the world in place of naïve visions of collective harmony, and in which the ambivalence and contradictions of modernism were favored over the deterministic worlds of naturalism. Eli Peck, Nathan Marx, Ozzie Freedman, and Neil Klugman each attempt to maintain their independence and penchant for self-questioning in the face of a community that has other ideas. Roth's heroes in these stories seem younger cousins to the protagonists of *Invisible Man* (1952), *The Catcher in the Rye* (1951), and *The Adventures of Augie March* (1953), each identified by R. W. B. Lewis in 1955 as part of the "Adamic tradition" in American literature: "the hero is willing, with marvelously inadequate equipment, to take on as much of the world as is available to him, without ever fully submitting to any of the world's determining categories" (199). Whereas Roth's early protagonists cannot be said to have the world-digesting energies of Augie March or Invisible Man, each occupies a place of resistance, opposing the persuasive certainty of his (American Jewish) community with "inadequate equipment": ambivalence, curiosity, and a paradoxical blend of self-questioning and self-belief. The stories of *Goodbye, Columbus* demonstrated that Roth's sensibility and allegiances fell in line with the mainstream of liberal intellectual thought in the 1950s—a mainstream shaped by a common narrative of disillusionment with the politics of the left, leading to a skeptical distrust of collective action, and thus to a veneration of the individual who must operate within, and often against, society. The stories, uncannily foreshadowing the controversy they would ignite among the book's Jewish readers, also show Roth's keen and specific understanding of the American Jewish community in flux, highly sensitive to individuals who would threaten its newfound, and ostensibly fragile, security and prosperity.

Whereas the "American Trilogy" does not focus on individuals and their communities in quite the same way as Roth's debut, each novel does feature a protagonist who attempts to "spring the historical lock," to set his own course in the face of "determining categories" which would restrict and impede his self-authored story, suggesting that Roth is still a product of the fifties sensibility that helped to form his literary character (*HS* 335). *American Pastoral*'s Seymour Levov strives for a postethnic American paradise, free from "that resentment stuff," the claims of ethnic belonging (*AP* 311). Ira Ringold, in *I Married a Communist*, escapes his modest beginnings as a Newark ditch digger and hoodlum to become a celebrity of sorts, a radio star married to a movie star, and a Lincoln-esque socialist and proselytizer for the common man. Coleman Silk makes the most dramatic escape of all in *The Human Stain*, dodging the restrictions of the race he was born into. However, Roth's treatment of each protagonist is characteristically "two-faced," even more so than in *Goodbye, Columbus*, and, as David Brauner points out, the audacity and ingenuity of each man's escape cannot erase the costs incurred along the way, nor prevent each man's tragic end:

> [T]heir attempts to recreate themselves are represented ambivalently: on the one hand as heroic feats of liberation, epitomising the quintessentially American ideal of the self-made man and the immigrant dream of successful assimilation; on the other hand as futile fantasies of escape, illustrating the limitations of American social mobility and the impossibility of transcending historical circumstances. (*Philip Roth* 151)

As in *Goodbye, Columbus*, the "American Trilogy" shows Roth again concerned with the complex of issues that grow up out of the individual who remains, in Brian McDonald's words, "ensnared in the conflict between the claims of self and social determination" (28). But because the canvas of the trilogy is much wider than that of Roth's debut, because it so deliberately and programmatically invokes three eras of American history, the conclusions to be drawn—and questions to be raised—from these individuals have a greater resonance, suggesting, sometimes explicitly, that the tragedies of these three protagonists may be the tragedies of twentieth-century America itself.

The Human Stain and "the tyranny of the we"

Roth begins *The Human Stain*, in Nathan Zuckerman's voice, with an invocation of the mania sweeping America in the summer of 1998, a two-page editorial on the scandal prompted by Bill Clinton's extramarital affair and the revival of "America's oldest communal passion [. . .] the ecstasy of sanctimony" (*HS* 2). Paralleling the censorious campus community that would end Coleman Silk's career, Zuckerman depicts an America of collective idiocy, of puritanical moralizing, everyone up in arms over the sexual activity of a man elected to lead the country's executive branch. As extraordinary evidence, Zuckerman quotes the conservative columnist William F. Buckley, who wrote of Clinton, "When Abelard did it, it was possible to prevent its happening again" (*HS* 2–3). Whereas Zuckerman draws a comparison between Buckley's implicit call for blood and the Ayatollah Khomeini's fatwa on Salman Rushdie, I hear echoes instead of one of Roth's earliest critics, a rabbi who wrote to the Anti-Defamation League after reading *Goodbye, Columbus*, asking, "What is being done to silence this man? Medieval Jews would have known what to do with him" (Roth, "Writing About Jews" 450). From the beginning of his career, Roth was made personally familiar with the extremity of such sanctimony; the conservative communitarian desire to subdue the individual whose independence might threaten the purported interests of that community is a force with few limits. As detailed in my first and second chapters, the fight against this powerful opposition became a defining battle for Roth in his early career, and he found himself forced "to assert a literary position and to defend my moral flank the instant after I had taken my first steps" (Roth, *Reading Myself and Others* xiii). Transmuted into opposition from Zuckerman's family, the coercive power of a community's interests was nonetheless recognizable as the force which Zuckerman had to reckon with from the outset of his career, as narrated in *The Ghost Writer*. And it is a similar force that renders Coleman Silk nearly paralyzed with rage on the occasion when he first comes over to Zuckerman's house in *The Human Stain*. Having spoken seemingly innocuous words about two absent students in his class ("Does anyone know these people? Do they exist or are they spooks?"), Coleman has been pilloried by the Athena College community, understandably sensitive over any perceived racism among its faculty, for the outdated pejorative term he used to refer to what turned out to be two black students (*HS* 6). What Zuckerman eventually learns is that this force—"the tyranny of the we"—is one that Coleman has attempted to evade his whole life, self-authoring a narrative that would leave him free of the nets of community demands (*HS* 108).

The secret of *The Human Stain*, Coleman Silk's secret, is that he is not, as everyone thinks, a Jew, but was born a light-skinned African-American. For Zuckerman, who only learns this after Coleman's death, the revelation of this secret, told to him by Coleman's sister Ernestine, leads directly to the writing of Coleman's story, which we are encouraged to believe is *The Human Stain* (*HS* 337).[3] Zuckerman's narrative of Coleman's life depicts an individual who quite blatantly and extraordinarily strives for self-determination. As Zuckerman tells it, growing up in East Orange, New Jersey, as an exceptional student and athlete (he is a boxer and a track star), Coleman never experienced his race as a hindrance or something to fight against: "he was of course a Negro, very much of their small community of five thousand or so, but boxing, running, studying, at everything he did concentrating and succeeding, [. . .] he was, without thinking about it, everything else as well" (*HS* 108). When he goes off to Howard University, however, he experiences the twin forces of racism and collective racial identity, two strong "determining categories" that threaten to subsume, and thus blot out, his individuality. First, upon his arrival in Washington, D.C., he is refused service at a Woolworth's and called a nigger. Immediately the effect is devastating, particularly due to the remark's inherent assumption about Coleman's individual identity: "At East Orange High the class valedictorian, in the segregated South just another nigger. In the segregated South there were no separate identities, not even for him and his roommate" (*HS* 102–3). What's more, in addition to the prejudice of white Southerners that would deny him his "separate identity," the university community works to take away his individuality in a different way. If in Washington, D.C., he is "a nigger," at Howard, an all-black college, he learns that "he was a Negro as well" (*HS* 108). To Coleman, "the greatest of the great *pioneers* of the I," this is unbearable. To be stubbornly, uncompromisingly singular, to resist the claims of the plural nouns "they" and "we," to evade all collective interests that would attempt to force him off of his own track, this is, in Zuckerman's imagination, to be Coleman's great project:

> You can't let the big they impose its bigotry on you any more than you can let the little they become a we and impose its ethics on you. Not the tyranny of the we and its we-talk and everything that the we wants to pile on your head. Never for him the tyranny of the we that is dying to suck you in, the coercive, inclusive, historical, inescapable moral *we* with its insidious *E pluribus unum.* Neither the they of Woolworth's nor the we of Howard. Instead the raw I with all its agility. (*HS* 108)

Coleman soon decides, upon signing up for the army, that he would "play his skin however he wanted, color himself just as he chose" (*HS* 109). For the rest of his life, he would keep this secret from the whole world, the lightness of his skin allowing him to escape the conditions faced by all others born to his race in America. Back before he went to Howard and discovered that the color of his skin subjected him to the "tyranny of the we," as a young boxer auditioning for a scholarship to the University of Pittsburgh, it is Coleman's Jewish coach, Doc Chizner, who first puts the idea in his head that he could be seen as something other than black. Crucially, Doc does not suggest that Coleman tell the Pittsburgh coach that he is white; rather, "If nothing comes up [. . .] you don't bring it up. You're neither one thing or the other. You're Silky Silk" (*HS* 99).[4] Doc's argument pays tribute to Coleman's singularity—he doesn't need to be black or white, just Coleman. Coleman rejects both the "we" and the "they," only embracing "the raw I"; what's at stake is not the matter of race, only the desire for total self-determination. "All he'd ever wanted, from earliest childhood on, was to be free: not black, not even white—just on his own and free" (*HS* 120).[5] But if Coleman will be neither black nor white, what will he be? His decision to pass as a Jew is a curious one; as David Brauner points out, if Coleman wishes to avoid the conditions facing a minority in America, "surely it would have made more sense to become part of the WASP establishment" (*Philip Roth,* 173–4).[6] But no, as Zuckerman imagines it, it is the milieu of Greenwich Village in the 1950s, and the flowering of the New York Intellectuals, which triggers Coleman's choice:

> [T]his was a moment when Jewish self-infatuation was at a postwar pinnacle among the Washington Square intellectual avant-garde, when [. . .] an aura of cultural significance emanated as much from their jokes and their family anecdotes, from their laughter and their clowning and their wisecracks and their arguments—even from their insults—as from *Commentary, Midstream,* and the *Partisan Review* (*HS* 131)

This is the same milieu that, I argue, prepared the ground for Roth's early fictional representations of the individual and community.[7] Even more than their "self-infatuation," "cultural significance," and their journals, it is perhaps the difficult cultural negotiation made by many of these figures that draws Coleman to them. To return to Jonathan Freedman's assessment, discussed in Chapter 1, the "earnest attempt" of the New York Intellectuals "to slough off immigrant garb and beliefs in order to pass as 'real' Americans," and their attraction to high culture as "a place where they could stake their own fates, make their own futures, outside the constraints both within and without the Jewish community" makes apparent what their appeal would be to Coleman (164, 166–7). For a man whose project entails self-transformation in the pursuit of self-determination, there were few better models than the Jewish members of the New York Intellectuals.

Alexander Portnoy, a highly self-conscious Jew in pursuit of the holy grail of gentile women, finds himself simultaneously attracted to and repulsed by the gentile culture he comes in contact with. Visiting "the Pumpkin" at her family's house in Iowa, Portnoy is both covetous and disdainful of the family's genteel manners and speech, feeling at once inferior and superior. Freedman names this negotiation, in referring to the Jews who became known as the New York Intellectuals, an "unstable amalgam of affect," describing the often tangled set of emotions that accompanied those Jews' entry into the world of high culture. For Coleman Silk, the entry into the white world is even more fraught, because the fact that he is a black man wishing to be accepted as an equal is a secret known to no one but himself. The psychological difficulty of gaining entry into the dominant culture is compounded by all the effort it takes to keep his secret. At first, he is "surprised at how easy it was. What was supposed to be hard and somehow shaming or destructive was not only easy but without consequences, no price paid at all" (*HS* 112). For an extraordinarily self-possessed character like Coleman, self-determination may be easy in and of itself, but it is in going out into the world, Zuckerman suggests, facing all that is outside of his control, that chinks in the armor start to show. It soon becomes clear that the effort ("the diligence, the discipline, the taking the measure of every last situation") to keep at bay the forces of social determination cannot succeed all of the time (*HS* 179). The fear of exposure comes to the surface, when he misreads his college girlfriend's poetic tribute to the back of his neck as "*the back of his negro*," and when each of his children are born—"[w]ith not a sign of his secret" (*HS* 112, 177). When a boxing promoter asks him to go easy on a black opponent in the early rounds of a fight, to "give the people their money's worth," Coleman refuses, knocking him out in the first round and snapping to the promoter, "I don't carry no nigger" (*HS* 116–17). Although, for Zuckerman, this is evidence of how committed Coleman is to his radical project of transformation, David Brauner points out that it is "precisely because Coleman is carrying the identity of a 'nigger' with him—that is to say, the consciousness of belonging to an ethno-racial group historically perceived as subhuman by many white Americans" that he lets the invidious term (Freudianly) slip out (*Philip Roth* 158). Similarly, in the wake of his dismissal from Athena, erupting with rage at his unhelpful lawyer, Coleman shouts, "I never again want to hear that self-admiring voice of yours or see your smug fucking lily-white face" (*HS* 81). It follows that Coleman's use of the outdated racist terminology "spooks" to refer to two absent students who later turn out to be black—the utterance that sets in motion his tragic fall—may be more than a cruelly ironic fate. It may be, as both Brauner and Mark Shechner suggest, the return of the repressed, the socially determined self returning with a vengeance (*Philip Roth* 159; *Up Society's Ass* 191).[8] That his words trigger the full force of another tyrannical "we"—the politically correct campus community of Athena College—signals the beginning of the end of Coleman's great self-making project.

Branded

On the second page of *The Human Stain*, Zuckerman makes reference to Nathanial Hawthorne, "who, in the 1860s, lived not many miles from my door," claiming that the country's sanctimonious interest in the Clinton scandal was another example of what the nineteenth-century author called "the persecuting spirit" (*HS* 2). Still, it seems, Roth is interested in "Studies in Guilt and Persecution." Coleman Silk's downfall, as it is engineered by a censorious campus community only too happy to ostracize the distinguished professor for his apparent transgression of the laws of political correctness, has been compared by a number of commentators to the fate of Hester Prynne in *The Scarlet Letter*.[9] Even if he is not paraded through town with a shaming letter sewn into his clothing, Coleman's experience at the hands of the eagerly judgmental faculty members and student organizations—"the charges, denials, and countercharges, the obtuseness, ignorance, and cynicism, the gross and deliberate misinterpretations, the laborious, repetitious explanations, the prosecutorial questions"—echoes Hester's at the hands of her neighbors (*HS* 12).[10] Elaine B. Safer invokes the scene in *The Scarlet Letter* when Hester is taken out from the prison to be brought in front of the crowd with her letter; for one matron in the crowd at least, this is not punishment enough: "At the very least, they should have put the brand of a hot iron on Hester Prynne's forehead" (Hawthorne 46; quoted in Safer 122). Branding, Timothy Parrish reminds us, although not with an iron or a scarlet letter, was also at the heart of a 1962 symposium on "The Crisis of Conscience in Minority Writers of Fiction," at which Roth was "grilled" with "inquisitorial pressure" by a crowd of Jewish readers ready to tar and feather him for his portrayal of Jews in *Goodbye, Columbus* ("Roth and Ethnic" 131). Roth describes the incident in *The Facts*, claiming that the confrontation with the symposium audience left him "branded" as a Jewish writer (127–30). Roth again spoke about being branded in a 1981 interview, and, although he uses a different connotation of the term, the sense of reduction and constraint remains—the definition of the self by society. Asked what changed for him after the huge commercial success of *Portnoy's Complaint*, Roth responds, "To become a celebrity is to become a brand name [. . .] Ivory is the soap that floats; Rice Krispies the breakfast cereal that goes snap-crackle-pop; Philip Roth the Jew who masturbates with a piece of liver" (*Reading Myself and Others* 98). In both cases, Roth's desire to define himself as a writer, to retain the freedom to write however he wants, is countered by a societal desire to brand the individual, to pin him down, to restrict his freedom of self-determination.[11] The branding of Philip Roth did not undo him—it was never a tight enough straightjacket to confine him for very long—but it does undo Coleman Silk, whose boldly constructed identity depends upon his self-determination remaining inviolate. His fate will resemble Hester Prynne's, for whom "[t]he effect of the symbol [. . .] was powerful and peculiar. All the light and graceful foliage of her character had been withered up by this red-hot brand, and had long ago fallen away, leaving a bare and harsh outline" (Hawthorne 147–8).

At the funeral of Faunia Farley, the lover with whom Coleman finds solace after the cataclysm of his resignation—a relationship seized upon as exploitative by the same community that ostracized him as a racist—Zuckerman reflects upon the "public stoning" that led up to both Coleman's and Faunia's deaths (*HS* 289). In the aftermath of the car accident that killed them both (in Zuckerman's imagining, caused by Faunia's insane, and anti-Semitic, ex-husband Les), Zuckerman reads an anonymous editorial on an internet bulletin board that amplifies the whispering campaign that labeled Coleman both a racist and an abusive misogynist; he is furious at the stupidity and illogic of the persecuting community:

> Only a label is required. The label is the motive. The label is the evidence. The label is the logic. Why did Coleman Silk do this? Because he is an *x*, because he is a *y*, because he is both. First a racist and now a misogynist. (*HS* 290)

The branding that Coleman is subject to in his final years, and after his death, should remind us of the branding that he fled from in his youth. Branding, whether it be "nigger" or "Negro" or "racist" or "misogynist" (without equating these terms), is a telling way that the "we" imposes its tyranny on the "I." This sort of labeling, by its very nature, is a restrictive and limiting force, aiming to deny the self-determining individuality that Coleman seeks. Seeking to flee from the historical and social forces that would determine him as a black man, he is mostly successful, save for the occasions, noted above, when he unwittingly betrays his own secret. But, and this is inevitable in the world of Roth's trilogy, he soon comes up against the tyranny of another "we," suggesting the inescapability of such plural nouns.

Zuckerman's focus on labeling points to one powerful way that communities function to restrict the individual—a subject of *Goodbye, Columbus* as well. Living within a community—living in society—involves being subject to claims from that community, and escaping from one community will only lead you into yet another. One version of the American dream, Lewis's mythic figure of the Adamic individual, seems embodied by all three protagonists in Roth's trilogy, but even more than the Swede and Ira, it almost exactly describes the ideal to which Coleman Silk aspires:

> an individual emancipated from history, happily bereft of ancestry, untouched and undefiled by the usual inheritances of family and race; an individual standing alone, self-reliant and self-propelling, ready to confront whatever awaited him with the aid of his own unique and inherent resources. (Lewis 5)

But from Zuckerman's perspective, no individual can be "emancipated from history," nor from ancestry, nor from society. In Zuckerman's imagining of Coleman's story (as well as the stories of the Swede and Ira), this particularly American tragedy follows from the pursuit of this impossible ideal. To live outside of history, to be without parents, children, colleagues—to be without entanglement with *other people*—is a pure distillation of the oft-represented American dream of innocence and individuality, and, in Zuckerman's estimation, it is a dream of not living in the world at all. Being in the world in any real way involves membership in at least some communities, and therefore necessitates subjection to the claims of those communities.

I Married a Communist: "the Ur of we"

When Zuckerman narrates Coleman's initial resistance to the claims of his racial identity and introduces *The Human Stain*'s central trope for belonging to a community, he tellingly reminds us of the first community we are born into, the community of our immediate family. In Coleman's exasperated tones, the family is figured as the first in a series of plural pronouns that imposes its demands on the individual: "You finally leave home, the Ur of we, and you find *another* we? Another place that's just like that, the *substitute* for that?" (*HS* 108). In *I Married a Communist*, the book that immediately precedes *The Human Stain*, the conflict between self-determination and social determination is explicitly framed in these terms, suggesting that the individual's susceptibility to the claims of pernicious social forces is directly connected to the individual's early experience in the nuclear family. Ira Ringold, the emotionally volatile former ditch digger who makes himself into a famous radio star in public and a steam-rolling activist for socialism in private, would seem to be, following the pattern of the trilogy, the book's tragic figure, and thus the individual whose attempts at self-determination are thwarted by forces beyond his control. And in some ways, he is, sharing with Coleman and the Swede "a life and career that rises on an edifice whose foundations are then undermined by the exposure of its faulty materials" (Brauner, *Philip Roth* 157). Debra Shostak highlights Ira's self-transformative urge, his continual attempts to remake himself—and to remake everyone around him in his image—reminding us that, when Zuckerman first meets Ira, he is not one man, but three: Abraham Lincoln, whom he impersonates to great effect on stage; Iron Rinn, his incarnation on the airwaves as an American model of patriotism and self-reliance; and Ira Ringold, "the redeemed roughneck from Newark's first ward" (Shostak 151; *IMAC* 23). But perhaps because so much of Ira's created identity derives directly from his mentor, the austere and demanding Communist Johnny O'Day, another American in a shack in the woods, because, as Mark Shechner points out, "Ira is the most unreflective of all Roth's unreflective characters," the individual whose negotiation of the claims of self and society is most illuminated in the novel is not Ira, but Nathan Zuckerman himself (*Up Society's Ass* 176). Conceiving of the battle to establish selfhood as an engagement with a series of allegiances, a series of substitutes for the original allegiance to family, Zuckerman eventually sees Ira as an illuminating contrast to his own path through the world.

It is Nathan Zuckerman's unexpected reunion with Ira's brother Murray, Nathan's high school English teacher, that sets in motion the narrative of *I Married a Communist*. Murray, now 90 years old, comes to Nathan's isolated cabin in the mountains for six consecutive nights, telling Nathan all the latter doesn't know about Ira's rise and fall. Interspersed with Murray's narrative are Zuckerman's own memories of his experiences with Ira, who was one of Zuckerman's first mentors. Mentors—especially Zuckerman's—fill the book. Both Murray, who first teaches Zuckerman that "Cri-ti-cal think-ing [. . .] is the ultimate subversion," and Ira, in whom "the America that was my inheritance manifested itself," help to shape Zuckerman's nascent character as he comes of age (*IMAC* 2, 189). "The Ringolds were the one-two punch promising to initiate me into the big show, into my beginning to understand what it takes to be a man on the larger scale" (*IMAC* 32). It is surely significant that this "one-two punch" takes the form of two figures who seem to represent the warring sides of the literary debates of the 1950s: high modernism and proletarian naturalism. Other mentors that Zuckerman tries out include Thomas Paine and the patriotic historical writers Norman Corwin and Howard Fast.[12] The combination of influences from the Ringolds and these three writers leads the budding novelist to write highly derivative radio plays that pay tribute to the American common man, plays that are, in turn, condemned for their simple-mindedness and political intent by another of Zuckerman's mentors, his college English instructor Leo Glucksman. It is Leo who, echoing Murray, tells Zuckerman, "You want to rebel against society? I'll tell you how to do it—write *well*" (*IMAC* 218). And, for a brief period, Zuckerman considers making himself a disciple to Ira's monopolizing mentor, Johnny O'Day, whose commitment to the socialist cause is so total as to blot out all other of life's concerns.[13]

The mentor-disciple relationship, and the very concept of swearing allegiance to someone else, is central to the novel, as is hinted at the first time Zuckerman meets Ira. Ira picks up Nathan's copy of Howard Fast's *Citizen Tom Paine* and quotes a passage in which Paine discusses George III: "I should suffer the misery of devils, were I to make a whore of my soul by swearing allegiance to one whose character is that of a sottish, stupid, stubborn, worthless, brutish man" (*IMAC* 27). Nathan, who had already written down and memorized the passage, admits that he particularly likes the phrase "a whore of my soul." The question of to whom allegiance should be sworn, the dangers of submitting yourself to the wrong master, is one that hangs over the novel, providing the terms for the book's dramatization of the conflict between self-determination and social determination. Zuckerman, like Augie March, is "[a]lways making [himself] eminently adoptable," and is initiated into becoming an American man through these educational transactions with his mentors (*IMAC* 106). Later in life, of course, as narrated in *The Ghost Writer*, E. I. Lonoff would become another of Zuckerman's mentors, the natural successor to Leo Glucksman, who, Lonoff-like, tells Zuckerman that "[y]ou must achieve *mastery* over your idealism, over your virtue as well as over your vice, aesthetic mastery over every-thing that drives you to write in the first place" (*IMAC* 219). In *I Married a Communist*, the role that Zuckerman's mentors play in making him into an American also calls to mind the Swede, who, as Zuckerman recounts in *American Pastoral*, is "the boy we were all going to follow into America, our point man into the next immersion," and thus a sort of wished-for mentor for the young Zuckerman (*AP* 89). In contrast to Zuckerman's mentor-promiscuity, Ira has only O'Day, who becomes his one and only mentor, telling Ira what to read, giving him 20 "Concrete Suggestions" for the writing of polemics, and telling him everything he needs to know about the socialist cause (*IMAC* 36). Ira's tragedy, Zuckerman eventually suggests, stems from his thralldom to a single mentor, the total control that he unthinkingly cedes to O'Day, instead of cycling through a number of such instructors, as Zuckerman does.

When Ira invites the young Zuckerman to spend a week with him out at his isolated shack in the New Jersey hills, Zuckerman's father insists upon meeting the radio actor before granting his permission. This permission is given after Ira reassures Dr. Zuckerman that he is not a Communist (he is lying) and that he is no threat to his son. At first the incident seems a great relief to Nathan, ecstatic that he is allowed to go. But soon he sees a "wound inflicted upon my father's face," and understands implicitly "the sense of betrayal that comes of trying to find a surrogate father even though you love your own" (*IMAC* 105, 106). After all that his father had done for him, Zuckerman is now "running off with another man" (*IMAC* 106). The exchange, one father figure for another, echoing Coleman Silk's comprehension of the black community at Howard as a substitute for his family, points to Zuckerman's eventual realization of Ira's shortcomings. A line is drawn between Nathan and Ira as contrasting figures on the spectrum that spans between self-determination and social determination. The week Zuckerman spends at Ira's shack is wonderful; Ira entrances his young disciple with tales of his youthful adventures as a rugged American roaming all over the country. But when Zuckerman returns the following summer for another week, Ira seems a different version of himself: paranoid and impotent with rage, he repeats over and over again his litany of warnings about America's foregone path to fascism. Zuckerman suddenly realizes that he is "savagely bored" by Ira and likewise feels "so much smarter than he" (*IMAC* 216).

He finally comes to understand what Ira's vividness and grandeur obscured: that Ira's early orphaning—his mother died when he was a child and his father was as good as absent, leading him to leave home at 15—has made him into, in Debra Shostak's words, "a giant suffering from stunted growth" (255). The betrayal that Nathan feels upon implicitly choosing Ira over his father points to the reason for the former's deformation:

> If you're orphaned as early as Ira was, you fall into the situation that all men must fall into but much, much sooner, which is tricky, because you may either get no education at all or be oversusceptible to enthusiasms and beliefs and ripe for indoctrination. (*IMAC* 216)

The situation that all men must fall into, it seems, is being forced to make connections in the world after you leave the original web of connections. This is the bruising entry into the world that all three of the would-be self-determining protagonists of the trilogy must negotiate. Because Ira never had the security that comes with the original family community, he is "an easy mark for the utopian vision" (*IMAC* 217). Utterly on his own, he was free "to connect with whatever he wanted but also left [. . .] unmoored enough to give himself to something almost right off the bat, to give himself totally and forever" (*IMAC* 216). This is the fatal mistake, in Zuckerman's telling. To give yourself "totally and forever" to a single person, idea or ideal, is to surrender any possibility for even partial self-determination.

Zuckerman comes to this realization as someone healthily socialized by a stable family home. Having never been abandoned as a child, never completely on his own, he was able to grow up normally, to be nurtured into his adolescence and then be "let go, ready to be a man, ready, that is, to choose allegiances and affiliations, the parents of your adulthood, the chosen parents whom [. . .] you either love or don't, as suits you" (*IMAC* 217). Zuckerman's ideal of manhood, as put forth here, is an active attempt at partial self-determination in a world in which totally escaping the forces of social determination is impossible—unless your life is to resemble Johnny O'Day's. It is an active ideal, the individual attempting to set his own path after passively accepting the one given to him by his parents. For, although Zuckerman conceives of these mentors and allegiances as substitute parents, they can, crucially, be picked up and put down at will. They are

> personalities to contend with, mentors who embodied or espoused powerful ideas and who first taught me to navigate the world and its claims, the adopted

parents who also, each in his turn, had to be cast off along with their legacy, had to disappear, thus making way for the orphanhood that is total, which is manhood. When you're out there in this thing all alone. (*IMAC* 217)

This is as close to a credo for Zuckerman's brand of self-making as you're likely to find in Roth's fiction: a willed engagement with a series of allegiances, a continued attention to the active work that is "navigat[ing] the world and its claims," ever mindful of the responsibilities of selfhood that ultimately cannot be evaded.

The Shack in the Woods

In his first appearance in Roth's fiction, in *The Ghost Writer*, Nathan Zuckerman flees the protection offered by his father—to whom he shouts, "I am on my own!"—only, immediately, "to submit myself for candidacy as nothing less than E. I. Lonoff's spiritual son" (*GW* 78, 7). Zuckerman's sustained and particular pursuit of self-determination as outlined in *I Married a Communist*, his recruitment of "all those extra fathers like a pretty girl gets beaux," only to abandon each father as it suits him, should come as no surprise to readers who know his history (*IMAC* 106). His refusal of the sort of abiding allegiance that Ira adopts has allowed him to set his own path, for better or worse, since the youthful days documented in *The Ghost Writer*. But his admission that he understands manhood as being "out there in this thing all alone" points to the dangers of such a rigorous promiscuity. At the end of the title novella of *Goodbye, Columbus*, Roth leaves Neil Klugman unsure of what path to follow, having abandoned both the provincial world of Jewish Newark embodied by his Aunt Gladys and the vividly materialistic new world of the Jewish suburbs embodied by Brenda Patimkin. Roth does not tell us where Neil goes from this solitary position, instead ending the novella with the ambiguous image of Neil gazing at the window of the Harvard library, looking both inward (at his reflection) and outward (through the window to the books inside). It is left to the reader to decide whether Neil is free and therefore ascendant, or rudderless and alone. Having delineated a similar path for Zuckerman, here Roth has Murray Ringold comment on the result.

Zuckerman's two-room cabin in the Berkshires—where he's written the three books of the trilogy—is his retreat from the world, the physical representation of his realization that he "[doesn't] want a story any longer. I've had my story" (*IMAC* 71). This retreat from the narratives of the self directly leads to his undertaking to tell the stories of the Swede, Ira Ringold, and Coleman Silk, but it also seems a continuation of the exhaustion with the self detailed in *Zuckerman Bound*, a different sort of solution than the exploration of the multifarious narratives of the self offered up in *The Counterlife*. The cabin is

[t]he place where you disrobe, molt it all, the uniforms you've worn and the costumes you've gotten into, where you shed your batteredness and your resentment, your appeasement of the world and your defiance of the world, your manipulation of the world and its manhandling of you. (*IMAC* 72)

What particularly Zuckerman is fleeing from is never made clear, but his utter seclusion is apparent to his old teacher. And after six nights of telling Ira's story, Murray is not sure the lessons to be learned from Ira's unwavering devotion to a doomed cause have sunk in for his pupil. As the two men ready themselves to say goodbye (for the last time, it turns out, for Murray dies two months later), Murray imparts a warning to Zuckerman: "Beware the utopia of isolation. Beware the utopia of the shack in the woods, the oasis defense against rage and grief. An impregnable solitude" (*IMAC* 315). What Murray recognizes is that Zuckerman's isolation, ostensibly a retreat from the expenditure of energy that self-making in the world requires, is just another utopian attempt at total self-determination. He recognizes that Zuckerman's cabin is an "upgraded replica" of Ira's shack in the woods, his "beloved retreat," the symbol of Ira's utterly unrealistic vision of himself as a morally pure dissenter from the evils of capitalism (*IMAC* 71).[14] Earlier, Zuckerman narrates his visit to Johnny O'Day's austere room, "the spiritual essence of Ira's shack" (*IMAC* 228). "What O'Day's room represented was discipline, that discipline that says however many desires I have, I can circumscribe myself down to this one room" (*IMAC* 227). Seemingly, Zuckerman has accomplished this difficult task, blocking out all of his desires to concentrate all of his energies on his writing. His existence is reminiscent of another secluded Berkshire figure from his past, E. I. Lonoff, whose own self-imposed asceticism makes its impact on Zuckerman in *The Ghost Writer*: "Purity. Serenity. Simplicity. Seclusion. All one's concentration and flamboyance and originality reserved for the grueling, exalted, transcendent calling. I looked around and I thought, This is how I will live" (*GW* 4). Now living like Lonoff, like O'Day, like Ira, Zuckerman finds that, having realized that Ira's mistake was to have given himself "totally and forever," he has himself given himself over to a singular version of the world. The implicit conclusion is that although Zuckerman has seemingly succeeded in his self-determination, in cutting himself off from all claims other than his own (unlike Coleman and the Swede, who discover that their self-determining projects are impossible), he is living a life that is no life at all.

I have suggested that the final image of "Goodbye, Columbus" offers up the community of literature as a refuge for those individuals, like Neil Klugman, who cannot reconcile the claims of unsatisfactory communities with their own desires for self-determination. No such balm is offered to the characters in the "American Trilogy." As we will see, the Swede, in *American Pastoral*, is a man without literature—he defines himself through sporting triumph and hard work—and it seems unlikely that high culture would save him from the cataclysm provoked by his daughter. Coleman Silk, of course, is a classics professor, a man devoted to the culture and literature of the ancient Greeks and Romans; this seems to offer him no protection against "the antagonism that *is* the world" (*HS* 315–16). As for Zuckerman, *The Human Stain* continues on from the end of *I Married a Communist* in suggesting that his willed solitude—a project specifically conceived as a retreat from life into a world of only reading and writing books—is untenable. His realization is triggered by the fact that he "had, without figuring or planning on it, fallen into a serious friendship with Coleman Silk" (*HS* 43). Having found that "the secret" to maintaining his solitude was "to find sustenance in *people* like Hawthorne, in the wisdom of the brilliant deceased," Zuckerman now finds that the entrance of Coleman Silk, with Silk's own brand of brilliance, into his life has made him "lonely [. . .] For life. The entanglement with life" (*HS* 44). Perhaps Murray Ringold's criticisms at the end of *I Married a Communist* are still ringing in his ears, or perhaps he's learned a lesson from the Swede, Ira, and Coleman about the dangers of utopian thinking, or perhaps, as is suggested at the end of *The Human Stain*, he simply fears for his life—Faunia Farley's ex-husband Les is still alive, and Zuckerman's book imagines that it is Farley who killed Coleman and Faunia—but the trilogy ends with Zuckerman resigned to the fact that "my five years alone in my house here were over" (*HS* 360).

American Pastoral: Living the Dream

As Brian McDonald points out, the chapter headings of *American Pastoral*— "Paradise Remembered," "The Fall" and "Paradise Lost"—immediately recall the Adamic narrative (28). And indeed Seymour Levov, the novel's protagonist, seems, almost as much as Coleman Silk, to be the embodiment of the "individual emancipated from history, happily bereft of ancestry, untouched and undefiled by the usual inheritances of family and race" (Lewis 5). Unlike Coleman, Levov has no need to radically re-author himself to achieve this ideal of self-determination. As Zuckerman narrates Levov's presence as the neighborhood celebrity of his childhood memories, he appears as a sui generis Adam, born with the looks, the confidence and the grace to appear untouched by all outside contingency. He acquires the nickname "the Swede" due to his strangely un-Jewish looks in a predominantly Jewish neighborhood, the "steep-jawed insentient Viking mask of this blue-eyed blond born into our tribe" setting him apart from his more darkly complexioned peers (*AP* 3). More than seeming to come from Sweden, the Swede seems totally alien and superior to everyone around him, "if not divine, a distinguished cut above the more primordial humanity of just about everybody else" (*AP* 5). His easy virtuosity in three sports, the way he seems to dominate every contest without even trying, becomes a microcosm of the ease with which he negotiates all of the world's claims, coasting through life on nothing more than an extraordinary "talent for 'being himself.' "

To Zuckerman, the Swede as an adolescent was "someone for whom there were no obstacles, who appeared never to have to struggle to clear a space for himself" (*AP* 19). This portrait of effortless self-determination, of an individual who does not even have to fight off the hindrances of society, history, or ancestry, is developed by Zuckerman's reconstruction of the Swede's ascent into untroubled manhood. Happily taking the reins at his father's glove factory, marrying Dawn Dwyer, a gentile candidate for Miss America, and moving out of Newark to the American pastoral setting par excellence, rural Old Rimrock, New Jersey, the Swede is "the man not set up for tragedy" (*AP* 86). Throughout this uninterrupted ascendancy, the Swede carries his nickname "like an invisible passport, all the while wandering deeper and deeper into an American's life, forthrightly evolving into a large, smooth, optimistic American" (*AP* 207–8). The "invisible passport" he carries is not merely his community's thralldom to his goyish looks or extraordinary prowess in sporting events—what the Swede carries is his unthinking talent for self-determination: his inherent ability to be unaffected—undeterred, undeformed—by the social conditions around him. He is a man with "this ability to imagine himself completely" and then miraculously—but easily—live as he imagines (*AP* 190–1).

Following the design of all three books in the trilogy, this picture of the easily achieved pastoral of self-determination is, as Zuckerman's description of the Swede as "the man not set up for tragedy" suggests, ripe for destruction at the hands of the exigencies of American reality. The Swede's pastoral, as David Brauner asserts, is "a mythical realm removed from—indeed specifically conceived as an escape from—the historical realities of American life" (*Philip Roth* 169). The historical reality that is most explicitly evaded, at least as recounted in the years before his daughter plants her bomb, is the reality of ethnicity, the inherited condition that outlasts even the attachment to parents. The American ideal that the Swede so effortlessly pursues—and seemingly achieves—is explicitly postethnic, as embodied for the Swede by the rural splendor of Old Rimrock. In trading in the Jewish Newark neighborhood of Weequahic—and bypassing his father's preference, the comfortable new suburb of South Orange—for Old Rimrock, the Swede transforms the town and the 100-year-old house in which he lives with his wife Dawn—herself fleeing her provincial Irish-American background—into a synecdoche for America itself, an America without ethnic identity. The Swede's project, in his attempt to leave the old neighborhood behind, surpasses even that of the Patimkins in *Goodbye, Columbus.* "Out in Old Rimrock, all of America lay at their door. That was an idea he loved. Jewish resentment, Irish resentment—the hell with it" (*AP* 310).[15] He becomes a "frontiersman," going beyond his father's trajectory, unconstricted by the claims of either ethnic belonging and ethnic discrimination—the tyranny of the "we"—to a new world in which "[n]obody dominates anybody anymore [. . .] This is a new generation and there is no need for that resentment stuff from anybody, them *or* us" (*AP* 310, 311). Ecstatically exclaiming to his wife, "Dawnie, we're free!" the Swede has seemingly fulfilled the American dream, discovering a paradise of absolute individual freedom, which is only as it should be: "Isn't that what this country's all about? I want to be where I want to be and I don't want to be where I don't want to be. That's what being an American is—isn't it?" (*AP* 308, 315). Of course, prefiguring the stories told in *I Married a Communist* and *The Human Stain*, this pastoral is soon destroyed, as the Swede's ingenuous question is unambiguously answered in the negative by his adolescent daughter Merry.

Merry Levov and the Uncontrollable

For Merry Levov, being an American is not about escape but about engagement, about being caught up in American history. Unlike her father, who seems to control his destiny without any effort at all, Merry is a passive object for conditions and forces outside of her control. Of her persistent and ineradicable stuttering, which the Levovs expend all of their resources of attention and money trying to remedy, Zuckerman notes that "[s]he was simply in the hands of something she could not get out of," a situation that, before his daughter's bomb, the Swede never finds himself in (*AP* 99). Never even noticing the obstacles that others have to negotiate in the establishment of selfhood, the Swede is wholly unprepared for the ease with which his daughter is taken from him. Foreshadowing Zuckerman's ideal of self-determination as outlined in *I Married a Communist*, Merry works her way through a series of allegiances throughout her childhood: a "Catholic phase," picked up from her maternal grandmother, is replaced by the 4-H Club, which in turn falls to astronomy and then Audrey Hepburn (*AP* 93). "She was a perfectionist who did things passionately, lived intensely in the new interest, and then the passion was suddenly spent and everything, including the passion, got thrown into a box and she moved on" (*AP* 94).[16] Although this series of fascinations initially seems to follow Zuckerman's pattern of allying himself with a substitute father, only to run off with another as it suits him, it turns out that Merry more closely resembles Ira.

Like Ira, she is "ripe for indoctrination," "an easy mark for the utopian vision." For the next passionate subject she is seized by, the replacement for the harmless fantasy of emulating Audrey Hepburn, is the "terrifyingly pure" dogma of the antiwar movement, soon leading her to the radical realm of domestic terrorism (*AP* 254). It is from this allegiance that she will not return, for all intents and purposes it is the allegiance to which she, like Ira, "give[s] [her]self totally and forever," for the bomb that she leaves outside of the local post office explodes and kills an innocent man dropping off his mail. It explodes, as well, the perfect life that the Swede had so effortlessly inhabited. To continue the analogy between Merry and Ira, both unprepared to fend off an allegiance that will deform or destroy their lives, is to be led to the question of why, if Merry was not an orphan, not "unmoored" like Ira, but instead the child of two seemingly faultless, loving parents, why does this happen? This question, actually a torrent of questions all probing the same mystifying problem, haunts the Swede for the rest of his life. "Once the inexplicable had begun, the torment of self-examination never ended. However lame the answers, he never ran out of questions, he who had nothing of consequence really to ask himself" (*AP* 92). For Brian McDonald, the question that hangs over the book centers on the connection between the Swede's pastoral innocence, his life set apart from the conditions of society, and his daughter's susceptibility to the tidal wave of history that carries her away from her father. "The issue which lies at the heart of *American Pastoral* is not the illusory nature of the Swede's innocence [. . .] but rather determining what role, if any at all, the Swede's innocence plays in his own tragedy" (37). For Zuckerman's part, a definitive answer to this question is never reached, as the book's final line, the last of the book's multitude of unanswered questions, asks, "What on earth is less reprehensible than the life of the Levovs?" (*AP* 423).

Merry's predisposition to the utopian vision of antiwar terrorism, although it is the engine of the plot, is not the story of *American Pastoral*. This is the Swede's story, as imagined by Nathan Zuckerman. Zuckerman "lift[s] the Swede up onto the stage" to try to understand "[t]he brutality of the destruction of this indestructible man" (*AP* 88, 83). The Swede's story, as Zuckerman tells it, is, like Coleman Silk's story, the story of a failed project of self-determination. The Swede "was fully charged up with purpose long, long before anyone else he knew, with a grown man's aims and ambitions, someone who excitedly foresaw, in perfect detail, the outcome of his story" (*AP* 192). And his greatest pleasure in life derives from the fulfillment of that purpose, the happy and wholly certain authorship of his own story. Authoring his daughter, however, is another matter entirely. As Johnny O'Day suggests in *I Married a Communist*, children introduce the uncontrollability of other people into the individual's immediate narrative, thus endangering the self-making project. Merry enacts upon the Swede's life what Coleman always fears his own children will do to his: if any of his children are born with signs of his (and thus their) African-American heritage, his self-determining project will be undone. He is saved from that fate, saved from his children dragging him back into the claims of historical conditions, but the Swede is not so lucky. It is his inability to author his daughter's narrative—his inability to grant her the same freedom from the forces of social determination that he enjoyed—that is his downfall. No longer Seymour, or the Swede, or even the husband of Miss New Jersey, he is permanently transformed into the father of the Rimrock bomber, his free and easy flight above the fray brought down with terrible violence.

In Zuckerman's long imagining of a dinner party held at the Levovs' house, that brings *American Pastoral* to a close, the table's conversation settles on the subject of the direction American culture had followed since the 1960s (the scene takes place in 1973). The Swede's father, a lifelong advocate of the value of hard work and moral rectitude, is predictably up in arms over the presumed relaxing of cultural norms: the rising divorce rate, *Deep Throat*, and the Newark riots all come in for his condemnation. What is unspoken, but firmly on the minds of both the Swede and the reader, is Merry Levov's place in this narrative of cultural decline. Mr. Levov declares that "[y]ou don't have to revere your family, you don't have to revere your country, you don't have to revere where you live, but you have to know you *have* them, you have to know you are *part* of them" (*AP* 365). Brian McDonald rightly points out that Mr. Levov is protesting against the apparent lack of limits in progressive politics and culture, pointing to the selfishness inherent in the radical movement Merry is caught up in: "a doctrine of individualism that seems to have absolutely no regard for the values which define his way of life, for his sense of decency, responsibility, patriotism, and respect for hard work" (35). Picking up on the sentiment expressed in Mr. Levov's words, there were some critics for whom *American Pastoral* was a political shift for Roth, a sort of mea culpa for the apparent allegiance to the permissive spirit of the new left expressed in *Portnoy's Complaint*.[17] But just as it is dangerous to see Alex Portnoy's *complaint* about the way he lives his life as a sign of support for any ascendant strain of the culture, I'd hesitate before assuming that Mr. Levov speaks for Philip Roth. The passage quoted above resonates as a statement about the mystifying destruction that Merry introduces to her seemingly unassailable home, but also, I think, as a warning—imparted too late—from a father to a son. The Swede, although he does revere his family and his country, seems to be caught unaware that he is a part of the dynamic country in which he lives, unaware that to live in America is to be subject to American history, to the inescapable conditions of living in American society. Like Coleman, the Swede seemingly escapes the condition of social determination, only to be blindsided by the forces of another in an endless series of tyrannical "we"s.

* * *

The three novels of the "American Trilogy" are, in this reading, not a break from Roth's earlier work, but a continuation, a deeper investigation of issues that have preoccupied him from the very start of his career. The conflict that springs up between the American ideals of innocence and individualism and the decidedly human need for community is one that Roth has explored throughout his career, and the similarities between the concerns of *Goodbye, Columbus* and those of these later works should make us skeptical of readings that posit late Roth as a changed man, a sort of late convert to the significant themes of the great novelists. And yet, Roth—and his reception—has certainly changed in the nearly 40 years between the publication of his debut and that of *American Pastoral*. Although the trilogy shares similar concerns with *Goodbye, Columbus*, the scope of the later works and their foregrounded focus on American history have worked to brand Roth yet again, this time as a grand old man of American letters. No longer branded as a purely Jewish writer, or "the Jew who masturbates with a piece of liver," Philip Roth is now introduced in article after article in the mainstream media as "America's greatest living writer."[18] Seemingly confirming this new standing, in 2005, Roth became just the third living author (after Eudora Welty and Saul Bellow) to have his entire oeuvre published in a "definitive edition" by the Library of America (the last of eight volumes is scheduled to be published in 2013). Although this new sense of Roth in the public imagination certainly fits into the narrative described above, in which the solipsistic, self-obsessed writer finally looks out at the world around him, it is also certain that the books of the "American Trilogy" themselves helped to create this new brand.

For much of his career, Roth has insisted that he is an American writer rather than a Jewish-American one; he claimed in a 1981 interview that "what the heart is to the cardiologist, the coal to the miner, the kitchen sink to the plumber, America is to me" (*Reading Myself and Others* 110). And yet, this formulation's implication—that Roth takes America as the subject of his fiction—was not truly confirmed until the "American Trilogy." Certainly, most of Roth's novels could have only taken place in America, and they tell us much about the nation over the past 50 years. But it is only beginning with *American Pastoral* that it can be said that Roth has taken America *as a subject*, with the trilogy's conceptual plan of tying the three protagonists to three eras of recent American history foregrounding a concern with the state of the nation. From the title of the first book (*American Pastoral*) to the last word of *The Human Stain* ("America"), the trilogy not only grounds its action in familiar eras of American history, it makes America—as place, as concept, as ideal—into a contested subject to be debated by nearly every significant character. In Zuckerman's imagining, the Swede "loved America. Loved being an *American*" (*AP* 206). But for his daughter, who "initiat[es] the Swede into the displacement of another America entirely," "being an American was loathing America" (*AP* 86, 213). In *I Married a Communist*, the adolescent excitement that Nathan feels when he first spends time with Ira and Murray Ringold stems from the sense that they are initiating him into America: "You flood into America and America floods into you" (*IMAC* 39). Murray is particularly alert to the American temptation of casting off your roots and becoming someone else: "You're an American who doesn't want to be your parents' child? Fine. [. . .] You've come to the right country" (*IMAC* 157). And, for the young Zuckerman, Ira seems to represent America itself: "I had never before known anyone whose life was so intimately circumscribed by so much American history, who was personally familiar with so much American geography, who had confronted, face to face, so much American lowlife" (*IMAC* 189). In *The Human Stain*, Coleman's downfall is explicitly paralleled with the political machinations of the summer of 1998, and the community that so viciously seizes upon his slip is indulging in "America's oldest communal passion [. . .] the ecstasy of sanctimony" (*HS* 2). For Zuckerman, Coleman's life itself dramatizes a narrative central to the American identity: "To become a new being. To bifurcate. The drama that underlies America's story, the high drama that is upping and leaving—and the energy and cruelty that rapturous drive demands" (*HS* 342). In the trilogy, then, America ceases to be merely a setting, but emerges as a central fictional subject for Roth to probe.

In *Goodbye, Columbus,* by contrast, the word "America"—so often debated and incorporated into grand statements by the characters of the trilogy—scarcely appears. Although Roth's debut, like the trilogy, is centrally concerned with the interaction between individuals and their communities—with the conflict between self-determination and social determination—it seems that these concerns are not examined outside of the context of the particular Jewish-American community that Roth grew up in. Roth has stated that he decided to go away to Bucknell University in central Pennsylvania as an undergraduate because "I wanted to find out what the rest of 'America' was like. America in quotes—because it was still almost as much of an idea in my mind as it had been in Franz Kafka's" (*Reading Myself and Others* 105). The "American Trilogy" sees the quotes well and truly falling away from Roth's vision of America, as he engages with America's myths of itself directly, daring to address unapologetically three wildly contested eras of American history. In doing so, he demonstrates that the concerns that preoccupied him in investigating his own community are just as vital and relevant when investigated in the context of the nation at large.

Conclusion

(There's no) Remaking Reality

The burden isn't either/or, consciously choosing from possibilities equally difficult and regrettable—it's and/and/and/and/and as well. Life is and: the accidental and the immutable, the elusive and the graspable, the bizarre and the predictable, the actual and the potential, all the multiplying realities, entangled, overlapping, colliding, conjoined—plus the multiplying illusions! This times this times this times this . . .

The Counterlife

Everyman, Roth's novel of 2006, opens with what is merely the first of a number of funerals the book will depict. In the book's chronology this is, in fact, the final funeral, as it is with the burial of the novel's unnamed protagonist that Roth begins his narration of the man's life. The protagonist's adult daughter Nancy, "like a ten-year-old overwhelmed," after delivering a brief eulogy, must face the difficult duty of throwing dirt onto her father's coffin:

Turning toward the coffin, she picked up a clod of dirt and, before dropping it onto the lid, said lightly, with the air still of a bewildered young girl, "Well, this is how it turns out. There's nothing more we can do, Dad." Then she remembered his own stoical maxim from decades back and began to cry. "There's no remaking reality," she told him. "Just take it as it comes. Hold your ground and take it as it comes." (*E* 4–5)

The protagonist's "stoical maxim" was coined as an attempt to console Nancy after his divorce from her mother: "That was the truth and the best he could do" (*E* 79). She refigures it here to refer to an acceptance of death as a part of life, an acceptance that however unfathomable and intolerable the fact of death is, "there's nothing [. . .] we can do," there is no escape from this universal fate. It's advice given from a daughter to her dead father, ostensibly admitting that there's nothing she can do to bring him back, nothing that he can do to "remake reality" and live another day. But Nancy is remembering her father's words to her and thus also advising herself that she has no choice but to take part in "our species' least favorite activity" (*E* 15). The act of throwing, or shoveling, dirt onto a grave is foregrounded again later on in the book, at the funeral of the protagonist's father, in which, as according to traditional Jewish rites, the grave is filled by the mourners. Still recovering from recent quintuple bypass surgery and too weak to take part in the heavy labor, the protagonist can only watch as his brother, sons, and nephews fill the grave:

> His father was going to lie not only in the coffin but under the weight of that dirt, and all at once he saw his father's mouth as if there was no coffin, as if the dirt they were throwing into the grave was being deposited straight down on him, filling up his mouth, blinding his eyes, clogging his nostrils, and closing off his ears. (*E* 60)

For the protagonist, watching the grave fill up with dirt is "like a second death, one no less awful than the first," and afterwards he tells his ex-wife, "[n]ow I know what it means to be buried. I didn't till today" (*E* 61).

Knowing what it means to be buried, and accepting that this fate awaits us all—that "there's no remaking reality"—is an imperative that seems to drive this brief and bleak book, which begins with the protagonist's funeral, moves backward through his life through the narration of a series of illnesses, and then forward again to his death. Roth's insistence on including such detailed descriptions of the physical reality of burial, as well as a scene in which a gravedigger painstakingly explains to the protagonist the ins and outs of digging a grave, seems to continue the stripping away of illusions in the face of death, emphasizing the fact that a dead body is buried in a coffin under six feet of dirt and will remain there forever. Roth's protagonist, as is indicated by his advice to his daughter, seems to uphold such realism in the face of death; we are told that he has no use for the consolations of religion and is determined to see death as nothing more than oblivion: "No hocus-pocus about death and God or obsolete fantasies of heaven for him. There was only our bodies, born to live and die on terms decided by the bodies that had lived and died before us" (*E* 51). And yet, he cannot help but to rebel against this bleak outcome. Late in life, besieged by heart problems that have required surgery after surgery, keeping the presence of death close at hand, he finds himself uncontrollably jealous and spiteful over his brother Howie's good health. Although "he was not without a civilized person's tolerant understanding of the puzzle of inequality and misfortune," he discovers in himself "the spiteful desire for his brother to lose his health," almost believing "that Howie's good health was responsible for his own compromised health" (*E* 100–1). He cannot keep himself from desperately wanting, and therefore "trying on," another fate. And despite his apparently clear-eyed resignation to the diminution of his health and potency, he can't subdue "his longing for the last great outburst of everything," submitting to the "folly" of pursuing a young and beautiful girl he sees jogging (*E* 134). Holding your ground and taking reality as it comes, it seems, is no easy matter.

Looked at from one angle, "there's no remaking reality" might be seen as an underlying maxim for Roth's whole career. As I've detailed in this book, his fiction has been defined by a refusal to commit himself to any one idea or position without taking up its opposite in turn. There is a sense in which this approach entails a refusal to impose a restrictive and reductive vision upon a reliably complex and unknowable world. *Everyman*'s unnamed protagonist echoes Uncle Asher, a character from Roth's early novel *Letting Go*, who councils Gabe Wallach to "let it flow" and vows to "take the shape the world gives me" (83). Ross Posnock seizes upon Asher's statements as central to Roth's sensibility, echoing Emerson's concept of abandonment, a way of being that admits that "[l]ife seems immune to our designs, and all we can count on is the unaccountable" (Posnock 190, 212–13). In this reading, Roth's interrogation of the communities in *Goodbye, Columbus* works to accurately reflect "our sense of reality," in Saul Bellow's phrase, as opposed to Jewish critics who would paint a different picture for the sake of "public relations" ("Swamp" 79). Peter Tarnopol's ultimate realization that he is "this me being me and none other!" seems, after so many attempts to rewrite the story of his self, to reflect a resignation to a reality that he is powerless to make over, as does the final image of Zuckerman in *The Anatomy Lesson*, wandering around a hospital, "as though he still believed that he could unchain himself from a future as a man apart and escape the corpus that was his" (*MLM* 330, *AL* 505). The books of Roth's "autobiographical" period can be seen as insisting upon the often messy consequences of the autobiographical move, consistently offering reminders that no writing takes place in a vacuum. And there is a sense in which the novels of the "American Trilogy," in Zuckerman's attempts to "dream" "realistic chronicle[s]," refute naïve and simplistic notions of American innocence and unfettered individualism. It is this Roth for whom the uproar over Bill Clinton's adultery was merely an example that "for the billionth time—the jumble, the mayhem, the mess proved itself more subtle than this one's ideology and that one's morality" (*HS* 3). An awareness—often, an awe—of the ways in which reality consistently frustrates our attempts to get a handle on it has been an element running through Roth's writing throughout his career.

But of course, in another sense, "remaking reality" is precisely the novelist's task. Roth reminds us that "[l]ife, like the novelist, has a powerful transformative urge," and much of his fiction has worked to emphasize the truth of this maxim, exploring the creation and consequences of self-willed realities ("Interview with Philip Roth" 12). Roth's imagining of Franz Kafka alive and teaching Hebrew in 1940s New Jersey and Zuckerman's transformation of Anne Frank from martyred victim of the Holocaust to the "Femme Fatale" of *The Ghost Writer* seem rooted in just such a fascination with remaking reality, as does Roth's imagining of a different historical fate for America under President Charles Lindbergh in *The Plot Against America* (2004). The structure of *My Life as a Man*, with Tarnopol's three versions—fictional and "autobiographical"—of his life's troubles, suggests that the book is most concerned with the protagonist's attempts to reimagine his reality. The presence of psychoanalysis in both *Portnoy's Complaint* and *My Life as a Man* offers Roth a series of fictional possibilities, as Portnoy and Tarnopol work to remake their realities on the analyst's couch. Each chapter of *The Counterlife* offers up a competing version of reality, with each character "writing fictitious versions of [their] lives [. . .] contradictory by mutually entangling stories that, however subtly or grossly falsified, constitute [their] hold on reality" ("Interview with Philip Roth" 11). And surely one of the reasons Zuckerman is attracted to the singular figures of the "American Trilogy" is their seemingly boundless energy for remaking their own realities. Zuckerman's awe at the self-transformative powers of the Swede, Ira, and Coleman is prefigured near the beginning of *American Pastoral*, in a speech he writes, but never gives, for his 45th high school reunion, in which he urges his classmates to "remember the energy" that was endemic to their American era: "the communal determination that we, the children, should escape poverty, ignorance, disease, social injury and intimidation—escape, above all, insignificance. You must not come to nothing! *Make something of yourselves!*" (*AP* 41). Thus Roth posits reality as provisional, subjective, and changeable. Seen this way, Roth's recurrent countermoves, his shifting between alternatives, can be seen as affirming Nabokov's famous dictum that "reality" is "one of the few words which means nothing without quotes," and thus invites challenges, reimaginings, and attempts at gaining a new way of experiencing the world (312).

So where does that leave us? Once again, Roth seems aligned with two opposing positions. Is he the clear-eyed realist, admitting and exposing the folly of attempting to understand reality as anything but unpredictable, immutable and ultimately unknowable? Or is he the playful postmodernist, extolling the power of the subjective in narratives that portray reality as constructed and mutable? It's quite easy to make a case for both of these arguments. It's much more difficult to argue against either, or both. In this book's introduction, I noted the tendency among recent academic critics of Roth's work to attempt to unify his vast career under the rubric of such ambiguous concepts as subjectivity, immaturity, willfulness, and comedy. I realize that my own reading tends similarly to a resistance to pin Roth down. If this is so, I'd argue, it is because Roth has himself resisted pinning himself down throughout his career, consistently running counter to his critics', and indeed his own, understanding of his central concerns and approach. If there is anything uniting all of Roth's writing, it is this restless, oppositional, fluid approach, an approach that resists the imposition of unity. Yet even this statement is difficult to wholly support, as the characters, connections, and threads that are shared by many of Roth's books seem to grant his career a unity attained by few other writers.

Beginning with *The Human Stain*, the front matter of Roth's books, which previously listed all of Roth's publications chronologically, now divides up Roth's prior work into four categories: "Zuckerman Books," "Kepesh Books" (both essentially self-explanatory designations), "Roth books" (including the four "autobiographical" works of the late 1980s and early 1990s) and "Other Books" (a sort of grab bag of everything else, including *Goodbye, Columbus, Portnoy's Complaint* and *My Life as a Man*). It is unclear whether this new organizing principle was Roth's idea or his publisher's, but in its attention to the presentation of a body of work, the move executes the particularly Rothian trick of giving a sense of unity (as if there was a plan all along) while dividing.

It certainly seems in line with a sense of lateness, as if Roth is tidying up his life's work for the ages. Almost as if to affirm the rightness of this categorization, the four works of fiction Roth published after *The Human Stain* cycled through all four categories one by one, each book adding another title to the individual lists. *The Dying Animal* (2001) completes Roth's trilogy about David Kepesh, begun in 1972 with *The Breast* and continued in 1977 with *The Professor of Desire*. *The Plot Against America* (2004), like *Operation Shylock*, is a work of fiction with Philip Roth as the main character and narrator, here as a child. A work of counterfactual history, Roth (the author) imagines what it would be like for Roth (the child) and his family if Charles Lindbergh had won the US presidency and aligned America with the Nazis. *Everyman* is this decade's contribution to "Other Books." And *Exit Ghost* (2007) is Roth's ninth (and apparently final) Zuckerman book, following Roth's sturdiest character as he makes his way out of his Lonovian exile to New York, back into the "Here and Now," and then back out again (41). Having added to each category, and having apparently completed both the Zuckerman and Kepesh sagas, Roth has continued to publish at a dizzying pace, putting out *Indignation* (2008), *The Humbling* (2009) and *Nemesis* (2010), three short novels that, along with *Everyman*, form a quartet of books that may well someday constitute their own category ("Death Books," perhaps). Roth's continued productivity ensures that we can't yet close the book on his career.

Speaking in 1984, Roth reflected:

> It's all one book you write anyway. At night you dream six dreams. But *are* they six dreams? One dream prefigures or anticipates the next, or somehow concludes what hasn't yet even been fully dreamed. Then comes the next dream, the corrective of the dream before—the alternative dream, the antidote dream—enlarging upon it, or laughing at it, or contradicting it, or trying to get the dream *right*. You can go on trying all night long. ("Art of Fiction" 236–7)

His formulation seems an appropriate way to conceive of the strange way his long career has been both unified and divergent. The dreamer's dreams, all the phases of a night's work, are all related—they may even be one long dream—but the way they are related is mysterious, not least to the dreamer. Correctives, alternatives, contradictions, enlargements, antidotes: each dream comments on the dreams that preceded it and lays some sort of groundwork for the dreams that are to come. The dreams continue on indefinitely, pursuing some ultimate end, but never reaching it. It is surely telling that Roth, a longtime student of Freud, conceives of his oeuvre as a series of dreams, for, like Freud's dreams, Roth's books, and his career as a whole, invite endless interpretation, but resist any ultimate, definite, explanation.

Notes

Introduction

[1] John N. McDaniel, in his 1974 monograph, argued that Roth was essentially a humanist, rather than a Jewish, writer. "As a writer who is a Jew, Roth asks for a literary rather than a narrowly religious evaluation of his fiction; as a social realist, he takes as his domain the society that he has seen and known—which includes but is not limited to Jewish life" (34). In his 1978 study, Bernard F. Rodgers Jr. sounds a similar note: "[S]o much of the commentary on [Roth's] fiction has continued to be preoccupied with determining the nature and extent of his relationship to Jewish-American religious and literary traditions that other elements in his work, which are just as important, have been consistently ignored or obscured" (7–8).

[2] Shechner's phrase is a derivation of Louis Smilesburger's justification for his work for the Mossad in Roth's *Operation Shylock*. Imagining what he will say in the event of a Palestinian triumph, Smilesburger "will offer no stirring rhetoric when I am asked by the court to speak my last words but will tell my judges only this: 'I did what I did to you because I did what I did to you.' And if that is not the truth, it's as close as I know how to come to it." (*OS* 351).

[3] My characterizations here—of Shostak's study as positing an inward-looking Roth and of Posnock's positing an outward-looking Roth—should be tempered by a few caveats. Shostak, despite her predominant focus on the problems of subjectivity, does engage with the ways in which Roth has turned outward to include history in his later work, arguing that this period "suggests that subjectivity is not just a narrative construct but also, inextricably, a historical product" (18). Posnock, for all that he shows that Roth is open to a wide variety of outside influences and unfamiliar discourses, tends to overly focus on literary intertextuality, leaving aside Roth's entanglements with Richard Nixon (in *Our Gang* and a number of essays in the 1970s), Prague (in *The Professor of Desire* and *The Prague Orgy*), Israel (in *Portnoy's Complaint*, *The Counterlife* and *Operation Shylock*), and London (in *The Counterlife* and *Deception*), to name a few of Roth's more notable outward turns.

[4] "Informing. There was the charge so many of the correspondents had made, even when they did not want to make it openly to me, or to themselves. I had informed on the Jews. I had told the Gentiles what apparently it would otherwise have been possible to keep secret from them: that the perils of human nature afflict the members of our minority" (Roth, "Writing About Jews" 450).

[5] When asked by Hermione Lee whether he writes with a Roth reader in mind, he answered, "No. I occasionally have an anti-Roth reader in mind. I think, 'How he is going to hate this!' That can be just the encouragement I need" (Roth, "Art of Fiction" 219).

Chapter 1

[1] It is also telling that Roth quotes this statement himself ("Kafka" 288). Mark Shechner points out that Roth uses Kafka, in the 1970s, as his "point of entry" to the historical inheritance of European Jewish culture, allowing him access to a richer, older Jewishness than his upbringing in New Jersey would allow (*Up Society's Ass 98*). Kafka's stated discomfort with ethnic belonging should make us skeptical of any straightforward alignment of Kafka with Jewishness, and yet Roth does use Kafka to refine his own sense of Jewish identity. I take up this issue in Chapter 3.

[2] It is worth noting that this movement to the suburbs was by no means confined to the Jewish community. As Catherine Jurca notes, "In 1950, the suburban growth rate was ten times that of central cities" (218). But, perhaps more than any other group, Jewish culture had seemed inextricably tied up with the urban landscape. For an analysis of how these ties were expressed in postwar fiction, see Brauner, *Post-War* 24–7.

[3] Although Bellow was based in Chicago, not New York, he was considered integral to the group—the New York Intellectuals' great hope among novelists. His frequent, long visits to New York in the 1940s established connections between the budding novelist and the milieu around *Partisan Review*. See Bloom 290–5 and Atlas, *Bellow* 81–93.

[4] Roth borrowed Bellow's terms when defending himself in his account of the controversy over *Goodbye, Columbus*: "The concerns of fiction are not those of a statistician—or of a public-relations firm. The novelist asks himself, 'What do people think?'; the PR man asks, 'What *will* people think?'" ("Writing About Jews" 448).

[5] Michael Rothberg, in his essay on the Holocaust in Roth's fiction, sees in the story a portrayal of a pivotal moment for American Jews, when "knowledge of the fact of the Nazi genocide has not yet become consciousness of the rupture the Holocaust would soon represent. But the proximity of the yeshiva to the town and Eli's deluded attempt to take over the identity of the Hasidic man also prophetically suggest that that consciousness is about to erupt and that, when it does, the results will sometimes be troubling" (56).

[6] Roth would go on to further caricature the rabbinical voice for more humorous purposes in *Portnoy's Complaint*, portraying a rabbi who pronounces the word "God" in three syllables (73).

[7] Victoria Aarons particularly sees Eli, with his "obsession with identity, with trying on and discarding selves," as a forerunner to many of Roth's later characters: "We hear, in Eli Peck's uncontrolled anxiety and in his phobic responses to conditions that he unwittingly creates, the prototype for Roth's later protagonists. Such characters may become more urbane, more sophisticated, and more self-ironic as his fiction develops, but they are no less comically and indelibly preoccupied and apprehensive as they attempt to negotiate the uncertain terrain of their American-Jewish lives" (10, 14).

[8] Much of my account of the New York Intellectuals' move toward the right comes from Wald's detailed study, which goes to great lengths to highlight the often contradictory political reversals of many in the group.

[9] In 1969, when the Newark City Council voted to cut off funding for the Newark Public Library, Roth wrote a piece for the *New York Times*, defending the library's place in the city's culture, arguing that when he was a child it taught him about the responsibilities of being in a community: "even more compelling was this idea of communal ownership, property held in common for the common good. Why I had to care for the books I borrowed, return them unscarred and on time, was because they weren't my property alone, *they were everybody's*. That idea had as much to do with civilizing me as any idea I was ever to come upon in the books themselves" ("Reflections" 30).

Chapter 2

[1] See Podhoretz, "Gloom"; Hyman; and Donaldson.

[2] "Some New Jewish Stereotypes" was given as a speech for a 1961 symposium on "The Needs and Images of Man," and later published in Roth's nonfiction collection, *Reading Myself and Others*.

[3] Of course, Trilling's first book, derived from his PhD dissertation, was a study of Arnold; Trilling expressed admiration for "the depth of [Arnold's] seriousness," (*Matthew Arnold* 28) echoing Arnold himself, in his formulation in "The Study of Poetry": "The substance of Chaucer's poetry, his view of things and his criticism of life, has largeness, freedom, shrewdness, benignity; but it has not this high seriousness. Homer's criticism of life has it, Dante's has it, Shakespeare's has it" (33). Arnold's discriminating evaluation seems a model for the sort of argument Roth mounts in "Writing American Fiction."

[4] Many Jewish writers, however, saw an implicit denial in Trilling's performed seriousness. Alfred Kazin, for example, has written that "I had from the very beginning written as a Jew; I never felt the way Lionel Trilling did. Trilling's manner amused me" (Rosenberg and Goldstein 204).

[5] Ross Posnock also calls attention to the revelations within Trilling's journal, contrasting Trilling's suppressed desire to be unserious with Roth's successful "embrace of irresponsibility." In Posnock's view, Roth "avoid[ed] the solution of elegant Anglophilia," and instead "devised a more complicated strategy, one that preserved irreverence but connected it to his canonical American predecessors": Melville, Whitman, Henry James and Emerson (53–4).

[6] For analysis of these two novels, see Donaldson; Cooperman; Atlas, "A Postwar Classic"; Girgus; and Tanenbaum.

[7] See also Sokolov and Goldman.

[8] Susann put in another cameo appearance in the cultural event that *Portnoy* became when she appeared on Johnny Carson's *Tonight Show*, saying that she would like to meet Roth, but wouldn't want to shake his hand (Roth, *Reading Myself and Others* 252–3).

[9] The editorial goes on to condemn "one current best-seller hailed as a 'masterpiece,' which, wallowing in a self-indulgent public psychoanalysis, drowns its literary merits in revolting sex excesses."

[10] Halio quotes from Murdoch's "Against Dryness: A Polemical Sketch."

[11] In Roth's archive, preceding one of the early drafts of *Portnoy's Complaint*, there is this epigraph from Kafka's "Metamorphosis": ". . . ought he really to call for help?

In spite of his misery he could not suppress a smile at the very idea of it" (Roth, "*Portnoy's Complaint*, Pages, n.d.,").

[12] That Portnoy's attraction to pop culture represented a shift in Roth's own sensibility is confirmed by Roth's memories of his friendship with the painter Philip Guston, begun just after *Portnoy's* publication. In a 1989 essay, Roth remembers that the two bonded over a shared interest in "crapola": "billboards, garages, diners, burger joints, junk shops, auto body shops." "Independently, impelled by very different dilemmas, each of us had begun to consider crapola [. . .] a blunt aesthetic instrument providing access to a style of representation free of the complexity we were accustomed to valuing" (*Shop Talk* 135).

Chapter 3

[1] Roth "'I Always Wanted You to Admire My Fasting,' or Looking at Kafka" (essay/story), *American Review* and *Lettre Internationale*, 1973–1975, 1984.

[2] Thomas R. Edwards, reviewing *The Great American Novel*, noted that Roth "has lately seemed an author in search of a subject," whereas Marvin Mudrick merely stated that "Poor Roth has lost not only his bearings but his marbles" (Edwards 27; Mudrick 547). For Sanford Pinsker, in the wake of *Portnoy*, "it became increasingly difficult to find a congenial home for [Roth's] sizable verbal talents" (71).

[3] Although there is no way of knowing whether Zuckerman's rage is a reflection of Roth's, it is interesting to find, among the correspondence in Roth's archive, a friendly letter from Howe to Roth written less than a year before the *Commentary* piece. It hints at, at the very least, a casual friendship between the two ("Yes, let's get together after your trip. By that time I will have, I hope, finished another story and will be in good spirits.") that could only have increased the sting that Roth felt after reading Howe's essay.

[4] In 1969, Howe published *A Treasury of Yiddish Poetry*, and then in 1973 *A Treasury of Yiddish Stories*, anthologies that seemed to signal a reconciliation between the New York Intellectual and his own inherited "personal culture."

[5] "No single interpretation," Mark Shechner writes, "will explain the mess Tarnopol is in, and nothing less than a symposium on the subject can begin to approach it." (*Up Society's Ass* 55).

[6] Roth, "*My Life as a Man*; Drafts; Early: Miscellaneous Pages and Notes, Set I; 1969–1970, n.d. (3 of 4)." 61, 61–2.

[7] Roth, "*My Life as a Man*; Drafts; Early: Copy A; 1968, Nov. 28 (2 of 3)." 360.

[8] Theodore Weinberger sees a connection between Roth's literary reading of Kafka's biography and the former's own increasing interest in playing with his own autobiography in fiction: "Kafka's life and work become a touchstone for Roth's own admixture of fact and fiction. [. . .] Roth is perpetually amazed by the fact that what he pointedly sets out to do is *done to* Kafka. The story of one Franz Kafka and his literary reputation is quite Kafkaesque" (250).

[9] Michael Rothberg argues that "it is less the Holocaust and its impact on American life that obsesses Roth than the unbridgeable distance between the Holocaust and American life—and the inauthenticity of most attempts to lessen that distance [. . .] [the Holocaust's] singularity is precisely not American" (53). It is along the same lines that Roth reverses his fantasy of Kafka's escape in

The Plot Against America (2004), in which he imagines a world in which America did not escape the threat of the Nazis.

10 I take the descent/assent distinction from Michael Krausz, in his essay, "On Being Jewish."

11 Mark Shechner argues that Kafka "does dual service for Roth, standing as a meta-phor for marital entrapment and sexual failure in some writing and elsewhere a metaphor for life under totalitarianism" (*Up Society's Ass* 63). I would merely add that, in many places, Kafka's presence works to both ends, simultaneously.

12 I cannot, for reasons of space, discuss them fully here, but Kafka has made a number of other appearances in Roth's writing. In 1974, prompted by President Ford's pardon of Nixon, Roth wrote an essay for the *Village Voice*, comparing con-temporary America to the world of Kafka's *The Castle* ("Our Castle" Rpt. in *Reading Myself and Others* 229–31). In *The Professor of Desire*, Kepesh dreams one night of going to meet "Kafka's whore," a seeming parody of his literary tourism of Prague (*PD* 187–93). And in *The Prague Orgy*, the final installment in *Zuckerman Bound*, Zuckerman travels to Prague; Olga, the desperate Czech woman who tries to seduce the American author, asks him, "Why are you in Prague? Are you looking for Kafka? The intellectuals all come here looking for Kafka. Kafka is dead. They should be looking for Olga" (*Zuckerman Bound* 529).

13 Lonoff, whom Zuckerman tells us is seen as "an out-of-step folklorist pathetically oblivious of the major currents of literature and society," whose "'translated' English" lends "a mildly ironic flavor to even the most commonplace expression," certainly bears some resemblance to Bernard Malamud, as many have remarked (*GW* 8,10). Zuckerman tells us of a Lonoff short story collection entitled *It's Your Funeral*, which is a line taken from Malamud's *The Assistant* (Malamud 67).

14 The judge also echoes Marie Syrkin, who famously characterized *Portnoy's Complaint* as being "straight out of the Goebbels-Streicher script" (64).

15 Many contemporary critics found fault with Roth's use of Anne Frank in *The Ghost Writer*, often seeing in Zuckerman's desire to be vindicated through a marriage a cheap ploy to further shock Roth's Jewish critics. Jack Beatty asked, "Is it worth bringing in the most famous symbol of the Holocaust just to add a clever touch, one, moreover, with a patently autobiographical reference? [. . .] Am I being a literary rabbi in saying that this use of Anne Frank seems to me a lapse of taste, a failure of aesthetic judgment?" (39). John Leonard accused Roth of using Anne Frank "as a sex object, as a wet dream, as a joke on his family. The *chutzpa* of it, appropriating the Ophelia of the death camps for his dark, libidinal purposes, his angry punch line. . . . He just can't help himself" (6). For Joseph Epstein, this is evidence that Roth "wants to shock yet still be adored," and the section "seems to call out for admiration—to want points for cuteness. See how clever I am, how imaginative!, it seems to say. Roth really ought to be better than this" (100).

16 Much of my brief portrait of Meyer Levin's involvement with the *Diary* is by now well-covered ground. For a fuller investigation, see Levin; Graver; and Doneson.

17 Frank wrote the letter on June 14, 1954. Qtd. in Doneson 69.

18 The Hacketts' letter is dated July 3, 1956. Qtd. in Doneson 70.

19 Sander L. Gilman, writing about the concept of the "self-hating Jew," argues that a crucial strand of Roth's thinking involves the distinction between American Jews' European past and their American present: "Roth sees the problem as

one with the myths of Jewish identity imported from Europe, myths that are inappropriate to the formation of the identity of the American Jew, especially the American Jew as writer" (355).

[20] As *I Married a Communist* informs us, a few years prior to the events of *The Ghost Writer*, Leo Gluckman, one of E. I. Lonoff's predecessors in the education of Nathan Zuckerman, enchants the young Zuckerman with the credo, "literature is the great particularizer [. . .] As an artist the nuance is your *task*. Your task is not to simplify" (223).

[21] R. Clifton Spargo is convincing in his assertion that "the invention of Anne Frank is only seemingly Nathan's peculiar trespass. At a deeper level the novel recalls several layers of cultural memory through which Anne Frank has been made a property of the American popular imagination" (89).

[22] She is inescapable for Roth as well; Anne Frank makes a number of other cameo appearances in his fiction, beginning with the original 1972 drafts of *American Pastoral*, which includes a fictional diary entry from Frank, who has fallen in love with Milton Levov (the precursor to the Swede, Seymour Levov) (Roth, "*American Pastoral*, Drafts"). For a fuller account of these drafts, see Shostak 123–5. Peter Tarnopol, in *My Life as a Man*, has an early story called "The Diary of Anne Frank's Contemporary" (itself one of the proposed titles found in the *American Pastoral* drafts), which fictionalizes a traumatic incident from his childhood, culminating in his relief that "we are Jews who live in the haven of Westchester County, rather than in our ravaged, ancestral, Jew-hating Europe" (248). And two books in *Zuckerman Bound*, *Zuckerman Unbound* and *The Prague Orgy*, each feature an actress who has performed in the role of Anne in *The Diary of Anne Frank*. When Zuckerman learns that Caesara O'Shea, the glamorous Irish movie star with whom he has a brief affair in *Zuckerman Unbound*, played Anne Frank, he thinks, "That Anne Frank should come to him in this guise. [. . .] life has its own flippant ideas about how to handle serious fellows like Zuckerman" (196).

[23] For example, Ozick has stated that "I am not in favor of making fiction of the data, or of mythologizing or poeticizing it" ("Roundtable Discussion" 284).

Chapter 4

[1] The title of *Zuckerman Bound*, ostensibly a play on both *Zuckerman Unbound* and the fact that it binds together all of the Zuckerman books to date into one book, also reflects something that I will discuss in this chapter: the increasing sense that Zuckerman is bound by his constricting (Freudian) view of his self. *Zuckerman Bound* was, in fact, one of the early titles for what would become *My Life as a Man* (before settling on Peter Tarnopol, Roth considered naming his character either Zuckerman or Zuckerborn). Other potential titles found in the early drafts point to Roth's interest in his characters' captivity and desire for freedom: "Zuckerman Unbound," "Zuckerborn Bound + Unbound" and "FREE ZUCKERBORN FROM HIS CAGE!" (Roth, "*My Life as a Man*, Drafts; Early; Miscellaneous Pages + Notes").

[2] In discussing psychoanalysis, I am concerned with Freud's writings and therapeutic project, and not the many ways in which psychoanalysis has evolved in practice over the past century. As Jeffrey Berman points out, "[Roth's] psychoanalysts

seem frozen in time, imprisoned by a rigid Freudian ideology that most analysts have long ago abandoned or sharply revised" (106).

[3] And yet it should be remembered that Dr. Spielvogel's famous closing line: "Now vee may perhaps to begin. Yes?" (*PC* 274) suggests that Portnoy's version of his story may be only part of the story—or only the start of the story.

[4] It is difficult to claim that the Nathan Zuckerman who appears in Tarnopol's stories is the same character who is the protagonist or narrator of nine of Roth's following books (the trilogy and epilogue of *Zuckerman Bound*, *The Counterlife*, *American Pastoral*, *I Married a Communist*, *The Human Stain*, and *Exit Ghost*). His biographical details, which vary between Tarnapol's two tellings, are modified again for *Zuckerman Bound*, and remain consistent throughout Roth's ensuing Zuckerman books. In this chapter, unless specifically noted, "Nathan Zuckerman" refers to Roth's Zuckerman, not Tarnopol's.

[5] We are reminded again of Lionel Trilling, whose inability to successfully move from critical work to fiction writing is figured by Adam Phillips as an attempt to sidestep his "conscious effort for dignity" ("Lionel Trilling's" 174). Phillips suggests that Trilling was only able to accomplish this required self-exposure in his psychoanalytic sessions. Similarly, in *The Human Stain* (2000), Zuckerman muses that Coleman Silk is unable to write his story because "[w]riting personally is exposing and concealing at the same time, but with you it could only be concealment and so it would never work" (*HS* 345).

[6] Both Jeffrey Berman and Debra Shostak have pointed out that this episode is based upon a remarkably similar article, published by Roth's analyst Hans Kleinschmidt in 1967, titled "The Angry Act: The Role of Aggression in Creativity." The piece, although it never names Roth (just as Spielvogel's article never mentions Tarnopol by name), nonetheless recounts a number of anecdotes from Roth's analysis that Roth would go on to fictionalize in *Portnoy's Complaint*, thus potentially exposing Roth, just as Tarnopol feels Spielvogel exposes him. If Roth was angered like Tarnopol is, there is no evidence of it in Kleinschmidt's letters to Roth in Roth's archive. A letter thanking Roth for an advance copy of *My Life as a Man* makes no mention of any conflict, in the past or present, and includes Kleinschmidt's assessement of the novel: "The book reads like a charm and shows you in top form." See Berman 94–110 and Shostak 163–4.

[7] Here we might be reminded of Roth's *Operation Shylock* (1993), in which much of the conflict comes down to the question of who is best suited to tell "Philip Roth's" story, "Philip Roth" or Moishe Pipik. For more on *Operation Shylock*, see Chapter 5 below.

[8] Roth, of course, will return to Zuckerman when he is older still, and his characterization in Roth's "American Trilogy" is of a man seemingly content to be without a story of the self—"I've had my story," he remarks in *I Married a Communist*. This will be taken up in my sixth chapter (*IMAC* 71).

[9] David Brauner reminds us that Roth's depiction of "the self as contingent, mutable, provisional, perenially improvised—as a performance and/or rhetorical construction—cannot be so readily associated with one particular figure or school. Nonetheless it has coincided with work by many theorists across a range of disciplines (sociology, philosophy, psychology, anthropology, linguistics, gender studies) that challenges and deconstructs the idea of a unified, sovereign, stable, core Cartesian self" (*Philip Roth* 116).

10 For an excellent analysis of Roth's treatment of embodiment, see Shostak 20–65.

11 See Polkinghorne; Payne; and Angus and McLeod.

12 For more on Roth's treatment of the pastoral, see Brauner, *Post-War* 74–7; Brauner, *Philip Roth* 148–85; Hogan; Lyons 120–7; and Royal, "Pastoral Dreams."

Chapter 5

1 David Brauner writes that the four books, as well as *The Plot Against America*, "constitute a sustained interrogation of the relationship between these two labels [fiction and non-fiction]" (*Philip Roth* 80). See also Turek and Goodheart.

2 Eakin continues: "once the narrative has been published, whatever the terms of the collaboration may have been, an act of appropriation has occurred, and the self who signs may well be led to reflect on the ethical responsibilities involved."

3 In the same interview, Roth explicitly ties the novelist's talent for impersonation to adultery: "Think of the art of the adulterer: under tremendous pressure and against enormous odds, ordinary husbands and wives, who would freeze with self-consciousness up on a stage, yet in the theater of the home, alone before the audience of the betrayed spouse, they act out roles of innocence and fidelity with flawless dramatic skill. [. . .] People beautifully pretending to be 'themselves'" (222). David Brauner has written about Roth's tendency to use legal language and metaphors in much of his work; see *Philip Roth* 21–8.

4 In an attempt to avoid confusion, I will follow other commentators in calling the author of *Operation Shylock* "Roth," the narrator "Philip" and the impostor "Pipik."

5 See Shechner, *Up Society's Ass* 132; Cohen 84–5; Shostak 142; and Brauner, *Philip Roth* 95, 101.

6 David Brauner notes that, at this point, Philip does defeat Pipik, by writing him out of the book, reclaiming his own novel, and authoring new developments that are perhaps even more absurd than those prompted by Pipik's presence (*Philip Roth* 104).

7 Philip is forgetting, if he is indeed Philip Roth, that he submitted the manuscript to *The Facts* to Zuckerman, for just this sort of scrutiny.

Chapter 6

1 "At age 73, Philip Roth is in the midst of what might be the most stunning 'late period' by an American writer since Henry James" (Bonca). Ross Posnock makes the same point, claiming that "[l]ate Roth is now beginning to deserve comparison with what is usually regarded as the summit of late turns of novelistic genius—Henry James's major phase at the start of the century" (5).

2 For a discussion of the ways in which *American Pastoral* continues *The Counterlife's* focus on the pastoral, see Hogan.

3 It is important to remember that both *The Human Stain* and *American Pastoral* are, each to a different extent, Zuckerman's suppositional attempts at telling the

accurate stories of Coleman Silk and Seymour Levov, respectively. In *American Pastoral*, having heard about Levov's death at his 45th high school reunion, Zuckerman "dream[s] a realistic chronicle" of Levov's life that takes up the final 350 pages of the novel (*AP* 89). Zuckerman's attempt at a written recreation of Coleman's life in *The Human Stain* is also prompted by his subject's death, with Zuckerman "standing alone in a darkening graveyard and entering into professional competition with death" (*HS* 338). In *I Married a Communist*, by contrast, the story of Ira Ringold is told to Zuckerman by Ira's brother Murray, and Zuckerman fills in Murray's narrative with his own memories of Ira from his youth. For an analysis of these narrative strategies, see Royal, "Pastoral Dreams" and Royal, "Plotting the Frames."

[4] Coleman's boxing nickname, reflecting as it does Coleman's smoothness and agility in the ring, carries connotations as well for his seemingly effortless escape from racial identity; the chapter that narrates Coleman's decision to pass is called "Slipping the Punch." It also has connotations of Silk's youthful sexual prowess and might remind us that one of Portnoy's nicknames for his penis is "the silky monster" (*PC* 127).

[5] As Ross Posnock points out, this is in some way Faunia Farley's project as well: "Analogously [to Coleman], Faunia is a middle-class woman who refuses to be one, a Yankee daughter of the Puritans who insists on a white-trash life. Her rejection of her original class membership is not an act of political solidarity with the lumpen but an act of aggressive disaffiliation from any collective 'we' with its expectations about 'what you're supposed to be . . . supposed to do'" (Posnock 221).

[6] Both Brauner and Posnock point out the incongruity of this decision and remind us that anti-Semitism was by no means a thing of the past in postwar America. Posnock further suggests that Roth's decision to have Coleman pass as a Jew "makes credible Coleman's belief that his decision is more about freedom than race" (Posnock 204–6).

[7] It is also the same milieu in which Anatole Broyard, whom many commentators see as the model for Coleman Silk, made his mark. Broyard, the long-time book reviewer for the *New York Times*, was of mixed-race descent, but passed as white his whole life. Henry Louis Gates, Jr., in an essay which revealed Broyard's secret after his death, paints a picture of Broyard in Greenwich Village in the late forties and early fifties that corresponds with Roth's portrait of the young Coleman Silk: "In the Village, where Broyard started a bookstore on Cornelia Street, the salient thing about him wasn't that he was black but that he was beautiful, charming, and erudite. In those days, the Village was crowded with ambitious and talented young writers and artists, and Broyard—known for calling men 'Sport' and girls 'Slim'— was never more at home. He could hang out at the San Remo bar with Dwight Macdonald and Delmore Schwartz." Gates's estimation of Broyard's passing is also telling: "Broyard was born black and became white, and his story is compounded of equal parts pragmatism and principle. He knew that the world was filled with such snippets and scraps of paper, all conspiring to reduce him to an identity that other people had invented and he had no say in. [. . .] Society had decreed race to be a matter of natural law, but he wanted race to be an elective affinity, and it was never going to be a fair fight" (Gates, Jr. 66).

8 Shechner has also described the Swede's downfall in *American Pastoral* in similar terms; here it is his daughter Merry who is the return of the repressed, representing the "Jewish fanaticism" that is her family inheritance, but that the Swede somehow escapes ("Roth's American Trilogy" 146–7). In addition, Debra Shostak spots the return of Ira's repressed in *I Married a Communist* in the form of Sylphid, Eve Frame's vindictive and vengeful daughter (253).

9 See Brauner, *Philip Roth* 118; Duban; Safer 121–2; and Shechner, *Up Society's Ass* 188. Ross Posnock also connects *The Human Stain* to *The Scarlet Letter*, but draws parallels instead between Coleman, a man who lives his entire adult life with a crucial secret, and Arthur Dimmesdale, whose "vigilance in maintaining his double life is strained near breaking" (235).

10 Also echoed, of course, is the fate of Bill Clinton. Speaking of his decision to set *The Human Stain* when he did, Roth has stated, "In 1998 you had the illusion that you were suddenly able to know this huge, unknowable country, to catch a glimpse of its moral core. What was being enacted on the public stage seemed to have the concentrated power of a great work of literature. The work I'm thinking of is *The Scarlet Letter*" (McGrath 7).

11 Circumcision, in *The Counterlife*, as an antidote to the pastoral, is also figured as a brand, "the mark of [Jewish] reality [. . .] The heavy hand of human values falls upon you right at the start, marking your genitals as its own" (*C* 327).

12 Both Corwin and Fast are heroes to the young Alexander Portnoy as well, with Portnoy, like Zuckerman in *I Married a Communist*, writing radio plays in the style of Corwin (*PC* 169, 130).

13 Tellingly, the claims of family life are explicitly anathema to O'Day's self-determining project: "O'Day was unmarried. 'Entangling alliances,' he told Ira, 'is something I don't want any part of at no time. I regard kids as hostages to the malevolent'" (*IMAC* 35).

14 Zuckerman mentions in passing that, after spending night after night sitting outside Ira's shack listening to Ira's stories, surrounded by citronella candles, "the lemony fragrance of citronella oil would forever after recall Zinc Town [where Ira's shack was] to me" (*IMAC* 188). Near the book's end, after driving Murray to his residence, thus signaling the end of his story, Zuckerman returns to his cabin to see that "[o]n the deck, the citronella candle was still burning in its aluminum bucket when I got back, that little pot of fire the only light by which my house was discernible, except for a dim radiance off the orange moon silhouetting the low roof" (*IMAC* 320).

15 In its formulation of a westward move to escape the claims of ethnic belonging, this passage confirms the bitter prediction made by Neil Klugman, reflecting upon the great Jewish migration out of the cities: "someday these streets [. . .] would be empty and we would all of us have moved to the crest of the Orange Mountains, and wouldn't the dead stop kicking at the slats in their coffins then?" (*GC* 83).

16 Timothy Parrish asserts that "[w]hat her father might dismiss as adolescent role-playing is thus a more extreme version of how he invents his life. Where Swede creates his self by imagining a single narrative future of Edenic bliss, Merry extends and multiplies her father's logic of self-identification and fulfillment. [. . .] An extreme version of her father's self-experimentation, Merry's innate

curiosity to explore the outer limits of the self's possibilities aligns her with the novelistic sensibility of Zuckerman and Roth" ("End of Identity" 91–2).

[17]　See Podhoretz, "The Adventures of Philip Roth" and Alexander.

[18]　See Thompson; Amidon; and Gray.

Works Cited

Aarons, Victoria. "American-Jewish Identity in Roth's Short Fiction." *The Cambridge Companion to Philip Roth*. Ed. Timothy Parrish. Cambridge: Cambridge University Press, 2007: 9–21.

Alexander, Edward. "Philip Roth at Century's End." *New England Review* 20 (1999): 183–90.

Amidon, Stephen. "A Guide to Philip Roth." *Sunday Times* [London] September 23, 2007: 6.

Angus, Lynne E., and John McLeod, eds. *The Handbook of Narrative and Psychotherapy: Practice, Theory, and Research*. London: Sage, 2004.

Arnold, Matthew. "The Study of Poetry." *Essays in Criticism*, Second Series. London: Macmillan, 1913: 1–33.

Atlas, James. *Bellow: A Biography*. London: Faber, 2000.

—. "A Postwar Classic." *New Republic* June 2, 1982: 28–32.

Beatty, Jack. Rev. of *The Ghost Writer*, by Philip Roth. *New Republic* October 6, 1979: 39.

Bellow, Saul. Interview by Gordon L. Harper. *Writers at Work: The Paris Review Interviews*. Ed. George Plimpton. Third Series. New York: Viking, 1968: 175–6.

—. "The Swamp of Prosperity." *Commentary* July 1959: 79.

Ben-David, Calev. "Guardian Angel." *Jerusalem Post Magazine* June 1, 2001: 10.

Berman, Jeffrey. "Revisiting Roth's Psychoanalysts." *The Cambridge Companion to Philip Roth*. Ed. Timothy Parrish. Cambridge: Cambridge University Press, 2007: 94–110.

"Beyond the (Garbage) Pale." *New York Times* April 1, 1969: 46.

Bloom, Alexander. *Prodigal Sons: The New York Intellectuals & Their World*. New York: Oxford University Press, 1986.

Bonca, Cornel. "Roth, Waxing." *OC Weekly*. Village Voice Media. June 29, 2006. Web. July 17, 2010. www.ocweekly.com/2006–06–29/culture/roth-waxing/

Brauner, David. "'Getting in Your Retaliation First': Narrative Strategies in *Portnoy's Complaint*." *Philip Roth: New Perspectives on an American Author*. Ed. Derek Parker Royal. Westport, CT: Praeger, 2005: 43–58.

—. "Masturbation and its Discontents, or, Serious Relief: Freudian Comedy in *Portnoy's Complaint*." *Critical Review* 40 (2000): 75–90.

—. *Philip Roth*. Manchester: Manchester University Press, 2007.

—. *Post-War Jewish Fiction*. Hampshire: Palgrave, 2001.

Brooks, Peter. *Reading for the Plot*. Oxford: Clarendon, 1984.

Broyard, Anatole. "A Sort of Moby Dick." *New Republic* March 1, 1969: 21.

Cohen, Josh. "Roth's Doubles." *The Cambridge Companion to Philip Roth*. Ed. Timothy Parrish. Cambridge: Cambridge University Press, 2007: 82–93.

Cooperman, Stanley. "Philip Roth: 'Old Jacob's Eye' With a Squint." *Twentieth Century Literature* 19 (July 1973): 203–16.

Crossley, Michele L. *Introducing Narrative Psychology: Self, Trauma and the Construction of Meaning.* Philadelphia: Open University Press, 2000.

Cryer, Dan. "Investigation of Life's Brevity Too Shallow." *Atlanta Journal-Constitution* May 28, 2006: 4K.

Donaldson, Scott. "Philip Roth: The Meanings of *Letting Go.*" *Contemporary Literature* 11 (Winter 1970): 21–35.

Doneson, Judith. *The Holocaust in American Film.* 2nd ed. Syracuse: Syracuse University Press, 2002.

Duban, James. "Being Jewish in the Twentieth Century: The Synchronicity of Roth and Hawthorne." *Studies in American Jewish Literature* 21 (2002): 1–11.

Eakin, Paul John. *How Our Lives Become Stories: Making Selves.* Ithaca: Cornell University Press, 1999.

Edwards, Thomas R. "The Great American Novel." *New York Times* May 6, 1973: sec. 7, 27.

Elliott, George P. "Real Gardens for Real Toads." *The Nation* November 14, 1959: 345–50.

Epstein, Joseph. "Too Much Even of Kreplach." *Hudson Review* 33 (1980): 97–110.

Farberow, Pearl. Letter to Philip Roth. Undated. MS. "Readers' reactions and reviews, 1959." Box 101, Philip Roth Collection. Library of Congress, Washington, D.C.

France, Alan W. "Philip Roth's *Goodbye, Columbus* and the Limits of Commodity Culture." *MELUS* 15.4 (1988): 83–9.

Frank, Anne. *The Diary of a Young Girl: The Definitive Edition.* Ed. Otto H. Frank and Mirjam Pressler. New York: Anchor, 1996.

Freadman, Richard. "Decent and Indecent: Writing My Father's Life." *The Ethics of Life Writing.* Ed. Paul John Eakin. Ithaca: Cornell University Press, 2004. 121–46.

Freedman, Jonathan. *The Temple of Culture: Assimilation and Anti-Semitism in Literary Anglo-America.* Oxford: Oxford University Press, 2000.

Freud, Sigmund. *The Complete Introductory Lectures on Psychoanalysis.* Trans. and Ed. James Strachey. London: Allen, 1971.

—. "Freud's Psycho-Analytic Method." *Collected Papers.* Trans. Joan Riviere. Vol. 1. London: Hogarth, 1956: 264–71.

—. "From the History of an Infantile Neurosis." *The Standard Edition of the Complete Psychological Works of Sigmund Freud.* Trans. and Ed. James Strachey. Vol. 17. London: Hogarth, 1955.

—. *The Interpretation of Dreams. The Standard Edition of the Complete Psychological Works of Sigmund Freud.* Trans. and Ed. James Strachey. Vol. 4. London: Hogarth, 1958.

—. "On the History of the Psycho-Analytic Movement." *Collected Papers,* Trans. Joan Riviere. Vol. 1. London: Hogarth, 1956: 287–359.

Gates, Jr., Henry Louis. "White Like Me." *New Yorker* June 17, 1996: 66–81.

Gilman, Sander L. *Jewish Self-Hatred.* Baltimore: Johns Hopkins University Press, 1986.

Girgus, Sam B. "Between *Goodbye, Columbus* and *Portnoy*: Becoming a Man and Writer in Roth's Feminist 'Family Romance.'" *Studies in American Jewish Literature* 8 (1989): 143–53.

Goldman, Albert. "Wild Blue Shocker: *Portnoy's Complaint.*" *Life* February 7, 1969: 56–65.

Goodheart, Eugene. *Novel Practices: Classic Modern Fiction.* New Brunswick: Transaction, 2004.

Goodrich, Frances, and Albert Hackett. *The Diary of Anne Frank.* London: Samuel French Ltd., 1958.

Gordon, Albert. *Jews in Suburbia.* Boston: Beacon, 1959.

Gordon, Ken. "Philip Roth: The Zuckerman Books." *Salon.com.* Salon Media Group. March 26, 2002. Web. July 17, 2010. http://dir.salon.com/ent/masterpiece/2002/03/26 /zuckerman/index.html

Graver, Lawrence. *An Obsession with Anne Frank: Meyer Levin and the Diary.* Berkeley: University of California Press, 1995.

Gray, Paul. "[America's Best] Novelist." *Time.com.* Time Warner, July 9, 2001. Web. July 17, 2010. www.time.com/time/magazine/article/0,9171,1000283,00.html

Halio, Jay L. "Fantasy and Fiction." *Southern Review* 7 (Spring 1971): 635–47.

Halkin, Hillel. "The Traipse of Roth." *Jerusalem Report* April 8, 1993: 54.

Hawthorne, Nathaniel. *The Scarlet Letter.* New York: Modern Library, 2000.

Hogan, Monika. "'Something so Visceral in with the Rhetorical': Race, Hypochondria, and the Un-Assimilated Body in *American Pastoral.*" *Studies in American Jewish Literature* 23 (2004): 1–14.

Howe, Irving. Letter to Philip Roth. January 18, 1972. TS. "Howe, Irving; 1973–1975, 1986–1988." Box 13, Philip Roth Collection. Library of Congress, Washington, D.C.

—. "Philip Roth Reconsidered." *Commentary* December 1972: 69–72.

—. "The Suburbs of Babylon." *Celebrations and Attacks: Thirty Years of Literary and Cultural Commentary.* New York: Horizon, 1979: 35–8.

—. *World of Our Fathers.* London: Phoenix, 2000.

Hyman, Stanley Edgar. "A Novelist of Great Promise." *The New Leader* June 11, 1962: 22–3.

Jumonville, Neil. *Critical Crossings: The New York Intellectuals in Postwar America.* Berkley: University of California Press, 1991.

Jurca, Catherine. *White Diaspora.* Princeton: Princeton University Press, 2001.

Kafka, Franz. *The Diaries, 1910–1923.* Ed. Max Brod. Trans. Martin Greenberg and Hannah Arendt. New York: Schocken, 1976.

Kakutani, Michiko. "Confronting the Failures of a Professor Who Passes." *New York Times* May 2, 2000: E1.

—. "A Postwar Paradise Shattered From Within." *New York Times* April 15, 1997: C11.

Kaplan, Justin. "Play it Again, Nathan." *New York Times* September 25, 1988: 3+.

Kapp, Isa. "What Hath Philip Roth Wrought?" *New Leader* March 3, 1969: 21.

Kazin, Alfred. *Bright Book of Life.* Boston: Little, 1973.

Kleinschmidt, Hans. Letter to Philip Roth. June 9, 1974. MS. "Kleinschmidt, Hans J.; 1964–1984, 1991, n.d." Box 17, Philip Roth Collection. Library of Congress, Washington, D.C.

Klemesrud, Judy. "Some Mothers Wonder What Portnoy Had to Complain About." *New York Times* March 31, 1969: 42.

Kramer, Judith R., and Seymour Leventman. *Children of the Gilded Ghetto.* New Haven: Yale University Press, 1961.

Krausz, Michael. "On Being Jewish." *Jewish Identity.* Ed. David Theo Goldberg and Michael Krausz. Philadelphia: Temple University Press, 1993: 264–78.

Krupnick, Mark. "'A Shit-Filled Life': Philip Roth's *Sabbath's Theater.*" *Jewish Writing and the Deep Places of the Imagination.* Ed. Jean Carney and Mark Shechner. London: University of Wisconsin Press, 2005: 15–39.

Lehmann-Haupt, Christopher. "So is the Hero Really Philip Roth, or Not?" *New York Times* March 5, 1990: C16.

Leonard, John. "Fathers and Ghosts." *New York Review of Books* October 25, 1979: 6.

Levin, Meyer. *The Obsession.* New York: Simon, 1973.

Levy, Adolph. Letter to Philip Roth. June 12, 1959. MS. "Readers' reactions and reviews, 1959." Box 101, Philip Roth Collection. Library of Congress, Washington, D.C.

Lewis, R. W. B. *The American Adam.* Chicago: University of Chicago Press, 1955.

Liehm, Antonín J. "'The Literature of the Other Europe': A Bit of Roth in Prague." *Philip Roth: Inventing America.* Spec. issue of *Du* 740 (2003): 82.

Lyons, Bonnie. "En-Countering Pastorals in *The Counterlife.*" *Philip Roth: New Perspectives on an American Author.* Ed. Derek Parker Royal. Westport: Praeger, 2005: 119–28.

Malamud, Bernard. *The Assistant.* London: Eyre, 1959.

Malin, Irving. "Looking at Roth's Kafka; or Some Hints about Comedy." *Studies in Short Fiction* 14 (1977): 273–5.

Mannes, Marya. "A Dissent from Marya Mannes." *Saturday Review* February 22, 1969: 39.

McDaniel, John N. *The Fiction of Philip Roth.* Haddonfield, NJ: Haddonfield House, 1974.

McDonald, Brian. "'The Real American Crazy Shit': On Adamism and Democratic Individuality in *American Pastoral.*" *Studies in American Jewish Literature* 23 (2004): 27–40.

McGrath, Charles. "Zuckerman's Alter Brain." *New York Times Book Review* May 7, 2000: 7–8.

Menand, Louis. "The Irony and the Ecstasy." *New Yorker* May 19, 1997: 88–94.

Miller, Nancy K. *Bequest and Betrayal: Memoirs of a Parent's Death.* New York: Oxford University Press, 1996.

Miller, Ross. "Chronicle of Life and Work." *Philip Roth. Inventing America.* Spec. issue of *Du* 740 (2003): 95–111.

Moran, Joe. *Star Authors: Literary Celebrity in America.* London: Pluto, 2000.

Morse, J. Mitchell. "Brand Names and Others." *Hudson Review* 22.2 (1969): 316–20.

Mudrick, Marvin. "Old Pros with News from Nowhere." *Hudson Review* 26.3 (1973): 545–61.

Murdoch, Iris. "Against Dryness: A Polemical Sketch." *Encounter* 16 (January 1961): 16–20.

Nabokov, Vladimir. "On a Book Entitled *Lolita.*" *The Annotated Lolita.* London: Penguin, 1995.

Ozick, Cynthia. "Roundtable Discussion." *Writing and the Holocaust.* Ed. Berel Lang. New York: Holmes, 1988: 277–84.

—. "Who Owns Anne Frank?" *Quarrel and Quandary.* New York: Vintage, 2000: 74–102.

Parrish, Timothy. "The End of Identity: Philip Roth's *American Pastoral.*" *Shofar* 19 (Fall 2000): 84–99.

—. "Roth and Ethnic Identity." *The Cambridge Companion to Philip Roth*. Ed. Timothy Parrish. Cambridge: Cambridge University Press, 2007: 127–41.

Payne, Martin. *Narrative Therapy: An Introduction for Counsellors*. London: Sage, 2006.

Phillips, Adam. "Lionel Trilling's Concentrated Rush." *Raritan* 21.4 (Spring 2002): 164–74.

—. "Philip Roth's Patrimony." *On Flirtation*. London: Faber, 1994: 167–74.

Pinsker, Sanford. *The Comedy that "Hoits": An Essay on the Fiction of Philip Roth*. Columbia: University of Missouri Press, 1975.

Plante, David. "Conversations with Philip." *New York Times* January 1, 1984: 3.

Plesur, Milton. *Jewish Life in Twentieth-Century America*. Chicago: Nelson-Hall, 1982.

Podhoretz, Norman. "The Adventures of Philip Roth." *Commentary* October 1998: 25–36.

—. "The Gloom of Philip Roth." *Show* 2 (1962): 92+. Rpt. in *Doings and Undoings: The Fifties and After in American Writing*. London: Hart-Davis, 1965: 236–43.

—. *Making It*. London: Cape, 1968.

Polkinghorne, D. P. *Narrative Knowing and the Human Sciences*. Albany: State University of New York Press, 1988.

Posnock, Ross. *Philip Roth's Rude Truth: The Art of Immaturity*. Princeton: Princeton University Press, 2006.

Pozorski, Aimee. "How to Tell a True Ghost Story: *The Ghost Writer* and the Case of Anne Frank." *Philip Roth: New Perspectives on an American Author*. Ed. Derek Parker Royal. Westport, CT: Praeger, 2005: 89–102.

Rahv, Philip. "Attitudes Toward Henry James." *Image and Idea* 77–86.

—. *Image and Idea: Twenty Essays on Literary Themes, Revised and Enlarged*. London: Weidenfeld, 1957.

—. "Paleface and Redskin." *Image and Idea* 1–6.

Raymont, Henry. "To Philip Roth, Obscenity Isn't a Dirty Word." *New York Times* January 11, 1969: 20.

Ricoeur, Paul. *Freud and Philosophy*. Trans. Denis Savage. New Haven: Yale University Press, 1970.

Rieff, Philip. *Freud: The Mind of the Moralist*. London: Gollancz, 1959.

Rodgers, Jr., Bernard F. *Philip Roth*. Boston: Twayne, 1978.

Rosenberg, Bernard, and Ernest Goldstein, eds. *Creators and Disturbers: Reminiscences by Jewish Intellectuals of New York*. New York: Columbia University Press, 1982.

Roth, Philip. "*American Pastoral*; Drafts, Original Version: Copy B (1 of 2); 1972." TS. Box 39, Philip Roth Collection. Library of Congress, Washington, D.C.

—. *American Pastoral*. London: Vintage, 1998.

—. *The Anatomy Lesson. Zuckerman Bound*. London: Vintage, 1998: 293–505.

—. "The Art of Fiction LXXXIV." *Paris Review* 26.93 (Fall 1984): 214–47. Rpt. as "Interview with *The Paris Review*." *Reading Myself and Others* 119–48.

—. *The Breast*. London: Vintage, 1995.

—. *The Counterlife*. London: Cape, 1987.

—. "*Deception*; Drafts, Second, Copy A, with notes; 1989, Feb. (1 of 2)." TS. Box 79, Philip Roth Collection. Library of Congress, Washington, D.C.

—. *Deception*. London: Vintage, 1990.

—. *Everyman*. London: Vintage, 2006.

—. *Exit Ghost*. London: Cape, 2007.

—. *The Facts*. New York: Penguin, 1989.

—. "From The First 18 Years Of My Life." *New York Times* October 24, 1971: 1+. Rpt. as "The Story of Three Stories." *Reading Myself and Others* 212–15.

—. *The Ghost Writer*. *Zuckerman Bound*. London: Vintage, 1998: 1–129.

—. *Goodbye, Columbus*. London: Penguin, 1986.

—. *The Human Stain*. London: Vintage, 2000.

—. "'I Always Wanted You to Admire My Fasting,' or Looking at Kafka" (essay/ story), *American Review* and *Lettre Internationale*, 1973–1975, 1984.' Box 245, Philip Roth Collection. Library of Congress, Washington, D.C.

—. "'I Always Wanted You to Admire My Fasting'; or, Looking at Kafka." *Reading Myself and Others* 281–302.

—. *I Married a Communist*. New York: Houghton Mifflin, 1998.

—. "In Search of Kafka and Other Answers." *New York Times Book Review* February 15, 1976: 6–7.

—. "An Interview with Philip Roth." Interview by Asher Z. Milbauer and Donald G. Watson. *Reading Philip Roth*. Eds. Asher Z. Milbauer and Donald G. Watson. New York: St. Martin's, 1988: 1–12.

—. "Interview with *The London Sunday Times*." *Reading Myself and Others* 111–18.

—. "Just a Lively Boy." *An Unsentimental Education: Writers and Chicago*. Ed. Molly McQuade. Chicago: University of Chicago Press, 1995: 123–30.

—. *Letting Go*. London: Corgi, 1972.

—. Letter to Mrs. Strausberg. July 22, 1959. TS. "Readers' reactions and reviews, 1959." Box 101, Philip Roth Collection. Library of Congress, Washington, D.C.

—. "My Life as a Man; Drafts; Early: Copy A; 1968, Nov. 28 (2 of 3)." TS. Box 142, Philip Roth Collection. Library of Congress, Washington, D.C.

—. "My Life as a Man; Drafts; Early; Miscellaneous Pages + Notes, Set I; 1969–1970, n.d. (2 of 4)." TS. Box 144, Philip Roth Collection. Library of Congress, Washington, D.C.

—. "My Life as a Man; Drafts; Early: Miscellaneous Pages and Notes, Set I; 1969– 1970, n.d. (3 of 4)." TS. Box 144, Philip Roth Collection. Library of Congress, Washington, D.C.

—. *My Life as a Man*. New York: Vintage, 1993.

—. "*Operation Shylock*; Drafts; First, Copy A; 1990, March 25." TS. Box 155, Philip Roth Collection. Library of Congress, Washington, D.C.

—. *Operation Shylock*. London: Vintage, 1994.

—. *Patrimony*. New York: Vintage, 1991.

—. "Philip Roth's Exact Intent." Interview by George Plimpton. *New York Times Book Review* February 23, 1969: 2. Rpt. as "On *Portnoy's Complaint*." *Reading Myself and Others* 13–20.

—. "*Portnoy's Complaint*, Pages, n.d." MS. Box 186, Philip Roth Collection. Library of Congress, Washington, D.C.

—. *Portnoy's Complaint*. London: Vintage, 1999.

—. *The Prague Orgy*. *Zuckerman Bound*. London: Vintage, 1998: 507–69.

—. *The Professor of Desire*. London: Vintage, 2000.

—. "Reading Myself." *Partisan Review* 15.3 (1973): 404–17. Rpt. as "On the *Great American Novel*." *Reading Myself and Others* 65–80.

—. *Reading Myself and Others*. New York: Vintage, 2001.

—. "Reflections on the Death of a Library." *New York Times* March 1, 1969: 30. Rpt. as "The Newark Public Library." *Reading Myself and Others* 216–18.

—. *Sabbath's Theater*. London: Vintage, 1996.

—. *Shop Talk*. London: Vintage, 2002.

—. "Whacking Off." *Partisan Review* 34 (Summer 1967): 385–99.

—. *When She Was Good*. London: Corgi, 1979.

—. "Writing About Jews." *Commentary* December 1963: 446–52. Rpt. in *Reading Myself and Others* 193–211.

—. "Writing American Fiction." *Commentary* March 1961: 223–33. Rpt. in *Reading Myself and Others* 165–82.

—. *Zuckerman Unbound*. *Zuckerman Bound*. London: Vintage, 1998: 131–292.

Rothberg, Michael. "Roth and the Holocaust." *The Cambridge Companion to Philip Roth*. Ed. Timothy Parrish. Cambridge: Cambridge University Press, 2007: 52–67.

Royal, Derek Parker. "Pastoral Dreams and National Identity in *American Pastoral* and *I Married a Communist*." *Philip Roth: New Perspectives on an American Author*. Westport: Praeger, 2005: 185–208.

—. "Plotting the Frames of Subjectivity: Identity, Death, and Narrative in Philip Roth's *The Human Stain*." *Contemporary Literature* 47.1 (2006): 114–40.

Safer, Elaine B. *Mocking the Age: The Later Novels of Philip Roth*. Albany: State University of New York Press, 2006.

Schaub, Thomas Hill. *American Fiction in the Cold War*. Madison: University of Wisconsin Press, 1991.

Shapiro, Edward S. *A Time for Healing: American Jewry since World War II*. Baltimore: Johns Hopkins University Press, 1992.

Shechner, Mark. *After the Revolution: Studies in the Contemporary Jewish American Imagination*. Bloomington: Indiana University Press, 1987.

—. "Roth's American Trilogy." *The Cambridge Companion to Philip Roth*. Ed. Timothy Parrish. Cambridge: Cambridge University Press, 2007: 142–57.

—. *Up Society's Ass, Copper: Rereading Philip Roth*. Madison: University of Wisconsin Press, 2003.

Shostak, Debra. *Philip Roth—Countertexts, Counterlives*. Columbia: University of South Carolina Press, 2004.

Sokolov, Raymond A. "Alexander the Great." *Newsweek* February 24, 1969: 55–7.

Solotaroff, Theodore. "The Journey of Philip Roth." *Atlantic Monthly* April 1969: 64–72.

Spacks, Patricia Meyer. "Male Miseries." *The Nation* October 15, 1977: 373–6.

Spargo, R. Clifton. "To Invent as Presumptuously as Real Life: Parody and the Cultural Memory of Anne Frank in Roth's *The Ghost Writer*." *Representations* 76 (Fall 2001): 88–119.

Spence, Donald. *Narrative Truth and Historical Truth: Meaning and Interpretation in Psychoanalysis*. New York: Norton, 1982.

Swados, Harvey. "Good and Short." Hudson Review 12 (Autumn 1959): 358–9.

Syrkin, Marie. "The Fun of Self-Abuse." Midstream April 1969: 64–8.

Tanenbaum, Laura. "Reading Roth's Sixties." *Studies in American Jewish Literature* 23 (2004): 41–54.

Tayler, Christopher. "America's Flight From Freedom." *Sunday Telegraph*, September 28, 2004, Review sec.: 11.

Temple Topics. Progressive Synagogue, Brooklyn, New York. December 30, 1963.

"'Writing About Jews' (essay/speech), Commentary, 1962–1964." Box 247, Philip Roth Collection. Library of Congress, Washington, D.C.

Thompson, Bob. "His Life as a Writer." *Washington Post* November 12, 2006: D1.

Trilling, Lionel. "George Orwell and the Politics of Truth." *The Opposing Self: Nine Essays in Criticism.* New York: Viking, 1955. 150–9.

—. *Matthew Arnold.* London: Allen, 1939.

—. "Some Notes for an Autobiographical Lecture." *The Last Decade: Essays and Reviews, 1965–75.* Ed. Diana Trilling. Oxford: Oxford University Press, 1982: 226–41.

Turek, Richard. "Caught Between *The Facts* and *Deception.*" *Philip Roth: New Perspectives on an American Author.* Ed. Derek Parker Royal. Westport, CT: Praeger, 2005: 129–42.

"Under Forty: A Symposium on American Literature and the Younger Generation of American Jews." *Contemporary Jewish Record* February 1944: 3–36.

Viderman, Serge. "The Analytic Space: Meaning and Problems." *Psychoanalytic Quarterly* 48.2 (1979): 257–91.

Wald, Alan. *The New York Intellectuals: The Rise and Decline of the Anti-Stalinist Left from the 1930s to the 1980s.* Chapel Hill: University of North Carolina Press, 1987.

Weinberger, Theodore. "Philip Roth, Franz Kafka, and Jewish Writing." *Literature and Theology* 7 (1993): 248–58.

Wershiba, Joseph. "Daily Closeup: Leon Uris, Author of 'Exodus.'" *New York Post* July 2, 1959: 34. "Readers' reactions and reviews, 1959." Box 101, Philip Roth Collection. Library of Congress, Washington, D.C.

White, Michael, and David Epston. *Narrative Means to Therapeutic Ends.* New York: Norton, 1990.

Index